2002 FISHING TIPS AND TRICKS

2002 FISHING TIPS AND TRICKS

Vlad Evanoff

TWO BESTSELLING BOOKS COMPLETE IN ONE VOLUME

GALAHAD BOOKS
NEW YORK

First Galahad Books edition published in 1999.

Galahad Books
A division of BBS Publishing Corporation
386 Park Avenue South
New York, NY 10016

Galahad Books is a registered trademark of
BBS Publishing Corporation.

This edition published by arrangement with the author.

Library of Congress Catalog Card Number: 98-75458

ISBN: 1-57866-058-0

Printed in the United States of America.

CONTENTS

1001 FISHING TIPS AND TRICKS

Contents

Preface

In recent years I have appeared at sports shows and have given lectures at fishing clubs where I met many anglers who had read my books and magazine articles. Time and again these anglers mentioned the fishing tips, tricks, and rigs in my columns in the *Salt-Water Sportsman* magazine and the *Jersey Angler's News*. They told me the advice was so helpful that they cut the tips and rigs out of the magazines and pasted them into scrapbooks for future reference.

When I heard this I got the idea of putting together a book including most of these tips and adding many new ones. The book grew and grew until I had over 1,000 tips and more than 100 drawings.

The result, I believe, is a concise and practical handbook that will help both the fresh- and saltwater angler, in all parts of the country, to catch more and bigger fish in a shorter period of time then he now does. A few of the tips included in the book have been around for a long time and are still valuable even if well-known to the expert. But the majority consists of recent research and the fishing experiences of myself and other anglers which every modern angler should be familiar with. It is hoped that this book, which represents thousands of hours fishing and conversations with scores of experts, will make better fisherman of us all. The screening and selecting of the best fishing advice has been done for you in this book. All you have to do is read, remember, and use these experience-proved methods in your own fishing.

I wish to thank the following editors and publishers for permission to use material which appeared in their publications: Henry Lyman and Frank Woolner for items and illustrations which appeared in the "Tip of the Month" section of *Salt-Water Sportsman* magazine. Also Fred Walczyk and Mike Zicarelli for tips used from the "Fishing Know-How" column which appeared in their weekly publication *Jersey Angler's News*. Also Dick Wolff and Robert Stankus of The Garcia Corporation for the use of tips and drawings published in their *Garcia Fishing Annual*.

And thanks are also due to the many anglers and readers who sent in tips and ideas which were used in the publications above and in this book.

VLAD EVANOFF

CHAPTER 1

Freshwater Fishing Tackle

Rods

When fishing shallow trout streams with spinning lures use an ultra-light outfit which can cast very light lures. Because such lures do not sink as quickly as heavier ones, they can be worked in shallow water without "catching" the bottom.

A spinning rod is best for steelhead if you have to fish deep water and make long casts in big, wide rivers where wading is impossible or dangerous. A fly rod with sinking line is best on the smaller, shallower rivers where wading is possible. A weighted head is helpful when casting for distance with the fly rod.

If you do a lot of bait-fishing for trout and use streamers and bucktails, very often you'll find the longer 8½ and 9-ft. fly rod best for such fishing. It can cast baits and bulky streamers, control the fly line and baits, and manipulate the streamers better than a short rod.

Catching black bass on a fly rod is a lot more fun than the heavier spinning gear and is especially effective in shallow waters early in the morning and in the evening. Although long, 9-ft. bass fly rods are

1

usually recommended, you can use your regular shorter 8 or 8½ ft. trout rod for bass bug fishing, provided you use a weight-forward, torpedo, or bug-taper fly line which matches the rod. Also, the shorter, lighter fly rods are not suited for casting large, bulky bass bugs. If you use such fly rods, get the smaller lightly dressed bass bugs.

If you fish mostly with big surface lures in weedy or snag-infested waters, you'll get best results with a bait-casting outfit. It casts accurately, and you can work the surface lures better than with a spinning outfit. Also, the stiffer rod action and heavier line used enables you to handle and boat big fish more often.

When using large lures for big fish, use a stiffer spinning rod than you use for smaller fish. The larger hooks are tough to set in the mouth of a big bass, pike, or muskellunge.

One rule that should be followed is to use a light, limber rod with small, fine-wire hooks and a stiff rod with large, heavy-wire hooks. If you use a stiff rod with fine-wire hooks, you'll straighten out the hook on a big fish.

There is a limit to the strength of the line which should be used with a particular rod. The line should break before the rod is strained to its maximum. If the line is too strong for the rod, you can snap your tip or have the rod break at a ferrule or at the reel seat. If you have to use a strong line get a stronger, stiffer rod.

A good rod should have enough guides so that the strain is distributed evenly along the rod. Usually, high-priced rods have enough, but cheaper models may need another guide or two to make them perform better. This can be quickly determined by running a line through the guides and then bending the rod. If the line follows the contour of the rod, there are enough guides.

It's a good idea to have two rods rigged in your boat when you go fishing. One rod can have a surface lure, while the other is equipped with an underwater lure. Not only do you save time otherwise spent changing lures, but you also have a spare rod and reel in case anything goes wrong with one outfit.

Before you join your rod together, rub the male ferrule through your hair or along your nose. This will leave enough oil on the ferrule to make it easier to take apart later.

REELS

A narrow-spool bait-casting reel will cast better than one of the standard or wide-spool reels, and a lightweight spool is a must for smooth backlash-free casting.

Which is better, an open- or closed-faced spinning reel? Get the closed-faced or push-button type if you are a novice or if you do a lot of night fishing. An open-faced reel is best for all-around casting, especially with light lines, light lures, and where distance is needed.

It's surprising how many anglers fish with reels which are only partially filled with line. This is a poor policy since it cuts down your casting distance and speed of retrieve—and there's the danger that a big fish may run off the remaining line on your spool. Also, a reel that is filled with the correct amount of line casts more efficiently and smoothly.

LINES

To be ready for most trout-fishing situations which arise, you should carry a floating fly line for dry flies and nymphs or wet flies which are fished on or just below the surface. A sinking fly line should be carried to work wet flies and nymphs deep or near the bottom. Have the lines on separate fly reels or on separate spools which fit the same reel.

To find out how much backing line your fly reel will need, first wind the fly line onto your fly reel. Then tie on the backing line and wind it on. When the reel is nearly full cut off the backing line. Now wind or remove all the backing line on the fly reel onto a line drier or another reel. Untie the backing line from the fly line, and then remove the fly line from your fly reel. Attach the backing line to the fly reel spool and wind it on. Connect the fly line to the backing line and reel it onto the fly reel. This gives you the correct amount of backing line needed without guessing.

Fly lines are now made in various tapers such as level line, bug taper, torpedo, or weight-forward tapers, but for day-in and day-out and all-around use, the double-tapered fly line is best for trout fishing. This line is a must for dry fly fishing.

When bait-fishing for trout, use a fly rod—but instead of a fly line fill your reel with a 6 lb.-test monofilament line. This line offers less resistance to the currents than a thick fly line and enables you to drift your bait deeper and more naturally.

When fighting a fish on a spinning outfit, do not crank the reel handle when the fish is running. This will create line twist; instead, let the fish run, without turning the reel handle. Then when it stops, retrieve line by pumping. This is done by raising the rod tip slowly, then lowering it quickly as you reel in the slack.

You can remove a twist from your line by letting the line out behind a moving boat. To remove a set in your line fasten the end to a stationary object, let out about 60 or 70 ft. of line, and then stretch it to get rid of the set.

If you are using braided nylon or Dacron bait-casting line, take a chunk of beeswax and rub it on the first few feet of the line. This will make the line wear longer since it will fray less.

To keep the free end of a fishing line or leader material on a spool from slipping off, simply tie a rubber band to the end of the line and snap it over the spool.

LEADERS

The length of your fly leader will depend on water conditions and the stream being fished. On small streams and for short casts a 7½ ft. leader is ample; for larger streams and longer casts a 9 footer is better. When the water is clear and low you may need a 12½ ft. leader. Also, when fishing pools or smooth runs you need longer ones than when fishing rough, broken water.

Avoid touching your fly leader with your hands as much as possible because your fingers usually have oil or grease from the fly or line which transfers to the fly leader making it float instead of sink.

A floating leader can scare trout because it casts a shadow on the bottom; for most fly fishing a sunken leader is best.

A shock leader should be used on most casting outfits such as spinning, spin-casting, or bait-casting. This shock leader should be long enough to just fall short of reaching the spool of a revolving spool type reel. On a spinning reel it should be long enough so that there are several turns of it on the spool. A shock leader should be stronger than the main fishing line itself. With light lines, the leader need only be 2 or 3 lbs. stronger; with heavier lines, it could be 5 or more lbs. stronger. A shock leader prevents line abrasion, prevents many line breaks when casting lures, and gives added strength for landing or boating a fish.

The leader material for tippets on fly leaders should be on the stiff side rather than soft and limp. Such a leader will turn over much better than one tied with the soft material.

On days when the surface of a lake is calm, try a long leader when trolling for landlocked salmon or trout. This can be up to 20 or 25 ft. of monofilament line, tied to the fly line.

OTHER TACKLE

If you are changing the hooks on your lures or replacing rusty hooks with new ones, try to match the size and weight of the old ones. Those that are too big or heavy may change the action of the lure, and heavy hooks may cause a floating plug to sink.

When fishing rocky or weedy areas, rig plastic worms or eels with light wire hooks and use an 8-lb. test line on your spinning reel. Then, when you get hung up on the bottom, a steady pull will straighten out the hook and you'll save your worm. Light wire hooks can be bent back into shape and they'll still land a good-sized bass if he swallows the worm.

For use with lures or for trolling, always rig with a straight hook which will not twist or spin like an offset hook. An offset or kirbed hook is fine for baitfishing or still fishing.

Surface bass bugs and plugs should have extra sharp hooks in order to hook striking fish. Carry a hook sharpener such as a small stone or file and use it on the dull points.

An ordinary safety pin makes a neat and useful hook holder. Simply string up to a dozen hooks of one size on a pin and close it. If you use several safety pins you can keep all your hooks separated according to size, and you will always know when you are running short of a certain size.

One of the easiest ways to carry a few hooks on your person is to lay them on a length of Scotch Tape. Then cover them with an equal length of the tape. The hooks can then be carried in your pocket without catching on to your clothes or body.

For bait fishing in fast, deep rivers you often need heavy sinkers up to several ounces or more to hold bottom. To make them hold even better drive nails into the lead as shown.

Heavy lines, leaders, snaps, and swivels will often kill the action of a light, delicately balanced lure. Do not use such heavy terminal hardware unless absolutely necessary, and then use only the lightest items.

Glue a thick sheet of cork to the bottom of your tackle box. This will protect the box from wet spots, sliding, and making a noise in a boat which will frighten fish.

An old wool or heavy cotton sock makes a handy reel bag. Just slip the reel into the sock and knot the open end. The sock acts as a cushion to protect the reel from banging around in your tackle box or car trunk.

CHAPTER 2

Freshwater Lures

DRY FLIES

MOST dry fly fishing is done by allowing the fly to drift naturally with the current. However, there are times when skating a dry fly on top of a quiet pool will produce strikes. The best flies for this purpose are those with long hackles such as the spiders.

If your dry fly is carried below the surface by drag or the current, try working it back in short jerks. Many times a trout will grab a sunken dry fly if it is given some rod action.

When fly fishing at night, you can use larger flies for trout than during the daytime. There are many moths and other large insects flying around then and large flies imitate them better. They are also seen more readily by the fish than tiny flies. You can use heavier leaders with big flies since the fish cannot see them—and you'll stand a better chance of landing the lunker trout which come out to feed at night.

When using dry flies and light leaders, hold your rod high: this helps prevent the leader from breaking when a big fish strikes.

Dry flies which have caught fish get slimy and soggy and don't float well. The best trick here is to spray or dip several flies of the same pattern and size and change them when they get too wet and soggy.

Trout rising at what seems like an invisible hatch of flies may be feeding on midges. These tiny flies are best imitated by flies tied on No. 18, 20, and 22 hooks.

Wet Flies

Two or three wet flies tied on a leader will often raise and hook trout which aren't interested in a single fly. One fly should be high up on the leader so that it daps on the surface when the rod is raised high.

An effective method of using a pair of wet flies on the leader is to cast across and downstream and then let them drift naturally. After the line straightens, twitch the flies or skip them on top, but do this in one spot. This will often draw a smashing strike from a good-sized trout!

Wet flies, as the name implies, are used underwater and the best flies of this type sink as soon as they hit the surface and stay down during the drift or retrieve. To do this, the wet fly should be tied on a heavy hook and be lightly dressed.

Trout in mountain lakes can often be taken on nymphs or wet flies trolled slowly from a boat with about 50 or 60 ft. of line out. Use oars or paddles instead of an outboard motor for best results.

Nymphs in real life are usually gray, brown, or black in color, so an assortment of flies in these colors will work in most waters.

Fly Combinations

Tie a big bucktail to the end of a leader and attach a heavily dressed dry fly to a dropper about 3 ft. ahead of the bucktail. This is worked in the current so that the bucktail swims under the surface

while the dry fly floats and bounces on top. A big trout thinks that the bucktail is a small fish chasing the dry fly and will try to beat it to the dry fly or turn around to grab the streamer itself.

Because it is difficult to detect strikes when fishing with nymphs, it's a good idea to attach a high-floating dry fly on a short dropper about 5 or 6 ft. above the nymph. This dry fly acts as a float or bobber which can be watched to indicate when a trout has taken the nymph.

Streamers and Bucktails

Streamer or bucktail? Which is better to use for freshwater fish? The streamer with its feather wings has more action at slow retrieves and is a good fly for panfish, trout, and bass. It is also better to use in quiet pools and lakes. But if you want to go after pickerel or pike, you'll find these fish will take a faster moving lure, and then you can use the bucktail which lasts longer when chomped by the sharp teeth of these fish.

Bucktails and streamers used for trout are often effective when fished in fairly shallow water. They imitate minnows or small fish, so use them where such baitfish are found. The tails of pools and shallow water along the shore or banks are good spots to try.

Water conditions determine the best way to work a streamer or bucktail. If the water is clear, flat, and shallow, work the fly fast in short jerks and closer to the surface. If the water is discolored and deep, work the fly slow and deep to give the fish plenty of time to see the lure.

Most bucktails and streamers are cast with a fly rod and are allowed to drift with the current before being retrieved. But these lures can also be used on a short line in small pools or along a deep-cut bank by merely lowering them to the water and skittering or dapping the surface. This is most practical where bushes or a thick tree trunk can hide the angler from the fish.

Use big streamers and bucktails when the water is high and roily, early in the morning and in the evening or at night. Also on dark, rainy, or stormy days. Use small bucktails or streamers when the water is clear and on bright days.

In fast water, you can fish a streamer fly directly downstream by merely holding the fly in the current. By gradually letting out line and moving the rod tip from left to right you can work many spots below you.

Hold your rod low and the line taut when using streamers or bucktails. Then you don't have to take up slack line to set the hook. Most of the fish will hook themselves and there will be fewer missed strikes.

Big trout are often cannibals that feed on their own kind or big minnow or other sizable fish. They will often ignore small flies or lures. When you see such a trout chasing smaller trout or big minnows, try a big streamer. And I mean BIG! Streamers up to 4 or 5 in. long can be used to catch huge trout.

An unweighted streamer or bucktail can be fished with a spinning rod if you add a light weight some 3 or 4 ft. ahead of the lure. (See illustration p. 14.)

Marabou streamers are great lures for locating fish. They raise a lot of trout or bass which often follow or swirl at the lure but do not hit. Then you can change to another fly such as a nymph or wet fly.

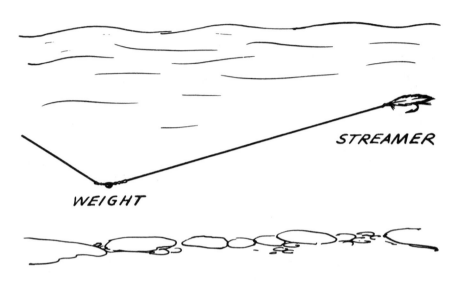

Streamer flies with big buoyant wings such as the Marabou do not sink readily, but float a while before becoming wet, or are pulled under by drag or the weight of the line. When this happens, try twitching the fly as it floats and drifts. Trout or bass will often grab it on the surface.

The fly called the Muddler Minnow is a killer for big trout. It should be fished as a dry fly, casting across and upstream. As it drifts downstream, it should be jerked lightly so that it dives under. It will rise to the surface and then the action should be repeated. The idea is to simulate a crippled minnow or disabled bug.

Bass Bugs

Although bass bug fishing is usually done with a fly rod, you can also use bass bugs with a spinning rod. You can buy weighted bass bugs made especially for use with a spinning rod. These can be cast a good distance. You can also take an ordinary fly rod bass bug and wrap some lead wire around the body or hook to provide weight for casting. These weighted bass bugs are most effective fished slowly close to shore, along lily pads and logs early in the morning and in the evening.

Trout will often take a small panfish or bass bug. Those that imitate beetles, grasshoppers, crickets, moths, or locusts are best, especially when used toward evening or at night.

PLASTIC LURES

The most effective way to use plastic worms and eels in fresh water is to reel them as slowly as possible along the bottom. This is best if the bottom is smooth. When fishing over a heavily weeded bottom or rocky bottom, a faster retrieve which keeps the worm just above the bottom is required. And on still other occasions you can just cast out and reel your worm or eel back at the normal speed used for other lures. Here an attractor like a spinner or a metal lip is often added to give the worm or eel more action and to provide casting weight.

There are two ways of hooking a fish when using plastic worms or eels. One way is to strike almost as soon as you feel a bite. This is best when using worms or eels rigged with two or more hooks or with weedless hooks. Bass are more apt to drop such worms if they feel the hardware. However, when using one small hook you can give the fish time to swallow the plastic worm before setting the hook.

At times, a plastic worm worked fairly fast on the surface with a rod whipping motion will take black bass. The worm makes a wake or ripple on top and bass hit it hard.

Take a plastic worm or eel and split the tail. This gives the lure more wriggle and draws more strikes.

Until you learn how to use a plastic worm or eel properly, it is best to add a weight about 2 ft. ahead of it. Then you can feel it hit bottom and know that the lure is down deep where it should be.

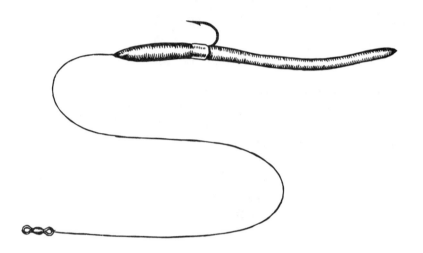

When using a plastic worm on top, it's a good idea to add a small barrel swivel about a foot above the worm. Sometimes a fish will grab the worm and get hooked, but most times when you see a swirl or feel a hit, you immediately flip open the bail and allow the bass to take line for several feet.

SPOONS AND SPINNERS

Although spoons are usually reeled fairly fast just below the surface or a few feet down, they are also effective lures for bottom scraping. Here you cast out and let the spoon sink to the bottom. Then you reel it in slowly with plenty of up-and-down rod action, making it rise, then sink and flutter back toward the bottom. Spoons worked in this manner will take big trout, bass, walleyes, lake trout, pike, and panfish.

When using spoons for steelhead, carry different sizes and weights to match the different conditions. Small, light spoons are good for shallow water, slow water, and for short casts. Larger, heavier spoons are better for deep water, fast water, and long casts.

Although spoons or spinners will occasionally take fish at night, the addition of a strip of pork rind or a plastic or rubber skirt will result in more strikes and more fish than the metal lures as they are.

Try adding a small bright-colored wet fly on the hook of the spoon by means of a tiny snap swivel. Bass, pickerel, and walleyes wil grab one or both of the lures, while panfish will go for the smaller fly.

JIGS

Jigs, as the name implies, are often jigged up and down under the boat or are given a whip with the rod tip during a retrieve. However, fish will also take jigs if they are cast out and allowed to sink to the bottom, then reeled slowly with a steady retrieve. Here you have to set the hook at the lightest tug, twitch, or movement of the line.

A good combination bait for walleyes is a jig and minnow. Simply hook a live or dead minnow through the lips with the jig and cast out and bump it along the bottom.

One of the most effective shad lures is a small jig with a fine-wire Aberdeen hook. The body is usually white or yellow with a red head. White or yellow bucktail or feathers are tied around the hook. Other good shad lures include shad flies, small spinners, and spoons.

A small jig can be worked in shallow water over a weed bed without getting hung up by attaching it below a float or cork. Measure the water depth over the weed bed; set your float a few inches less. For best results, move the jig very slowly in short jerks and pauses.

Another deadly combo lure is a weedless type jig with a plastic worm or eel added to it. This is used in deep water for big bass. It is dragged or bounced along the bottom or dropped from ledge to ledge along a rocky shore. (See top illustration, p. 19.)

VARIOUS LURES

A spinner and fly combination is most effective when fished slowly and allowed to settle at regular intervals. Reel it slowly a foot or two, then stop and let it sink, then reel again and let it sink. A light blade is best for such a retrieve.

A good lure for pickerel and bass is a bucktail or streamer fly with a short length of pork rind on the hook.

A thin-gauge spoon or similar metal lure can be bent out of shape after you catch a big fish on it. This can change or ruin the action of the spoon. Bend it back into shape with pliers and test its action alongside the boat by casting and retrieving before using it again.

It's a good idea to carry some aluminum foil in your tackle box or fly vest. You can wind a strip of foil around your leader ahead of a hook, wet fly, or streamer. The added glitter and flash will often bring more strikes than a plain bait or fly.

Cut a plastic worm in half and attach it to the hook on a spoon or spinner. The wriggling worm, if flexible, adds more action and draws strikes. (See illustration, p. 20.)

Where salmon eggs are illegal, anglers use all kinds of imitations to catch rainbow trout in the spring. They have used jelly beans, tapioca, corn, cheese, and bits of sponge. Most of these are dyed pink, orange, or red to imitate the color of natural salmon eggs.

Carry an assortment of plastic skirts in the smaller sizes for freshwater fishing. You should have some in white, yellow, red, and black. They can be added to the tail hook of a plug, spoon, or behind a spinner. Or you can attach them above a live bait such as a worm or minnow. When cast and reeled or trolled, the plastic streamers provide added action and visibility which attracts fish.

A short length of pipe cleaner about ⅝ in. long can be cut off and tied on both ends around the shank of a hook. This makes a fair imitation of a caddis larvae on which trout feed. Or try wrapping several turns of the pipe cleaner around a hook and add some hackle to the body to imitate a smaller caterpillar.

You can create your own plastic worms and eels by combining sections from them. Simply cut a worm in half or quarters, then hold the ends over a flame or burner. When they start to burn, blow the flame out and press the burnt parts together where they are to be joined. Hold until cool and they will stick together.

You can quickly make shirts for your lures by cutting ordinary balloons into long, narrow strips. They are thin and flexible and have a lively action when attached to a spoon, spinner, jig, or plug.

Experiments with black bass have shown that these fish prefer red over all other colors; yellow is their second choice. So when choosing lures, it's a good idea to have some with these colors.

A beginner in fishing is better off if he carries only 1 or 2 lures and uses them constantly until he can work them effectively. Later he can add other lures and learn how to use them. Experts, of course, should carry a wide assortment of lures and know how to use most of them.

When the surface of a lake is disturbed by strong winds and waves, underwater lures are usually best. If you use a surface lure, work it loud with plenty of commotion to attract fish.

As a rule, it is easier to work a lure in a current than in still water. The current provides a lot of movement and action. But in still water you have to work the lures yourself. Also, fish tend to strike faster and harder in the moving water than in the quiet water.

When spinners or spoons become tarnished, try painting them white, yellow, red, or black. There are times when trout, bass, and other freshwater fish prefer these colors over the nickel, chrome, or gold metallic finishes.

CHAPTER 3

Freshwater Rigs

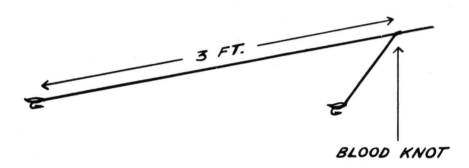

3 FT.

BLOOD KNOT

WHEN using two wet flies, the quickest way to make a dropper strand for the higher fly is to tie a blood knot. But pull out about 6 or 8 in. of the heavier leader end while tying the knot. Then attach your wet fly to the end of the dropper. The distance between the two flies should be about 3 ft.

12"   3"

One of the best methods of adding a weight to a worm rig used for trout is to tie a short 3-in. monofilament dropper about a foot above the hook. Then clamp your split-shot sinkers to this dropper. The dropper enables you to add or remove the shot without damaging

22

the leader. Also, if the sinkers get caught on rocks they will usually slip off the end of the dropper, thus freeing your leader.

BAIT

4 OR 5 SPLIT SHOT ABOUT 6 INCHES APART

To use natural baits such as stonefly nymphs, larvae, grasshoppers, salmon eggs, and worms, the rig above is a good one. It distributes the split-shot sinkers along the leader about 6 in. apart and enables the bait to drift naturally near the bottom.

A tricky way to cast a plastic worm, get it down to the bottom fast, and work it deep, is to attach it on a short leader behind a jig. The same idea works with other lures and even natural baits.

STREAMER

WET FLY

Another gimmick is to tie a streamer or bucktail on the end of your leader and a wet fly on a dropper above the streamer. This gives the impression of a minnow or small trout chasing an insect.

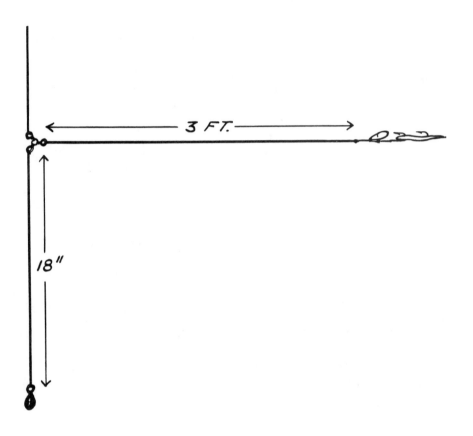

This walleye rig can be used for slow trolling down deep in rivers and lakes. A June-Bug spinner with tandem hooks and a worm or minnow is attached to the 3-ft. leader. The line from the three-way swivel to the sinker can be weaker than the leader holding the lure or the main fishing line on the reel. Then, if the sinker gets snagged, it can be broken off, saving the rest of the rig. Trolling is done very slowly by bumping and feeling bottom with the sinker to make sure that the lure is down deep enough.

Here's a steelhead rig that can be used with a wide variety of wet flies, streamers, wool yarn, salmon eggs, and other baits. The snap swivel makes it easy to change weights to match the currents and depth of the water being fished. The rig is fished, slowly raising and lowering the rod as it bumps bottom, reeling it only when the rod is being lowered. It has the advantage over a dropper-leader-sinker-rig in that it doesn't twist and tangle as often.

Make a loop using monofilament, and tie a knot so that a short length is on top and a longer leader is on the bottom. Then impale a small minnow on the short or upper leader and a larger minnow on the longer leader. This rig can be used with either live or dead minnows for trout, bass, and panfish.

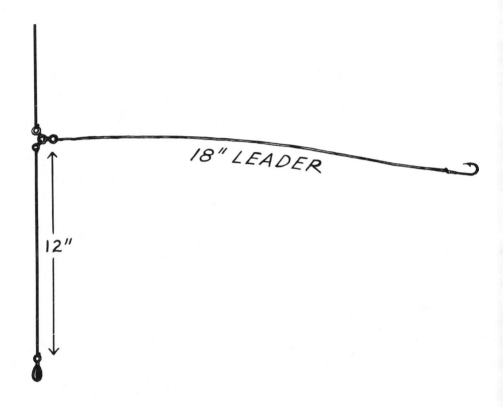

Catfish usually hug the bottom and your bait should be down there to catch these fish. Shown here is one of the best rigs to use when casting or when fishing a river with a strong current. You tie an 18 or 20 in. leader to one of the 3-way swivel and the sinker is attached about 10 or 12 in. from the other eye of the swivel. The hook is then tied to the end of the longer leader. This can be a 1/0, 2/0, or 3/0 for small catfish, and as big as 7/0 for the larger catfish.

The rig shown on top of p. 27 is good for pike and walleyes in cold weather or when they are feeding at depths of 10 to 30 ft. A 3 or 4-in. live minnow is hooked through the back, and a cork float is used to keep the minnow above weeds where it can be seen by the fish.

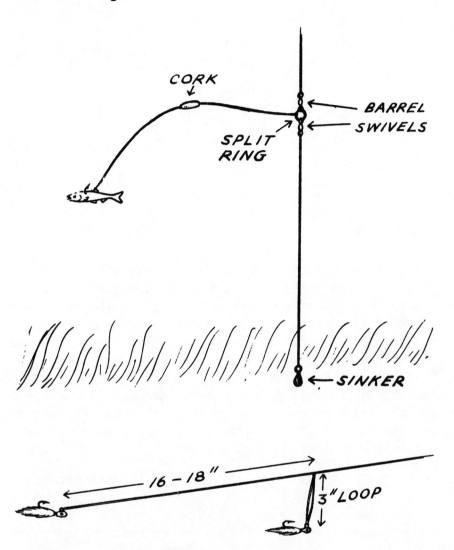

Two jigs on the end of a line often work better than one. They can be trolled slowly, or cast and bumped along the bottom. Bass, pickerel, and panfish will go for them, and you'll often hook two fish at a time.

A buoyant underwater plug such as the balsa wood and hollow plastic type can be used near the bottom with the aid of the sinker rig drawn here. Attach a 3-way swivel to the end of your line; then attach a leader anywhere from 10 to 20 in. to one eye of the swivel. Attach the plug to the end of this leader. Then attach the sinker to the remaining eye of the swivel. This rig can be cast out until you feel the sinker hit bottom. Raise the rod tip quickly to activate the plug, then drop it, allowing the sinker to settle back to the bottom. Keep repeating this at a slow pace as you reel in the slack. The buoyant plug will stay above the rocks and weeds and will foul less than a deep-running or sinking plug.

To make this rig, place a light egg sinker on your line, then tie a small barrel swivel on the end of the line. This keeps the sinker from sliding down. Then tie on a 3-ft. leader to the barrel swivel and a small No. 6 short-shank hook. Cover the hook with 2 or 3 salmon eggs.

This rig is fished in a river or lake by casting out and letting it lie on the bottom. When a fish picks up the bait let it swim off a few feet then set the hook.

When using a spinning or casting outfit for small panfish, it is difficult to cast small bass bugs or panfish bugs because they are too light. This can be solved by putting a small cork stopper or tying a small surface lure ahead of the bass bug, as shown in the drawing. Use a nylon leader about 15 in. long to tie the small bass bug or panfish bug to the lure or cork.

WEAK LINE

If you don't like to fight a fish with a sinker or trolling weight on the line when doing deep trolling, use the rig shown. The weak line will break when you set the hook and the sinker will fall off.

When a bobber or cork float is too high up on the line, it makes for difficult casting. This can be easily solved by this sliding bobber rig. You simply tie a knot on your line with a short, separate piece of cord at the spot where the bobber should stay. Then you slip a button on the leader or line, then the cork float or bobber, then a small clincher sinker, and finally tie on the hook. The cork will slide down to the sinker when you cast but will move back to the knot when at

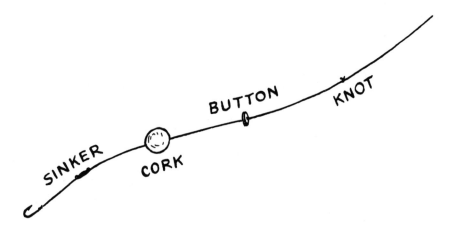

rest in the water. Make certain that the hole in the cork or bobber is big enough for the line to move through it freely.

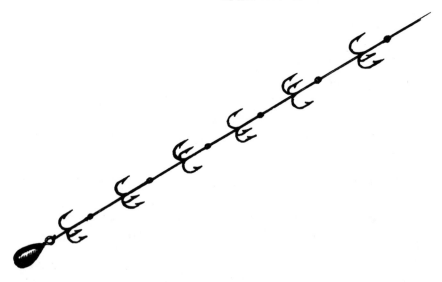

For snagging suckers, carp, or other fish which are not protected by laws, use the rig shown above. Tie up to 6 or more treble hooks about 3 in. apart above a sinker. Lower or cast the rig out and jerk it fast through a school of fish to snag them.

CHAPTER 4

Freshwater Natural Baits

WORMS

A SURPRISING number of trout anglers using worms will fish with the same worm for long periods of time even though it is almost dead. If a worm isn't lively and doesn't wriggle or is cut or torn, take it off and replace it with a fresh one.

The secret of catching trout early in the year when the season opens is to drift a worm naturally down deep right in front of a trout's nose. Because of high water and fast currents it is difficult to get a long drift. You can help by raising the rod slowly, then dropping it quickly as you feed some slack line. If the water is roily or discolored, you should work each pocket or hole slowly so that your bait will eventually drift in front of a trout.

For trout and panfishing use the smaller earthworms rather than the larger nightcrawlers. However, nightcrawlers are fine for bass, pickerel, walleyes, and catfish.

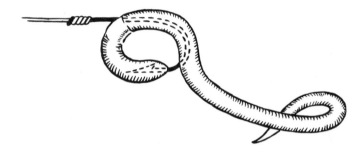

The illustration above shows a good way to hook a single worm when fishing for trout or bass in a stream or lake where there are a lot of weeds. By turning the head of the worm and pushing it onto the point and barb of the hook, you have a bait which is weedless.

A worm can be fished by wading downstream and letting it drift on a slack line into pockets, holes, and pools where trout lie. By feeding slack line, you can make the worm drift naturally for a good distance.

INSECTS

One of the commonest foods found in trout streams is the caddis larvae. These are the tiny grubs which build a case around themselves from sand, pebbles, or twigs. You can use two or three of the tiny grubs on a small hook to catch trout.

A good bait for yellow perch is a wiggler which is the larvae of the mayfly. They are found in the mud or silt along river banks. To catch them, get a fine wire screen and wash the mud through it. The wigglers will be left on the screen.

One of the top live baits for smallmouth bass in streams or rivers is the hellgrammite. This black larvae of the Dobson fly lives under stones in fast water or shallow rapids. To catch them, you hold a window screen under the rocks which are turned over. The best size for bait are those from 2 to 3 in. long. The smaller ones should be thrown back into the water. The hellgrammite should be hooked through the collar and allowed to drift through the pockets and holes where smallmouth bass are present. In the deeper pools they can be fished near the bottom. If the current is strong, you may need a sinker to get the bait down.

During the late summer and early fall grasshoppers start to reach a good size, and fish in streams, rivers, and lakes begin to feed on them. You can use an artificial fly such as a muddler or similar imitation with good results. But the natural grasshopper on a hook is hard to beat. Care should be taken in hooking the live insects so that they stay alive. Use a small, fine-wire hook and hook the 'hopper lightly behind the head. Cast it out carefully and let it kick around on the surface. If the fish aren't taking them on top, you can let the grasshopper sink.

An easy way to catch grasshoppers is to spread a blanket of fleecy wool in a field and chase the 'hoppers onto it. Their feet will get caught in the wool and you can pick them up. If you have no blanket, you can still catch them by hand if you get up early before the sun has dried the grass. Grasshoppers are frozen and stiff early in the morning and less active than later on when the sun thaws them out.

Catalpa worms which are found feeding on the leaves of catalpa trees make a fine bait for bluegills. To gather them, place a blanket or canvas under a tree and shake the branches. You can keep worms or caterpillars in a container filled with green catalpa leaves for a few days.

MINNOWS

To make a minnow livelier and more active in the water, cut part of the tail off with a pair of scissors. The minnow will have a more difficult time staying upright and this crippled action will attract gamefish fast.

When using preserved or dead minnows in fresh water, they should be given some movement. In streams or rivers, cast them upstream and let them drift and tumble in the current. In quiet pools, retrieve them slowly with a stop-and-go action.

When using live shiners for big black bass in Florida waters, hook them through the nose and troll them slowly along a shoreline or edges of lily pads or hyacinths.

An effective bait for catfish is a chub about 4 or 5 in. long. Run the hook into the minnow's mouth, then through the body, and out of the side near the tail.

If you are going after lake trout through the ice, try using several minnows on one hook. Run the hook through the eyes of the minnows.

The best place to keep live minnows for ice fishing is a spring hole or small pool just below a spring. Such springs rarely freeze even in the coldest weather. Just sink the minnow cage in the spring water and the baitfish will stay lively and healthy.

Use small minnows when ice fishing for yellow perch. These fish have small mouths and have trouble swallowing any minnow over 2

or 2½ in. long. For pickerel and walleye, of course, you can use larger minnows up to 3 or 4 in., and for pike and lake trout, even larger minnows can be used.

When using live minnows for ice fishing, best results are obtained if you get down near the bottom or just above a weed bed. Some minnows go down and stay there, but others do not. Then you should add a couple of split-shot sinkers or clincher sinkers to the leader to get them down.

Dead or preserved minnows require rod action or movement to bring strikes. One way to give a preserved minnow some flash and glitter is to add a single spinner blade in front, and reel or troll it slowly.

If you have a choice when using dead minnows for casting or trolling, get live ones and kill them just before you put them on the hook. They are a far better bait in appearance and scent than preserved minnows in jars, which may have a smell that is offensive to many fish.

A strip of meat cut from the side of a sucker can be used to catch big trout. It should be about a half-inch in width and about 4 or 5 in. long. Attach it to a hook, add a split-shot or two about 2 ft. above, and drift it into pools with the current.

Put some live minnows in a glass jar and punch some holes in the cover. Tie a line around the neck of the jar and lower it under the boat toward the bottom. The minnows will act as decoys and attract larger fish. Then you can lower a hook baited with a live minnow down next to the jar.

The saltwater killie which is often used for fluke or summer flounders also makes a good bait in fresh water for pickerel and black bass. Killies are hardy and live a long time. Hook them through both lips, and fish them over sunken weed beds, but use a cork float or bobber to prevent the killie from hiding in the weeds.

FROGS

There are two ways to hook live frogs. One is through the lips as shown in the top drawing. The second is in the leg near the crotch. There are also special frog harnesses which can be used. The main thing to watch when fishing with live frogs is to give the bass or other fish plenty of time to swallow the whole bait before trying to set the hook.

When other baits fail to interest largemouth bass, try live frogs. Almost any kind such as the leopard frog, pickerel frog, green frog, or a small bullfrog can be used. Cast the frog near the shore or a log or edges of lily pads and let it swim around naturally.

To catch frogs for bait along a lake or pond shore chase them into the water and watch where they hide in the mud or weeds. Then reach under the water and grab them quickly.

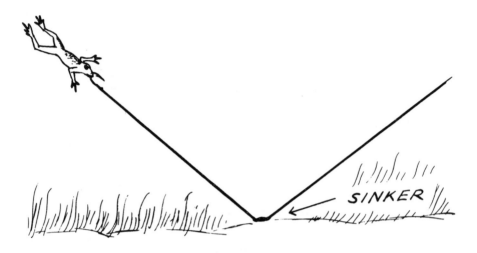

To fish a frog in a deep hole near the bottom, add a couple of split-shot or a small clincher sinker about a foot or so ahead of your hook. The frog will sink slowly to the bottom but will float and kick above the bottom where it can attract a bass.

When using a frog for bait, a dead one is often as good if not better than a live one. In fact, some anglers kill the frog and even break its back and leg bones to make it more limber. Naturally, such a frog must be fished with some rod action to make it look alive.

CRAYFISH

Crayfish make good bait for smallmouth bass and big trout. Two ways of hooking them are shown on p. 39. In the top drawing, the hook is run through the hard back carefully so as not to make too large a hole. In the lower drawing, the hook is run through the tail starting from the bottom, bringing the hook out on top.

If you use hard-shelled crayfish, break off the two big claws. This makes the bait more attractive and easier for the bass to swallow, and the crayfish is also less likely to hide under a rock or in the weeds.

Soft-shelled crayfish are used in rivers and lakes for smallmouth bass. One way to do this is to cast out the crayfish and let it sink to the bottom. Then pull some line off the reel and coil it in the bottom of a boat or on shore if that's where you are fishing. When you get a bite, let the bass take all the loose line. When the slack is gone you can set the hook.

Another effective way to use crayfish for bass is to cast out, let it sink to the bottom, then creep it very slowly back.

In certain rivers, big carp and catfish can be caught on soft-shelled crayfish as bait.

OTHER BAITS

Brook lampreys make fine bait for bass and walleyes. They are found in creeks or brooks where the bottom is a mixture of mud and sand. A coal shovel is best for digging them.

To catch leeches or bloodsuckers use a wire trap with small funnel holes. Bait the trap with liver or meat and lower it into a pool of a stream. It also helps if you stir up the bottom and make the water muddy. Leeches make good bait for trout, bass, and catfish.

Salamanders or newts often make an excellent bait for big trout or black bass. These small lizardlike creatures are found under logs, rocks, in springs, shallow brooks, and along the banks of streams. They should be hooked at the base of the tail.

A strip cut from the white belly of a fish makes a good bait. Simply cut a long, narrow, tapering strip and insert a hook at the head. It can be used with a light spinning rod or a fly rod. You can work it in many ways, fast on the surface, over or under lily pads, slow, down deep near the bottom, or at mid-depths with a stop-and-go action. Sometimes a fish will hit the strip near the head and get hooked immediately, but most of the time they grab it in the middle and you have to give the fish time to swallow it.

Ordinary white bread can be used to catch a wide variety of fish. Just knead or roll the fresh bread into a ball around a hook. Bread will catch trout, sunfish, carp, bullheads, and catfish.

A quick doughball bait for carp which requires no cooking can be made by using an equal mixture of cornmeal, oatmeal, and graham flour. Flavor this with vanilla, cinnamon, and nutmeg, add some milk and then mix into a dough.

If there are berry bushes or trees growing alongshore in waters where carp are found, try using these berries for bait. Mulberries are especially good, but carp will feed on many kinds of berries and vegetables.

Canned corn of the whole kernel type often makes a good bait for carp. Put 4 or 5 kernels on a small but strong hook. It's also a good idea to scatter a can of corn in the waters you will fish. If done a day or two ahead of time, it will attract more carp to the area.

One bait which can often be used to catch sturgeon is the "moss" or green algae found growing on rocks near shore. A large ball or chunk of this moss is placed on a big hook and used with a sinker to get it down to the bottom where the sturgeon feed.

A quick, handy catfish bait which often works is a cube of soap on the hook. Simply cut the soap into small cubes and put them on the hook.

A good substitute for salmon eggs is a yellow or orange cheese such as cheddar. Roll some of the cheese into small balls and put 2 or 3 on the hook.

Ordinary cottage cheese makes a good chum in lakes for trout and panfish. All you have to do is scatter it in the water around the boat.

You can usually find some kind of live bait at your feet. Turn over stones in shallow water for crayfish, hellgrammites, and nymphs. Turn over stones on land in damp spots to find worms. Turn over dried leaves, grass, hay, and straw to find crickets. Kick the grass alongside roads and in the fields to locate grasshoppers. Break up rotten logs and remove the bark from dead trees to find grubs.

To hold such slippery natural baits as leeches, lamprey eels, and common eels securely while putting them on a hook, dip them into a container filled with sand. Then you can get a firm grip on them since the sand sticks to their skin. But when you drop the bait into the water the sand washes off.

A loaf or two of white bread can be taken along on a fishing trip if you want to catch some minnows or to chum for panfish. To catch minnows break up a slice of bread and scatter it over an umbrella type net. When minnows gather over the net lift it quickly. To chum for panfish scatter pieces of bread near shore or around a boat. This will attract minnows, sunfish, yellow perch, crappies, bullheads, and carp. These fish will often interest a bass or pickerel in turn.

A quickly made chum for fishing can be made from a minnow, sunfish, or yellow perch by chopping or cutting these fish up into small cubes and scattering them around the boat. However, check your state laws to see if such chum is legal in the place where you fish.

Natural baits used for black bass should have plenty of life and movement. Only rarely do these fish take a dead or stationary bait. If the bait gets sluggish or dies replace it with a fresh one; if you must use dead baits give them some action with the rod.

If you are fishing with natural or live bait, make sure that it is fresh and clean. By clean, I don't mean a little dirt or sand on the bait. This will wash off quickly. But if you have handled gasoline, oil, insect repellent, or some chemical, wash your hands thoroughly before you handle any bait. Fish have a keen sense of smell and even a trace of such foreign substances will repel them.

When bait fishing, use the smallest and lightest wire hooks that are practical for the tackle you are using and the fishing you will be doing. A small, light wire hook allows the bait to live longer and to act more naturally and lively.

CHAPTER 5

Trout

Brown Trout

Big brown trout are big because they are smart and wary. They are also lazy and rarely rise to a small dry fly. They like plenty of meat and feed on minnows, crayfish, or smaller trout. So the best baits and lures for them are minnows sewn on a hook, big streamers and bucktails, spoons, spinners, and tiny plugs. During the summer months big brown trout move and feed more at night. Another good time to catch them is when a shower or rain raises the water level and discolors it a bit.

One of the most effective ways to take big brown trout on spinners and spoons is to cast upstream and retrieve slowly so that the lure hugs the bottom. The trick here is to retrieve just fast enough to give your lure action. Usually reeling just a bit faster than the current will be the right speed.

When fly fishing for big brown trout at night use large and bulky or bushy flies. The larger wet flies, streamers and bucktails are best.

The color of the fly is not as important as its general outline, shape, and size.

A brown trout that is feeding will often lie just ahead of a rock where there is a good view of any food drifting down toward him.

RAINBOW TROUT

In most large rivers emptying into a lake or reservoir, the best rainbow trout fishing for big fish takes place in the spring when the fish move up the rivers to spawn. This run usually starts soon after the ice breaks up and lasts only 3 or 4 weeks, so timing is very important.

When fishing western lakes for rainbow trout, try casting a small spoon and let it sink until it hits bottom, then lift it quickly off the bottom and reel it back slowly as deep as possible.

Rainbow trout can be taken in many lakes late in the afternoon when they rise to the surface to feed on insects. You can cast wet flies, dry flies, and streamers. Or you can troll a wet fly or streamer behind a boat. Do this slowly and jerk your rod every so often.

Rainbow trout like fast, white water and are often found in such sections of streams and rivers. But even here they usually lie behind boulders or in the slicks and glides around them.

BROOK TROUT

One of the best times to catch big brook trout, or "squaretails," in Maine and Canada is right after the ice thaws in the early spring. The big trout are then feeding on or near the surface and can be caught on cast or trolled streamers, bucktails, spinners, and spoons. One hot spot for big brookies in a lake is where a stream or brook enters the larger body of water.

Look for brook trout in a small stream under submerged logs, tree roots, log jams, undercut banks, and under waterfalls. They usually lie behind a rock, log, or other obstruction.

Occasionally brook trout will rise to a dry fly and can be taken on top. This usually happens during a hatch of insects. Most of the time, though, the brookie is an underwater feeder and the best action is obtained by using wet flies, smaller streamers, and nymphs. Natural baits such as worms, minnows, grasshoppers, and crickets are also good.

TROUT METHODS AND TECHNIQUES

Trout usually feed either on the surface or just below it, or down deep near the bottom or just above it. The middle area is usually barren of food and trout.

Big trout choose the best spot in a river or stream. If you catch the fish, another one will move into the same spot. Many such spots have produced big fish year after year.

When using tiny flies such as midges it is difficult to see them and know when to strike. Here it's a good idea to watch your line and leader near the fly. If there's a rise which appears to be in the vicinity of your fly you should set the hook.

Nymphs are deadly early in the year because they are present in most streams and form the bulk of a trout's diet. They are fished somewhat like wet flies in that they are cast across or upstream and allowed to drift naturally with the current. Then you can retrieve the sunken lure in short jerks.

NYMPH

Early in the season when trout are sluggish and on the bottom, nymphs should be fished deep and slow. In fact, you can even try letting the nymph settle to the bottom in the deeper, quieter spots of a stream. Let it lie on or near the bottom for several minutes before you retrieve it.

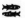

Most of the time trout will face the current which is coming from upstream. However, in the case of an eddy the current may turn and reverse and here a fish will often face downstream.

Early in the spring soon after "ice out" in lakes, big trout are often found in the shallows. Then small spoons are very effective lures. The best way to fish them is to cast and let them sink to the bottom; then work them back deep and slow so that they stay near the bottom.

Bait fishing in a lake for trout can be done by using a sliding sinker rig with a worm, dead minnow, or salmon eggs. Cast out as far as you can; when the sinker hits bottom let it lie there for a minute or two; then if there are no bites, lift the rod and slowly reel in the bait. Keep reeling it in slowly along the bottom.

If you want big trout, fish the tail ends or lower portions of pools with streamers or bucktails. Big trout will often come into such waters in the evening to chase and feed on minnows.

During the hot months of July and August, concentrate on the heads of pools and the white-water rapids where there is fast water. Trout stay in such places because it is cooler and the water contains more oxygen.

When the trout streams are low and clear, wait for a rainy day. When the rain raises the water level of the stream, start fishing. The rain cools the water and washes food into the stream. Trout will be at their feeding stations on the lookout for tidbits, and nightcrawlers, earthworms, and plastic worms will work well in a rising stream.

When there are several trout rising in a pool or run, cast to the nearest one first. Keep working on that fish until he is put down or fails to respond—then try for the next nearest fish. If you hook a trout, try to lead him away from the other fish so that his fight won't frighten them.

Even if you prefer fly fishing to using lures for trout, it is still a good idea to toss a small, hookless spoon or spinner into a stream. You'll see trout flash and rush or follow the lure. Thus, a good-sized trout will often reveal its position or hiding place, and you can go after it later with a fly.

When trout fishing on quiet, flat water, a delicate delivery is a must. Use such dry flies as the spiders, bivisibles, and variants which fall slowly and lightly on the water. A fine, long-tapered leader and the lightest double-tapered fly line you can cast with your fly rod also aids in a delicate delivery.

If you know a big trout is lying in a pocket or other spot and you are fly fishing, don't cast the fly beyond him. Instead, cast the fly to the edge of the spot just short of the fish. This way there is less chance that the fish will see the leader.

Usually on most trout streams there will be two periods when fish will rise to floating or hatching natural flies. One will occur in the morning and the other in the evening. These are the best times to use dry flies for trout.

Lakes often contain lunker trout, but they aren't the easiest places to fish for them or to locate the fish. Sometimes you'll see trout rising for flies on lakes and you can use dry flies; this usually happens in the evening when there is a hatch and when the water is calm. Most of the time, however, you have to use underwater lures. With a fly rod, try wet flies, nymphs, and streamers; fish these at various depths from top to bottom. With a spinning rod try small spinners, spoons, and underwater plugs. Natural baits such as worms, minnows, grasshoppers, and crickets fished deep near the bottom are often good for trout in lakes. One of the best times to fish is when a heavy rain discolors the streams and brooks flowing into the lake. Then, trout will often be found waiting for food being washed into the lake by these tributaries.

If you know the location of a big trout, you can sometimes tease him into striking a bucktail. First, drift the bucktail toward the fish, and when you think he sees it, pull it away as fast as you can. Do this several times until you see the fish follow the bucktail or swirl behind it. Then on the next cast, slow down your retrieve so the big trout can catch it.

Trout can often be "chummed" into feeding and rising by dropping grasshoppers, crickets, or Japanese beetles into the water so that they drift toward their resting or hiding places. Once the trout comes up and takes a few of these insects, you can cast a lure which imitates the particular bug and let it drift over the trout.

Lead head jigs are often effective for trout, especially early in the season and in deep waters. The lighter, $\frac{1}{16}$ or $\frac{1}{8}$ oz. sizes are best. Jigs can be cast across stream and bumped slowly along the bottom; you can also pause and let the jig rest on the bottom every so often.

Fast rapids with pockets contain many trout, but to take them here you have to make short, accurate casts. These pockets are often small in area and your fly has to float right through them to raise fish. Drag is a problem here, so a long leader and short cast will allow the fly to float longer drag-free than a short leader and long cast.

Trout in flat runs often move around feeding on hatching flies and do not rest or lie in one spot. Here it's best to cast your fly well above a rising fish. Such a fish is heading upstream and if you cast too close to the rise he'll move up and the fly will drift behind him instead of in front of him.

To catch trout that are down deep during the summer months in lakes or ponds, try trolling with weighted or lead-core lines. When using a lead weight or lead-core line, attach a monofilament leader no less than 10 ft. long between the line and the lure.

During the summer months, trout streams get warm and low and fishing goes into a slump. However, there is one location which remains good even during the hot months. This is a stream or river just below a reservoir where water is released every day. Such streams or rivers remain cold and trout congregate and feed there all summer long.

Big trout in a stream usually stay in the deeper, slower waters where they don't have to fight the current. They will rarely move far when resting in such places. Your best bet is to drift a bait or lure right in front of their noses. That is why wet flies, nymphs, natural baits, streamers, spoons, and spinners are better than dry flies for the lunkers.

If grasshoppers are being blown into a lake from shore on a windy day, trout may go on a feeding spree. Then grasshopper imitation flies such as Joe's Hopper, Michigan hopper or the Muddler will often take the fish.

Dry fly fishing for trout in lakes is usually best in the late afternoon and evening, especially at sunset and if the water is calm. Then there may be a hatch or insects hovering over the water and trout will be seen rising and feeding.

Many of the crystal-clear lakes in our western mountain areas contain big trout but they are shy and spooky. The secret is to get within casting distance of the fish without being seen; then your fly must be cast exactly the right distance in front of the fish. If it's too close the trout will be frightened; if it's too far the fish won't see the fly.

If you want to find out the best way to drift a fly or bait for trout in a stream, just drop a leaf, twig, or even a live insect in the current and watch the route it takes. Then drift your fly or bait over the same drift.

In the spring when trout season opens, there is no need for an early start. In fact, you'll generally do best if you wait until the afternoon to do your fishing. If the day is sunny, the water temperature will rise and trout are more apt to become active and feed then.

Even if you are thoroughly familiar with a trout stream it is still a good idea to check it in the spring before going fishing. Winter storms and floods may have shifted around the logs, gravel, sand, and rocks and changed the stream.

In rivers and streams you'll often find that trout lie in deep holes or undercut banks close to shore. The current is slower here and the water is cooler in the deeper hole.

When fishing for trout in rough, broken water you can use larger, heavier-hackled flies since they float better and are more easily seen both by the fish and the angler. But when fishing smooth, quiet water a smaller, thinly-hackled fly is better.

When trout are chasing minnows or small fry on the surface, a fast retrieve of a streamer or bucktail is effective. Stripping the line in fast and causing the fly to break the surface imitates a frantic minnow or small fish.

Good-sized trout will often lie in surprisingly shallow water along a shoreline if there is cover overhead. Look for overhanging banks, rocks, roots, and bushes where trout can conceal themselves from the bright sun and enemies.

A good general rule is to cast a long line in calm, clear water and a short line in fast, broken water.

When fishing small trout brooks or streams, do not approach too close to the banks of such waters. Trout often like to lie close to shore or under the overhanging banks or bushes and you will scare them. The best procedure is to sneak up quietly and stand a few feet from the water's edge to fish. Even better is to hide behind a tree trunk or bush while you fish.

Spoons and weighted spinners are excellent lures early in the year for trout. They cast far and sink quickly to reach sluggish trout which are hugging the bottom when the water is cold. One way of making them go even deeper is to cast slightly upstream and let them sink on a slack line. Then reel in just fast enough to stay off the bottom.

The spider dry fly is a great fish locator which often stirs up a trout to fed. Trout will sometimes rise to a spider fly but refuse to take it, merely jumping over, swirling around, or bumping it, but not really grabbing it. When this happens, change to another dry fly pattern such as an Adams, Light Cahill or Quill Gordon. Chances are good that the trout which was stirred up will take one of these.

Plastic worms are good lures to use after a shower or rain which raises the water level and washes food into the stream. In shallow water, drift the worm naturally down with the current; in deeper water and pools, retrieve it slowly along the bottom.

If your dry fly floats over a fish and he continues feeding or rising, you can make other casts and present the fly again. But if you see a trout stop feeding, hold your cast; he's suspicious and it is best to wait until he has started feeding or rising again before you cast.

When casting to a rising trout, try to place the dry fly directly in front of the fish. Trout rarely move too far to the left or right when in a feeding lane.

A trout lying under a grassy bank is usually on the lookout for insects falling into the water. Here a fly can be cast onto the shore and then dropped into the water.

Trout can often be teased into striking a fly even on a hot, bright day by using a big spider fly. The fly should be tied on extra-long hackles and on a small hook. To use it, cast it out and then "skate" it across the top of a pool by stripping in about a foot of line with your left hand and twitching the rod tip. This should be repeated until a new cast is made.

Trout found in many of our coastal streams and ponds feed on young herring. Since herring have a blue-green back and silvery sides, any lure such as a streamer, spoon, or small plug which imitates a young herring can be used in these waters.

Trout can sometimes be teased into striking in hot weather by using a small streamer fly with a couple of split shot about a foot above on the leader. Sink this streamer into a deep pool or hole and jerk it back and forth against the current. Keep this up for at least 10 or 15 min. before giving up and trying another spot.

On a big, deep trout river try trolling a tiny plug, spoon or spinner as the boat floats downstream with the current.

Fishing a worm for trout isn't always easy—there are many times when you have to study the currents, eddies, pockets, and rocks so that you can drift the worm naturally to the spot where a trout is lying. Depending on the speed of the current, you have to cast your worm anywhere from a few feet to 15 or 20 ft. upstream from the spot to be fished.

Trout in lakes often cruise around searching for food. If you find a spot where many fish move by, you can anchor the boat or stand on shore and cast to each fish. The fly should be presented well ahead of the fish in order to prevent the line or leader from scaring the fish.

Beginners in trout fishing will find that bivisible dry flies are easier to use than the regular lightly dressed dry flies. Bivisibles are easier to see, float better and higher, and can be fished in fast, broken water.

During the summer and low-water periods, try small streamers for trout. They are especially good on small streams and in clear water. They match the small "fry" or young trout and tiny minnows. Patterns tied to imitate baby brook trout, brown trout or rainbow trout are best. So are such standard patterns as the Black Nosed Dace, Gray Ghost, and Mickey Finn. These small streamers should be tied on No. 10 hooks.

Small trout are fast and quick and strike in a flash. Here you must be alert to set the hook as soon as possible. But big trout are slower in their actions and take a fly more deliberately. Here a pause of a second or two before setting the hook will hook more fish.

If you plan to try night fishing for big trout, choose the quiet nights with little or no wind. There is more insect activity on such nights and trout are more apt to be on the move feeding. Also, if you are using a fly rod, it will be easier to cast and work your lures on a quiet night than on a windy one.

Big trout will often strike small plugs, especially underwater models which imitate the minnows or small trout. The slim balsa-wood types about 2 or 2½ in. long are the kind to use.

Trout are in the usual hide-outs during the daytime, but at dusk and during the night they leave these places and can then be found cruising and ranging in the most unlikely spots.

If you are fishing small trout streams, it pays to go easy—take your time and approach or wade slowly so that you don't frighten or alert the fish; plan your casts so that each one counts; work each pool or run carefully and methodically for best results.

For fishing western waters where trout come big, carry some large, bushy, dry flies tied on No. 6, 8, or 10 hooks. They will raise and hook (and hold) big rainbow and brown trout which are not interested in small flies.

The best procedure when fishing a big river for trout is to keep on the move until you locate fish. There is a lot of water to cover so don't waste time fishing places where you don't see or raise any fish.

Look for a spot where you see fish feeding or where they rise to your fly.

For trophy trout, fish the lakes or reservoirs that contain these fish. A big river or stream is also a good bet. Most of the trout found in the smaller streams are small or medium sized.

If you are interested mainly in catching big trout, choose the dark, cloudy days over the bright, sunny ones. If you must fish on such clear, bright days, fish early in the morning or late in the afternoon and evening.

The majority of trout anglers fish the easy spots in a stream. Those where they can wade without difficulty, have plenty of room for casting, and places which can be reached or fished with no work or effort. The trouble, though, is that trout soon become wary in such spots and are scared away by constant fishing. You'll do much better in most heavily fished waters if you fish spots which are harder to reach and which most anglers avoid.

CHAPTER 6

Black Bass

LARGEMOUTH BASS

ONE of the most dependable spots for largemouth bass is a large patch of lily pads in a lake. Bass will be found here most of the year. If the lily pads extend into fairly deep water, fishing will be good even during the hot, summer months among the pads.

When you hook a big bass among lily pads, the safest procedure is to pull hard to skate the bass along the top of the pads into open water where you can fight the fish better. For this fishing, you need a stiff rod and strong line.

Largemouth bass prefer shorelines with plenty of cover. Thus you'll find them under lily pads, weeds, duck-weed, algae, logs, or stumps and brush. Often to get results you have to cast your lure right into the middle of such weeds and pads. For this, you need lures with weedless hooks.

While largemouth bass usually prefer weed beds, lily pads, and other vegetation, they will also be found around rocks and boulders in lakes where vegetation is absent or scarce. In such waters, it is best to fish the rocky points and around submerged rocks and boulders.

Most anglers using surface plugs for largemouth bass retrieve them too fast. In fact, it is safe to say that it is almost impossible to retrieve a surface lure too slowly. Cast it out and let it lie without moving. Some anglers believe that the plug should lie still for a minute or longer. But you can wait until the first ripples die, then twitch the lure; then let it lie still again; keep doing this all the way in.

When the sun is bright and high, fish the shady spots for large-mouth bass. Toss your lure under overhanging trees, along the edges, and into the pockets among lily pads and the shady sides of stumps and rocks.

During the summer months, you can often find largemouth bass under duckwort also called duckweed, duck-wart, and scum. These tiny plants form a carpet which provides shade for the bass and they lie under the patches. Use a pork frog or chunk with a weedless hook to fish the duckwort, since such a lure slides over the top of the growth without getting fouled.

Not all the big bass are on the surface or in shallow water at night. Many are caught in our southern reservoirs and lakes in deep water up to 30 ft. deep. A jig and eel, or plastic worm combination is a top lure for such fishing.

When casting a surface plug or bass bug, try to drop it on a rock, log, or lily pad; then after a short wait pull it into the water. Bass usually lie waiting under such spots for any insect or small creature to fall into the water.

Bass bugs used with fly rods are most effective on the smaller, shallow lakes. Here you get best results by fishing the shoreline in water from about a foot to 3 or 4 ft. deep.

When bass are feeding on dragonflies or damselflies, imitations of these will often take bass even in midday when these insects are numerous. Cast them on lily pads, and let them rest on the edge until a fish rises for it. Try casting the fly over a branch or bush so that it dangles in mid-air a few inches above the water.

SMALLMOUTH BASS

Smallmouth bass in rivers spend most of their time in the deeper eddies. However, when feeding they move up to the head of the eddy where the rapids or riffles enter it. They will also move into the shallow rapids themselves when on the prowl for food. Look for them along the sides or below sunken or exposed rocks or boulders. Rocky ledges alongshore which have underwater caverns are hot spots for river bass. Another good spot is the tail of an eddy where the still water begins to speed up. These shallow waters are especially good for evening fishing.

Smallmouth bass fishing in northern waters is usually fastest during the spawning period if the season is open then. June is a good month. Then the bass are over the shallow gravel or sand bottoms and will usually strike surface plugs, bugs and shallow running plugs, spinners, and spoons.

In our northern lakes in Maine and Canada cold weather will often drive smallmouth bass away from shallow water and the shoreline. Then, trolling deep near the bottom will bring better results and so will bait-fishing with minnows, frogs, or crayfish.

When looking for smallmouth bass in a lake, look for rock bars, reefs, shoals, and boulders in deeper water, especially if they have the type of bottom which attracts crayfish or minnows.

When smallmouth bass are feeding underwater, try a floating bass bug imitating a small frog. Use it on a sinking-type fly line and jerk it slowly to imitate the swimming motions of a frog.

Smallmouth bass will sometimes bite in water that is discolored. Best baits are minnows or nightcrawlers drifted slowly along the bottom. The bass can't see a lure or bait any distance in muddy water, but will strike a lure or bait that comes close to them. Lures that give off vibrations are good at this time. Muddy water fishing also requires a knowledge of where bass hang out and a slow, methodical pace of fishing.

Smallmouth bass feed on insects a lot, and fly-rod lures such as bass bugs imitating grashoppers, crickets, beetles, and moths are deadly, especially when fished in the late afternoon and at dusk.

Trout-size streamers or bucktails rarely take big bass. If you want to catch big bass, use large streamers or bucktails. They are especially effective during roily water and at dusk or night.

Look for big smallmouth bass in a river near the main currents and in the deeper, rockier water.

When damsel flies are hatching on a smallmouth bass river, these fish often go on a feeding spree. Then a large No. 8 dry fly will often take them. Wait until you see a bass rise—then cast the fly just above him.

One way to locate smallmouth bass in a big river is to sit quietly toward evening and watch for feeding fish. You'll often see the bass rising to floating insects or chasing minnows. Then you can cast to the fish.

Smallmouth bass often come into shallow water to feed at night. Here you'll find them along the outer edges of bullrushes, weedbeds or over rocky gravel bars and reefs in water from 2 to 6 ft. deep.

A good place to find smallmouth bass in a river is at the head of a pool where there are bubbles or froth created by falls or rapids above.

Pools and deep water below rapids and waterfalls are good hangouts for smallmouth bass, especially during hot weather. The water is cooler here and the fast-moving current brings food into the pool. A quick-sinking lure such as a weighted spinner, spoon, or jig should be used here and cast upstream and allowed to sink to the bottom before being retrieved slowly, so that it stays deep.

When smallmouth bass are lying deep in a lake during the hot summer months, you have to work your lure right past their noses to interest them. Such fish are lethargic, not feeding, and won't move for a lure or bait; but if it is reeled close enough or dangled in front of them, they may make a swipe at it.

When using surface bass bugs for smallmouth bass, work them more quietly than you do for largemouth bass. Let them lie still, then twitch them or work the rod tip or line so that the bugs quiver in the water like a struggling insect.

If smallmouth bass are actually chasing minnows in the shallows (which is indicated by frantic minnows leaping or skipping out of the water), use a tiny surface plug such as a popper or darter.

When fishing in a lake or river, look for rocky bottoms where crayfish are abundant. This is a favorite food of the smallmouth bass. A softshell crayfish in such areas is deadly. If you can't get soft-shelled crayfish, use the smaller hardshelled ones.

Smallmouth bass will often take a nightcrawler or several smaller worms if they are cast out and allowed to sink to the bottom where they can lie and squirm.

On the larger, northern lakes look for smallmouth bass in the shallow bays, coves, shores, and around islands where there are rocks.

When fishing a river for smallmouth bass, it's a good idea to troll upstream, then drift downstream and cast. Of course, if you see a promising spot you can hold or anchor the boat; or you can beach the boat and fish from shore.

After a shower or rain which muddies a stream or river entering into a lake, try to fish the edge of the muddy water, casting into the clear water alongside. Bass will often be cruising here, looking for food washed into the lake by the rising river or stream.

MORE BASS TIPS

A good general rule to follow when bass fishing is to use lures with bright and shiny finishes early in the morning, in the evening, and when the water is discolored. On bright days and in clear water, use lures with dull-colored or natural scale finishes.

One deadly way to use a jig for bass is to cast out and let the lure go down to the bottom; then reel in and lower your rod tip almost to the water. Now yank hard and raise your rod over your head, then quickly lower it so that the jig settles on the bottom again. Keep on doing this as you slowly retrieve line. This up-and-down fluttering of the jig attracts fish which usually strike and get hooked when you raise your rod.

One trick used to hook more bass with a plastic worm or eel is to let the fish run freely with the lure, but to twitch it very lightly ever so often. This makes the bass believe that the fake worm or eel is alive and he's less inclined to drop it than when the lure is lifeless.

During the hot summer months if fishing is slow, keep an eye out for a cold front or radical weather change. If it becomes cloudy and rainy, it usually cools the water and fish start feeding actively.

If you are fishing at night for bass, work your lures much slower than you do in the daytime. Bass do not see as far then and may also lose the lure if it goes by too fast. When using surface bugs or plugs, let them rest at least 2 or 3 min. after the cast, then retrieve them with plenty of stops.

Early in the season in April and May, black bass are still sluggish and are best caught on deep-running or sinking lures or bait. From about June 1st to the middle of September they become more active and can be caught on surface lures. Then during October and November they again head for the deeper water where underwater lures and bait can be used once again.

In the summer, bass spend most of their time in the deeper holes
or resting places. They leave these deeper waters and move along
specified migration routes into shallow water to feed. This usually
occurs at dusk, during the night, and early in the morning. Your
best bet is to locate a hole or resting place during the day and fish
it with spoons, deep-running or sinking plugs, rubber or plastic
worms, jigs, or natural baits.

Sometimes a bass will strike a plastic worm or eel hard and then
you can set the hook quickly. But most of the time the bass will
grab part of the bait and hold on. Then the best thing to do is lower
the rod tip and give the fish plenty of slack line; then wait until the
fish starts to move away and the line becomes taut before trying
to set the hook.

When you catch a big bass from a deep, underwater spot, play
him carefully to avoid frightening other bass which may be present.
Usually you can catch more big bass from the same spot. Then you
can come back a few days later and catch other bass which replaced
those that have been caught.

If you are using a sinking lure in deep water for bass, you can give
it some lively action by working your rod tip up and down as the lure
slowly sinks. Many big bass will watch the agitated lure sink and
then pick it up as it settles on the bottom. If you feel the line
tighten, or the lure feels like it's caught on the bottom, strike hard
to set the hook. It could be a lunker bass with the lure in its mouth!

Once the fish are located, or the spot being fished is known to
contain bass, then the secret of taking them with artificial lures lies
in the correct "manipulation" of the lure. Each lure has its own
special action and works best at a certain speed of retrieve, depth,
and rod action. The best freshwater anglers usually carry a big tackle

box filled with dozens of lures. But usually they stick to one or two favorites which catch most of the bass. These are the lures in which they have the most confidence and which they have used so often that they can make them look alive.

Fly-rod bass bugs usually raise and catch more black bass than other lures, but these fish will run smaller than those caught on plugs.

One reason why many anglers fail to catch more bass is because they avoid fishing around rocks, weeds, sunken trees, logs, and snags where they get hung up often and lose lures. These are actually top bass hangouts and if you want to catch them you have to accept the fact that you'll hang up often and lose a lure from time to time.

A surface lure landing close to a bass may scare the fish away. If this happens, let the lure lie still for a while. The bass will usually return and watch the lure. Then you can twitch it and make it look crippled. If you succeed in making your lure look like an easy meal, the bass may forget his earlier fright and come up and grab the lure.

When bass are chasing gizzard shad or other minnows on the larger reservoirs or man-made lakes, look for the smaller bass on top and the larger ones down below. To get the bigger ones, cast a spoon and let it sink deep before starting the retrieve.

Black bass soon become familiar or conditioned to certain lures which are used often by many anglers in a specific lake. Then something unusual or unfamiliar in the way of lures may draw a strike. No matter how crazy a lure looks, don't rule it out. Give it a fair trial on different days and under varying conditions.

During the hot weather, head for your favorite lake or river before dawn. Bass often start feeding around daybreak, since the water has cooled in the shallows during the night.

When night fishing for bass, pick the quiet nights over the rough, windy nights. At night you can't see where you're casting and must depend on hearing to know where your lure lands. On quiet nights you can often hear fish breaking or feeding. And last but not least, a calm lake is safer to fish at night than a choppy one.

Most of the big bass caught in the deeper lakes and reservoirs are taken on underwater lures. Small bass often rise to surface lures, but the big boys prefer the depths. Such lures as jigs, plastic eels or worms, and deep-running or sinking plugs, together with spoons and spinners, account for the majority of the big bass caught in these waters.

To catch big bass, choose the lures which work well at slow speeds. Big bass are lazy and don't move far or fast like the younger ones do. So lures that barely crawl or wriggle at a slow retrieve are the best ones to use.

When fishing deep for bass early in the year, late in the year, or when the water is cold, you have to be alert to feel a strike since the fish are sluggish and pick up a lure lightly. Set the hook at the slightest indication of a pick-up.

The real secret in using a surface lure or bug for bass is to fish it as slowly and thoroughly as possible. Cover a small section of shoreline foot by foot, rather than haphazard casts along a long shoreline.

One plug and retrieve which drives bass crazy and makes them hit furiously is the deep-running plug with big lip which bumps bottom. Use this in a moderate depth so that the plug reaches bottom when cast and retrieved or trolled. The plug should bump bottom and kick up sand, gravel, or mud.

The balsa-wood and light plastic plugs of the natural minnow type can be twitched and worked slowly on the surface, then retrieved a bit faster just below the surface. Bass are often attracted by the surface ripple, but don't hit the plug until it is moving below the surface.

When fishing for bass, try wading instead of casting from a boat. This way you can usually approach the fish without frightening them. Also, you will cover the water more thoroughly than from a boat.

If you want to catch big bass on many of our larger reservoirs and impoundments in the South, fish at night and concentrate your efforts in the deeper water from 10 to 40 ft. deep. Rocky points which run underwater for quite a distance are especially productive spots to try.

When trolling for bass, keep feeding or taking in line, depending on the depth. The lure should occasionally bump bottom or run through the tops of the weeds in order to interest the fish and draw strikes. If you don't hang up every so often or feel the lure bump bottom, you are not fishing where you should.

One way to wake up and excite lethargic bass into striking is by tying a rock or other weight to a rope long enough to reach bottom. Then you troll slowly dragging the rock on the bottom at the same time letting a lure out behind it. The bass will be attracted to the area by the disturbance and seeing the lure in back will often attack it with a vengeance.

On a large lake or river, the angler who moves around often catches more bass than the guy who anchors in one spot and sits there all day. Bass tend to gather in certain areas. If you know the location of several such areas, try to spend some time fishing each one. Some of the best bass anglers make only a few casts in one spot and if they get no strikes, they move quickly to the next spot. Sooner or later, if they know enough spots they will find one where the fish are hitting.

CHAPTER 7

Muskellunge, Pike, Pickerel, and Walleyes

MUSKELLUNGE

To LOCATE good muskie spots in a lake or river, look for points of land, or islands which extend into the water. If there's an underwater bar running out that is covered by weeds, chances are good that muskies will feed here.

If there's a wind or current, a good way to cast for muskies is from a drifting boat. This is quiet and doesn't scare the fish. You also cover more territory then when fishing from an anchored boat.

A top muskie spot is a deep channel between islands or between the islands and the main shore.

Muskies are more likely to be in shallow water on windy, overcast days and in the evening or during the night.

A limber rod is not much use for pike or muskie fishing. These fish have tough, bony mouths and jaws and you can't strike hard enough with a soft, limber rod to set the big hooks found on most muskie or pike lures. A stiffer rod will do a better job of setting the hook; it will also cast the heavier lures much better than a soft rod.

You'll catch more muskellunge if you retrieve your lure at a fairly fast pace. This goes for both surface and underwater lures. These fish will also strike slow moving lures, but they have more time to examine and look over the lures at the slower speeds. They'll follow it, but not take; a fast moving lure, on the other hand, is less readily examined at close range and stands a better chance of being hit by a muskie.

When choosing lures for big muskies, pick the larger spoons, plugs, and spinners. Spoons and plugs up to 7 or 8 in. will attract big muskies, when the smaller lures won't interest them. These lures also have larger, stronger hooks which are more apt to stand up than the smaller, weaker hooks found on the average bass plug.

A bullhead often makes a good bait for big muskies. You can use them up to a foot long and hook them in the back. They live a long time, but it is best to use a large float to keep the bullhead just off the bottom so that it won't hide or rest.

Muskies can be taken in water up to 20 or 25 ft. deep, but there will be more fish of various sizes in shallower spots such as reefs, weed beds, and coves.

A dead sucker will catch muskies if it is given plenty of action. Cast it out and work it back with a pumping action which causes the sucker to skip and dart on the surface. When a muskie grabs the bait, let him take it and give plenty of slack line and time to swallow it.

If you want to land big muskies, use a long, 3 ft. wire leader when trolling. Muskies have sharp teeth and gill covers. They also roll and thrash, and their long bodies can break a line. For casting, a shorter 18 or 20 in. wire leader is needed.

Probably the best chance of catching a muskie is to take plenty of hours off to fish, day after day. One or two day trips are usually a waste of time unless you are lucky to hit right. If you do take a short fishing trip, hire a guide. Best bet is to take 2 or 3 weeks off and spend the entire time just fishing for muskies.

PIKE

Look for pike in coves with grass, along edges of lily pads, and shores filled with stumps, logs, driftwood, and fallen trees.

The top lure for pike is a medium-sized spoon, preferably in a red-and-white finish. For big pike, cast out the spoon and let it sink almost to the bottom before you start to retrieve.

Where pike are numerous and strike often, it's a good idea to re-place the treble hook on your spoon with a single hook. You'll save time and effort required for removing the treble hook from the pike's jaws.

A prime spot for pike is a sudden drop-off from a shallow weed bed. Pike like to lie along the edge of the shallows waiting for smaller fish to venture out from the protection of the weeds.

When pike follow a lure but do not strike, try giving it even more rod action and speeding up the retrieve. This often results in a smashing strike.

Pike will often hit a surface plug if it creates a lot of commotion on top. When you cast, let the plug hit the water, then jerk it hard so that it makes a big splash. Then reel it fast to leave a big wake. Let it rest a few seconds, then repeat the fast retrieve right up to the boat.

Pike often gather at a stream or river mouth emptying into a lake. Here they feed on minnows or small fish going up and down the river or stream.

Fishing for pike in northern waters is usually best from about 9 A. M. to late afternoon. It is especially good in the late spring or early summer right after the pike have finished spawning.

In rivers, look for pike in the deep, still pools, eddies, backwaters, quiet coves, and shorelines with cover, such as weeds and overhanging branches.

Float fishing, which is usually done for smallmouth bass or trout, is also a good method for pike on the larger rivers. Here you drift with the current and cast into the deeper pools, backwater coves, and eddies.

When trolling for pike near shore in shallow water, you'll get more strikes and more fish if you use a long line up to 100 ft. or more.

A good way to retrieve a lure in a river for pike is to cast downstream and retrieve it against the current, straight upstream.

Occasionally a big pike will be taken in shallow water, but generally the fish found in a foot or two of water will be the small pike. For big pike, try depths from 6 to 20 ft. over weed beds, and along sand and rock bars and reefs.

Pike will take a spoon that is sinking and fluttering toward the bottom. No rod action is needed—merely raise the rod slowly when the spoon nears the weeds or bottom and let the lure flutter and sink again.

Big bass bugs, especially those made from hair, are effective lures for pike. They should be much bigger in size than the regular bass bugs and have larger, stronger hooks.

PICKEREL

Pickerel are easier to catch than black bass and can provide a lot of fun and sport. To get the most out of these fish, use a light or ultra-light spinning outfit. A fly rod is also good. Pickerel will hit small plugs, bass bugs, spoons, and spinners. Fly rodders can use streamers and bucktails. Cane pole or still fishermen can use live minnows.

Pickerel will often strike at a surface lure, such as a small popper, crippled minnow, swimmer or crawler, which makes a commotion on top. A lot of fun can be had with a fly rod and a bass bug. You can often see the pickerel streak just under the surface toward the lure.

Big pickerel feed in the shallows most often during the spring and fall months. During the summer, they go into the deeper water during the middle of the day, but come into the shallows early in the morning and toward evening.

Pickerel are very active during the fall months and will hit small surface and underwater plugs, spinners, and spoons. And live minnows are always a dependable bait. Look for pickerel over submerged weed beds, in coves, along the edges of lily pads, and around logs and tree stumps close to shore. In rivers, they are found in the deeper pools, eddies, and slower-moving sections.

Skittering is a time-honored method of catching pickerel which still works. Here you use a long cane or glass pole about 18 or 20 ft. long and attach an almost equal length of line. For bait you can use a frog, minnow, strip or pork rind, or a strip cut from the belly of a yellow perch or pickerel. Such baits are flipped out and then worked across the surface in short, frantic spurts. Best results are obtained among lily pads, weed beds, and around stumps and logs.

WALLEYES

As a general rule, you'll find most walleyes over sandy, rocky, or gravel bottoms. However, these fish are usually in schools which move around a lot. So the best procedure is to become familiar with several good walleye spots and try as many as possible to locate the fish.

In rivers, look for walleyes below dams, rapids, and alongside eddies; they also frequent the deep water along undercut banks and deeper pools.

KEEL
SINKER

A good walleye rig to use with a shallow running, floating plug is made by using a short, wire leader about 8 in. long. Attach the plug to this leader and a keel-type sinker to the other end, then the line. The sinker should be heavy enough to sink the lure and bump bottom in the current of a river. Then station yourself above a hole where walleyes are found and drift the lure back, bouncing bottom. By letting out line and shifting locations, the entire hole can be covered. (See illustration, p. 75.)

When walleyes come into shallow water toward evening, at night, or on cloudy days, a live minnow makes a good bait. You can hook a minnow through both lips, add a couple of split shot sinkers to the leader, and cast it out. Let the minnow sink to the bottom. Instead of just letting it lie there, reel it in slowly with short pauses; if a fish picks up the minnow let him run with it until he stops. When he starts off once more, set the hook.

Walleye fishing in streams and rivers is usually best during the spawning runs in the spring. These may start as early as February in southern states or as late as May in our northern areas.

Walleyes in lakes will be found feeding on gravel and sand bars, over rocky reefs and ledges. They will come into shallow water near shore early in the morning or evening during the spring and fall. Look for schools of minnows in the spots mentioned above, since walleyes feed mostly on these small fish.

Walleyes are great night feeders and can be caught at this time, often in shallow water near shore. Use live minnows or cast an underwater plug, and reel slowly. For trolling, a June-Bug spinner with a minnow, lamprey eel, or nightcrawler is a good combination.

A good way to get down to the bottom with a lure where walleyes are is to use a lead-core line. Add a monofilament leader of about

3 or 4 ft. and put your plug, spinner, or spoon on the end. Let out the line until you feel the lure bump bottom. Troll slowly for the walleyes.

You can catch walleyes on jigs if they are worked slow and deep. The best method is to cast and wait until the line goes slack, indicating the lure has hit bottom; then raise your rod tip. Reel in the slack as you drop the rod tip so that the jig hits bottom again; then raise it again. Keep doing this all the way in.

Walleyes often have the habit of following a lure and nipping at the trailing pork rind, plastic worm, or eel. So it's a good idea to add a "tail" hook to the rind or plastic lure which will hook these short strikers.

CHAPTER 8

Panfish

BLUEGILLS AND SUNFISH

BLUEGILLS can be caught the year-round in most waters and in most states the season is always open on them. They'll bite in the spring, summer, fall, and even through the ice in winter. Best fishing, however, is usually around spawning time in the late spring and again in the early fall.

Bream or bluegills go for small panfish bugs or rubber-legged spiders fished with a fly rod on top. They should be worked very slowly with short twitches. Too much action or disturbance will frighten the sunfish rather than attract them.

In some lakes during the hot summer months, bluegills go into deep water and can be caught in depths up to 20 or 30 ft. However, they will come into shallow water early in the morning and again in the evening.

Bluegills tend to stay in small schools or groups but do not wander too far or too wide. They have a limited range and move back and forth over it. They tend to stay in weedy areas most of the time, but some fish prefer shady spots such as docks, piers, overhanging trees, and big rocks or boulders.

Bluegills will hit a dry fly if it is allowed to remain motionless for a while, then moved very slightly and slowly. Such gentle twitches should be made during the entire retrieve.

A good winter bait for bluegills for ice fishing is the small, white grub found in the stem of goldenrod plants. Look for the swellings along the stem and break them open to get at the grubs. If you want to keep the bait for future use, store the stems in a cool place.

PLASTIC FLOAT   PANFISH BUG

One of the most effective combinations for bluegills in ponds or lakes is a plastic bubble-float or a small popping plug with a short 12 or 14 in. leader tied behind it. To the end of the leader attach a small panfish bug or bushy dry fly. Cast this toward shore or some lily pads and work it back slowly with alternate twitches of rod tip and rests in-between.

In southern swampy waters, if you see any floating moss islands cast your bait or lure up to the edge and let it sink. Sunfish and warmouth and even bass like to hang around under such floating islands.

Big bluegills will often hit small surface plugs, underwater plugs, spoons, spinners, and jigs. The lures can be made even more effective for these fish by adding a small worm to the tail hook.

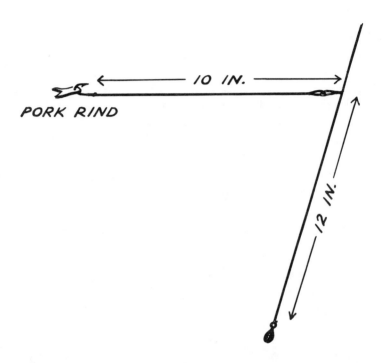

A good rig to use for drifting for bluegills in deep water (from 8 to 20 ft. deep) in hot weather is shown above. It can also be cast out and retrieved slowly. Use a tiny piece of pork rind and a small No. 6 hook to hold it.

YELLOW PERCH

Yellow perch feed on the surface only rarely when certain hatches of insects appear or insects are blown onto the water in great numbers. Most of the time you'll do best if you work your lures or baits below the surface.

One of the most effective lures for yellow perch is a small spinner. For best results, it should have a fly or small strip of pork rind or a worm on the hook.

To catch big yellow perch during the summer months, fish the deeper water anywhere from 20 to 50 ft. deep. Most of the perch found in shallow water at this time will be the smaller "runts."

When ice fishing for yellow perch, try using the eyes of the first perch you catch to take other perch.

Yellow perch are usually the most active panfish during the winter months. They move around in schools to favored spots such as sunken weed beds, stream mouths, bars, coves, and channels. Ice fishing for them is usually sporadic with waits in between.

When fishing through the ice, it's a good idea to stick it out until dark. Yellow perch and walleyes often become active toward evening, and if a big school moves in, you can have fast action.

WHITE PERCH

White perch are often found in brackish water where a river flows into the ocean or bay or where a brook merges with salt water. Here they'll take seaworms, grass shrimp, pieces of clam, and small spearing or killifish.

When white perch come closer to shore in the evening to feed on insects or minnows, they can be readily caught at this time. In fact, these fish will often bite well at night too. Good baits are earthworms and tiny minnows.

You can easily locate white perch in a lake by watching for dimples caused by surface feeding fish; this usually occurs at dusk.

At times, white perch will take artificial lures, such as wet flies, tiny streamers, spinners, and spinner-and-worm combinations. Small spoons in silver finish are very good also.

CRAPPIES

In the spring, crappies will move inshore into shallow water to feed on warm, calm, sunny days. But if the weather turns cold and windy, they will move out to deeper water.

Crappies hang around weed beds, under lily pads and hyacinths, around sunken brush and trees; often they will be confined to a very small area. If you learn the location of several such spots, you can try them until you locate one where the crappies are present and biting.

Crappies usually take a live bait, such as a minnow, lightly, and a bite is often undetected by the angler. It pays to be alert and to strike at the proper moment so that the crappie is hooked before he steals the bait.

Trolling for crappies is an effective way to catch them. Top bait is a small minnow trolled behind a spinner as slowly as possible—just fast enough to keep the spinner blade revolving.

Actually, you can't work a lure too slowly for crappie. When using a fly, tiny streamer, jig, or spinner, work them as slowly as possible, and twitch the rod a bare inch or two to give it slight action.

Crappies move into shallow water near shore to spawn. This movement often begins early in the spring in March, and they stay in shallow water until May. They hug the shoreline, flooded coves, and weed beds. A good trick here is to anchor right near shore and cast your lure so it travels parallel to the shoreline.

In the summer, look for crappies in shady spots. Docks, piers, houseboats, and rafts are good locations, especially if they are in fairly deep water.

Minnows—tiny ones—are one of the best baits for crappies. The rig drawn here offers a quick way to get 2 minnows down to the level where crappies are feeding.

Crappies will go for cut bait, such as small chunks or strips cut from a sunfish, yellow perch, or crappie itself. Fish these baits about 4 or 5 ft. under a light float or bobber, and give the bait an occasional jerk; then let it settle back.

To create your own crappie hangouts, sink an anchor some dead trees, branches, or brush in a lake containing these fish. The best depth for sinking these shelters is from 8 to 20 ft. deep. Anchor them with a heavy rock so that they stay in place.

You'll find crappie fishing best when the water is calm or slightly rippled. When it is windy and there are big waves, try to find a quiet cove or a protected place where you can fish.

Where legal, a bright light hung over the side of a boat or dock will attract insects in the air and minnows in the water. This in turn will often attract crappies, which can then be caught.

White Bass

White bass often chase minnows on the surface and create a disturbance which is easily spotted. They usually show best early in the morning and again late in the afternoon and evening. At such times, a small plug, spinner, spoon, or jig will take them.

When the white bass do show on top, they are spooky and a boat will put them down. The best procedure is to approach the school and cut your motor some distance away; then cast toward the fish.

Even when white bass are showing on top, you can still fish deep. Use a small jig and cast out, letting it sink toward the bottom. Then retrieve it close to the bottom in short jerks. Most of the bigger white bass will be found down deep and not near the surface.

You can catch white bass on or near the bottom during the winter and early spring. They are sluggish at this time, but if you cast a small spoon or jig, let it sink to the bottom, then reel in and jig it so that it bumps bottom on the way in.

White bass are great night feeders—especially under a light. This is a popular way to fill a stringer with them during the summer months. Bring along a lantern or lamp, and rig it so that it shines into the water from the end of a pier or a boat. Use a small minnow for bait, and lower it under the light.

OTHER PANFISH TIPS

Most panfish have small mouths and tend to follow and nip at the end of a lure. That is why the smallest lures are best for these fish, and the hook or hooks should be as near the end of the lure as possible.

Rock bass got their name from the fact that they hang around rocks and that's where you can locate them. They also stay under overhanging trees, bushes, banks, rock ledges, and logs—almost anywhere they can find some cover and shade.

Carry some white bread, crackers, oatmeal, or boiled rice with you when you go panfishing. Scatter this around the boat, and soon you will see a gathering of minnows, sunfish, yellow perch, or other panfish around this chum.

Where lily pads or hyacinths are thick, your best bet for catching bream or sunfish, crappies or pickerel, is with a long cane or glass pole. By reaching out from a boat, you can lower the bait into the openings between the growth.

CHAPTER 9

Other Freshwater Fishes

STEELHEAD

STEELHEAD runs in particular rivers, depending on the time of year, the weather, and water conditions. To find out if the fish are running, read the local rod-and-gun columns in newspapers, and drive up and down the steelhead rivers to see if anglers are catching fish. Local fishing tackle stores are also good sources of the latest information.

Steelhead often move fast in a river on their way upstream, and a stretch which is productive one day may be barren the next. That is why it's a smart idea to locate several spots in a river and hit as many as possible in one day. Of course, once you locate a productive spot or stretch, you can work it as long as there is action.

The steelhead are apt to strike at any time of day, but generally the best fishing takes place on cloudy days, and early in the morning and evening.

Dry fly fishing for steelhead is most effective in the faster or moderate stretches and shallow sections of a river.

A steelhead rarely smashes a bait such as salmon eggs, but takes it quietly, and the angler barely feels the bite. Therefore, if your bait stops drifting, or your line tightens, immediately set the hook. It may be .hung up, but then again, it could be a fish.

When drifting a bait, such as a nightcrawler, for steelies, let the bait move freely; but when it comes to the end of a drift, let it stay or hang there for a minute or two before reeling in. Steelhead will often follow a bait and watch it for quite a while before deciding to grab it.

You can sometimes tease a steelhead into striking a dry fly by skipping it upstream against the current. To do this, you stand at the head of a fast run and make a cast across the current. When the fly has drifted directly below you, bring it in slowly so that it skips on top of the water. Then you can let it drift back and repeat the skipping technique.

To catch steelhead on flies during the winter months, use weighted flies and sinking fly lines that get down to the bottom where the fish lie. Flies used for winter fishing should be larger and bulkier than those used during the summer. Fluorescent red, orange, and yellow flies are especially effective if the water is discolored.

Steelhead like to lie and rest in the slower sections of a river, especially during the fall, winter, and spring months. During the summer months, however, when the water warms, they'll move into the faster water which contains more oxygen.

One way to catch steelhead on a large, deep river is to hold a boat in the current by rowing and letting out about 100 ft. of line with a spoon on the end. The current will work the lure, and by rowing from one side of the river to the other you can cover the entire pool.

Summer steelhead will hit a wet fly if it is cast across and slightly upstream. A weighted fly and sinking line is best in a fast, deep current. Let the fly and line sink, then hold it so that it swings and the line and leader straighten out. This is the moment when a steelhead will often strike.

Most of the time, a fly for steelhead should drift naturally with little or no rod action.

One good way to locate steelhead in a strange pool or run you haven't fished before, or one that may have changed due to recent floods, is to start at the upper end. Then you work your way downstream, drifting the bait in the likely spots right down to the lower end of the pool or run.

In the summer when fly fishing for steelhead, look for them in the fast, narrow runs—especially those at the head of a pool. Other narrow, shallow areas to try are found between rocks or boulders and along the edges of pools.

When drifting baits or lures for steelhead, it is important to always have a taut line so that you can feel a light pick-up or strike.

Salmon eggs and other baits used for steelhead should be cast across and upstream and allowed to drift downstream as close to the bottom as possible. When the drift is completed and the line straightens, reel in, and make a new cast. Pencil sinkers of various weights are required to keep the eggs or other bait down deep and drifting naturally.

When drifting a dry fly for steelhead or cutthroat in shallow water, don't remove the fly from the water if the fish fails to rise to it. Many times such fish ignore the fly when it passes over them, but will turn and follow it downstream and take it a good distance from their original resting spot.

Drag should be avoided when using a dry-fly for trout or steelhead. One way to do this is to mend the line as soon as it starts to form a belly. Here you throw a loop on the opposite side or upstream side. While doing this, your fly may give a short skip or hop. Be prepared for a sudden strike when this happens.

ATLANTIC SALMON

Atlantic salmon are found in so few spots in a river that it is usually a waste of time to cast at random, as in trout fishing. Most of the time it is best to cast to a salmon that you can see, or fish a spot where they are leaping or showing.

The best Atlantic salmon fishing periods usually take place in the late spring or early summer when the rivers are normal or still a bit high. Fishing becomes more difficult later on when the water level drops and rivers are low.

Although most Atlantic salmon are fished for in the deeper water or pools, they can also be caught at times in fast, shallow stretches with only 2 or 3 ft. of water.

Atlantic salmon will often start hitting a fly just before and during the first rise of a river, during a rain—especially if the water has been low.

A salmon which rises to your dry fly, and misses, is interested in the lure. Cast over him again and chances are good he'll take the fly.

Many salmon are lost by trying to set the hook too soon. A good rule is to wait until you feel the pull of the fish's weight on the line or rod. In many cases, the hook will set itself due to the friction of the line.

It is difficult, if not impossible, to predict exactly when Atlantic salmon will rise to the fly. They have their days and moods and periods, and these often fluctuate from hour to hour. The most successful anglers spend many days and hours fishing, in order to be on the river when the salmon decide to take.

If you see a salmon leap out of the water, wait about 2 or 3 minutes for the fish to settle down before you make a cast.

LANDLOCKED SALMON

One of the best spots for landlocked salmon early in the spring is the mouth of a stream where smelt are spawning. The smelt are usually running up the stream at dusk and return downstream at daybreak. So two good fishing periods are the hours just before dark and the first hour or two after daybreak.

Landlocked salmon usually bite better on windy, cloudy, bad-weather days, than when the weather is good. When the water is rough, you'll find them on the windward shore in shallow water. Then, trolling or casting a streamer, spoon, or spinner near shore is often productive. (See illustration, p. 92.)

TROLL OR CAST ALONG
THIS SHORE

Landlocked salmon like a fast moving lure. When casting, retrieve your lure rapidly. When trolling, don't creep along, but move at least 4 or 5 mi. per hour. Another trick when trolling is to hold the rod and twitch it, or hold the line and jerk the lure.

When the water is calm, you should also troll faster than when the water is rough. In calm water, it pays to keep your flies or lures close to the boat in the wash of the boat's propeller.

Good spots for landlocks are the drop-offs near shore which are cruised by these fish. Submerged sand bars and gravel bars also attract minnows and smelt, and these also attract the salmon.

Landlocked salmon go deep during the summer months and like to stay in water with temperatures between 40 and 50 degrees. This means trolling at depths from 30 to 150 ft., depending on the lake.

Weighted lead-core or wire lines are required to get the lures down into the deep holes and cold water, where landlocks are feeding on smelt and other small fish.

It is usually best to troll for landlocks using two fly rods with streamers, or two spinning or bait-casting rods with lures; but if you locate a school of fish, you can stop the boat and cast for them.

Lake Trout

Lake trout come into the shallows in the spring soon after the ice is out, and great sport can be had casting for them. Best days for fishing are usually cloudy ones. If the day is bright and sunny, fish for lake trout early in the morning and in the evening.

The top lure for lake trout is a spoon. This can be trolled near shore in the spring and fall, and down deep during the summer months. You can also cast a spoon from a boat or shore; let it sink and flutter and work it back in an erratic manner.

When choosing spoons for lake trout trolling, pick the lightest, thinnest ones you can. Thin-gauge spoons have more action at very slow speeds and flutter more, but do not sink as fast as the heavier ones.

Lake trout can be caught through the ice in lakes where they are present. In most cases, you have to let your bait down deep up to 100 ft. or more to get results. Best baits are minnows, smelt, ciscoes, and pieces of fish.

A spoon can also be used to catch lake trout through the ice. Here, you let the spoon down until you feel it hit bottom, then reel in about a foot, and start jigging it up and down. Do it gently to make the spoon flutter up and down in an imitation of a small, crippled fish.

SHAD

Shad are not supposed to feed much, if at all, during their upstream spawning migration. But they will strike at lures such as jigs or darts, small spoons, spinners, and flies. This may be mostly a reflex or instinctive action, but they do it often enough to provide persistent anglers with fun and sport. Meaning that if you want to catch shad, you have to keep on casting until they decide to hit.

Shad moving upstream usually follow the main channels and strongest flow of water. You can sometimes see them moving or flashing in such spots. The best fishing is usually found where there are obstructions such as falls, dams, shallow rapids, or narrow runs which concentrate the shad in a small area.

Shad usually lie deep in a river and rarely rise to a lure near the surface. So when fishing for them with a fly rod, use a sinking line. With a spinning rod, tiny spoons, weighted spinners, and jigs or darts will do the job.

In order to work your lures deep for shad in fast water, it may mean casting well upstream or up current to get the lure down. Or, you may have to add some weight above the lure to get it down to the proper depth.

West Coast shad fishermen use a trick which often stirs up these fish and makes them hit. They work hard to catch the first shad; then they take it upstream above the spot they are fishing and scale it. The scales are thrown into the water and flicker and flash as they drift in the current and stir up lethargic shad.

Most shad are caught by casting from shore or boats, but they can also be taken by trolling. Use a small weighted spinner or tiny spoon and let it out anywhere from 100 to 150 ft. behind the boat.

CATFISH

Big catfish often feed at night close to shore, where they forage for small fish, frogs, and other animal food. Dark nights are usually better than moonlit ones.

Channel catfish in rivers are active fish, and more will be caught on baits which are drifting or moving with the current than those that are lying still. Earthworms and minnows are both good baits for these fish.

In a lake which has a stream or river entering it, wait until there is a rain; then after the rain, fish at the mouth of the stream or river. The rain will make the river muddy and also wash food into the lake. Catfish gather there to feed at such times.

When fishing a small river or stream for channel catfish, look for the deeper holes and pools and drop your baited hook into these spots.

When catfishing in a lake, fish the side toward which the wind is blowing. The waves carry natural foods toward that side, and the fish move in to feed.

A top bait for big catfish is a bullhead about 7 or 8 in. long. Hook one in the back with a 7/o or 8/o hook and let it down to the bottom. The bullhead not only attracts its larger relatives, but also stays alive longer than other baits.

Catfish, bullheads, and eels in rivers and streams usually bite best at night. But if the water turns brown from a heavy shower or rain, these fish will often feed well during the daytime, and good catches can be made.

CARP

Many anglers who have never fished for carp on light tackle are in for a surprise. They are not fast or flashy like trout or bass, but are powerful and pull like a mule. And carp are not easy to catch. Best baits include doughballs made from cornmeal and flour, and canned corn kernels. Look for carp in the shallower, weedy portions of lakes, and quiet pools of rivers and streams.

The best time of year to fish for carp is in the spring—May and June. Carp start to feed avidly then after a long winter fast, and they also come into shallow water to spawn. You can usually hear them splashing around near shore.

Carp fishermen have to be patient and quiet. This means do not let the fish see or hear you; walk softly, and sit down or hide behind a bush. You may have to wait many hours for a bite. Don't give up just because nothing is touching your bait—sooner or later a carp will show interest if you stick it out.

In the spring and fall, you can catch carp most of the day. But during the summer months, they either move into deeper water or sun themselves just below the surface. They do not bite well at such times. Best bet then is to fish early in the morning, in the evening, and during the night.

To detect light nibbles and bites when carp or sucker fishing, split the end of a short 3-in. stick or branch, and attach it to your line just below the rod tip.

When baiting a hook for carp, you should try to hide the entire hook as much as possible.

When carp fishing, look for a mulberry tree that has branches hanging over the water, growing along the shore of a lake or river. Carp like to eat mulberries and will hang around where the berries fall into the water.

OTHER FISHES

Sturgeon caught in our western rivers bite best on smelt, lamprey eels, and strips of salmon. Heavy tackle, such as saltwater surf fishing gear, is required to cast the heavy sinkers needed to hold the bait on the bottom and to fight the big sturgeon in a strong current.

Chinook or king salmon will often hit a lure such as a spoon in freshwater rivers. Look for concentrations of the fish in a pool. They usually reveal themselves by rolling or even leaping clear of the water. The spoon should be cast across and upstream and allowed to sink deep, where it is retrieved close to the bottom.

Whitefish will take a dry fly when they are feeding on the surface, or if you locate them in shallow water. Such fishing is best in the evening when flies hatch and the whitefish rise to the top to feed on them.

Suckers are beloved by hundreds of thousands of kids and older anglers because they are one of the first freshwater fish to bite early in the spring. They usually become active as the water warms and rises from spring rains, moving up the rivers, streams, creeks, and brooks to spawn. You can catch them on worms, and small earthworms are better than the larger nightcrawlers. One lively worm on a small hook is good, but often 2 or 3 small worms on a single hook are better. The baited hook should lie on the bottom without moving; in a strong current this may require a sinker on the end of the line to hold it in place.

CHAPTER 10

Other Freshwater Tips

A DRY fly will float longer without drag if you make a short cast and hold your rod high so that most of the line is off the water.

When using popping lures or other surface lures in shallow water, don't work them too vigorously or pop them too loud. You're more apt to scare the fish away than attract them in clear, shallow water. However, when fishing in deeper water or on days when the water is rough or roiled, you can yank hard to cause the surface lure to make a loud noise and create a big disturbance.

A heavy or prolonged rain which raises the level of a lake creates new feeding areas for the fish. As the water floods grassy shallows, the fish tend to scatter far and wide, gorging themselves. At such times, the best procedure is to fish these new areas, but to keep moving from one spot to another. Surface lures or shallow running lures are usually best, since there will be grass and weeds in the flooded areas.

Farm ponds are usually shallow and small in size, so the water warms up more quickly than in the larger, natural lakes. Bass do not feed much in such warm water, and fishing is usually poor. But by dragging a lure along the bottom in the deepest part of the pond, you can often tease a bass into nipping the lure. You can also try fishing at night when bass are bolder, less discriminating, and more likely to be in the shallows.

You can fish with a lure and natural bait at the same time. Get a surface plug, such as a popper, and remove the tail treble hook. Tie on a short 12 or 15 in. leader, and bait hook to the tail of the plug; then bait the hook with a worm or other bait. The plug provides casting weight and can also be twitched to attract attention to the bait. Most of your fish will be caught on the live bait, but every so often a bass may decide to sock the plug instead.

When fly fishing and your backcast hits a tree, rock, or other object, check your hook before you resume fishing. Chances are that it has been broken, bent, or the point has been dulled.

If you must fish during the middle of the day during the summer months, choose the cloudy or rainy days rather than the bright, sunny ones.

On hard-fished streams, look for the spots which most anglers avoid or pass up. Brush, logs, overhanging trees, hard-to-reach spots, etc., are passed by most anglers for easier-to-reach spots; yet, these very same places are likely to harbor big trout which want cover and undisturbed locations.

When you are ice fishing, it's a smart move to clear any snow from the ice all around the hole. Do this in a circle at least 10 or 12 ft. in diameter. The light will shine through the clear ice and attract fish to the area.

If you have hooked a big trout on a fly rod which makes a long run and threatens to take all your line off the reel, there is one trick which often works. Strip the backing line off the reel as fast as you can to create slack line and take the rod pressure off the fish. This usually stops him and then you can recover some line and continue the fight.

At night, you can use larger, heavier lures than in the daytime. Trout will go for bulky flies, large streamers, and even small plugs. Bass will hit big surface and underwater plugs, long plastic worms, and eels. Such big lures are easier to cast and feel when you work them.

If you frighten a trout or bass, wait at least 15 or 20 min. before trying to catch it. Fish that are put down or frightened rarely strike too soon after such an experience. But if you wait or leave and return later, you stand a good chance of catching that fish after he gets over his fright.

Carry some paper cups with you when using live bait that's too light to cast, or when fishing spots where casting is impossible. Place your baited hook attached to your fishing line into the cup, and let it float out to the spot you want to fish. A pull on the line will tip over the cup and free the bait.

One trick which can be used to stir up fish is to go upstream and throw some earth into the water above the spot to be fished: this muddies the water and often arouses the trout or bass.

If you plan to do any night fishing, get acquainted with the shoreline during the daytime first. Learn the location of logs, lily pads, weeds, so that you can cast just short of them at night.

Extra care should be taken when working a surface lure in calm, clear water. Try to keep your line off the water by holding your rod tip high as you work and retrieve your lure.

Fish quickly accept an object, shadow, or light if it is stationary; but a quick, sudden movement of a person, boat, shadow, or light will scare them and make them dart away or hide.

One reason why many fishermen do not catch big fish is that they spend most of their time fishing for the smaller fish which are easier to catch. If you want big fish, you have to concentrate your efforts on the big ones and ignore the small ones.

Any disturbance on the surface of a lake or river should be investigated. A school of minnows skipping or even a single minnow flipping may mean fish are chasing them. Swirls, breaks, or dimples on the surface may indicate fish feeding on insects.

Surface lures can be worked among lily pads if they aren't too thick and have openings or narrow channels between the pads. A weedless plug or bug is best, and you have to shift the rod from one side to the other to guide the lure through the openings.

One effective way to cover a lot of area when casting a lure from an anchored boat is to cast in a circle all around the craft. Each cast should be made about 15 or 20 ft. apart so that you cover the water all around the boat completely.

Canny freshwater fishermen often spend hours, or even days, locating fish in different spots of a stream or lake. Then they catch 1 or

2, but leave the rest for another day—or they may just play the fish, then release it to live for another day. In this way they have a steady, dependable supply of fish which can be tapped when fishing gets tough.

If you are trolling deep with a level-wind bait-casting reel, you can tell how much line to let out by counting the number of times your level-wind goes back and forth. Then when you get a strike, you can remember how many times to count the next time you let out line to reach the same depth.

Although surface bass bugs and floating plugs are used on top, try adding a clincher sinker about 18 or 20 in. ahead of such lures, and work them along the bottom. They float clear of weeds and obstructions and often take bass, walleyes, panfish, and even catfish.

When fishing a weedless spoon among lily pads, pull it over the tops of the pads. If it comes to an opening, let it sink to give the bass that may be following the spoon a chance to grab it. Usually a slow or moderate retrieve is best, but there are times when a fast retrieve across the tops of the lily pads is best.

A shore angler using natural baits can reach a distant spot if the wind is blowing from land. All you need is a small inflated balloon attached to the end of your line. Then tie a shorter leader and hook next to the balloon, add your bait, and toss the rig out into the water. As the wind blows the balloon, you feed slack line. The balloon will also act as a bobber and show if you have a bite. (See illustration, p. 105.)

Jigging a jig or spoon in a lake is a good way to locate a fishing spot. Let the boat drift, and then lower the lure to the bottom; after which you jig the rod up and down, letting the lure quickly rise and flutter down. If you get a strike or hook a fish, drop the anchor and give the spot a good work-out.

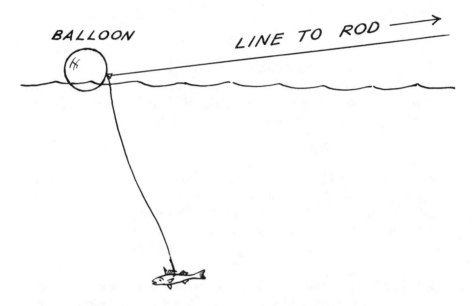

When fishing a wet fly for trout, cast across and slightly upstream, then follow the drift of the fly with your rod tip. The fly should drift naturally with no drag or too much slack in the line or leader. When the fly is downstream, you can let out some more line and let it drift a few more feet. Keep an eye on your leader or the end of your line, and if it moves or sinks quickly, set the hook.

In addition to imitating minnows, streamers and bucktails can also be tied to imitate young trout or salmon. Trout, steelhead, and big Pacific salmon are often cannibals and feed on the young of their own kind.

When using bass bugs or panfish bugs, many strikes are missed. You'll hook more fish if you hold your rod tip low, just over the water in front of you. Then, instead of giving your bug action with the rod tip, use your left hand to strip in line, twitching the bug slowly. If a fish strikes, you can then quickly set the hook by a short, quick pull

on the line. Of course, once the fish is hooked, you raise your rod tip
to fight him.

Trout, steelhead, and Atlantic salmon fishermen must pay close
attention to the rise and fall of the stream or river water level. A rise
or drop of a few inches can change the feeding locations and lying
or resting places of these fish.

Standing in a boat when fishing can frighten fish. If you are sitting
and low, you can approach closer to a fish than when you are standing and waving your arms while casting. This is especially true when
fishing shorelines where the water is shallow and clear.

When fishing freshwater lakes, always look for underwater weed
beds. These are good hangouts for black bass, pike, pickerel, and
even muskies. Minnows, small yellow perch, and crayfish hide in the
weeds, and gamefish look for them there.

One of the most important techniques in fly fishing with dry flies
is how you pick your line off the water for the next cast. Too many
anglers have the habit of picking a long line off the water and creat-
ing a disturbance which puts down fish. The best method is to pull
in slack line with your left hand until only about 10 or 12 ft. of line
remains on the water; then raise your rod high, and quickly pick the
few feet of line and leader remaining in the water off the surface, with
as little disturbance as possible.

On many of the larger freshwater lakes and reservoirs, gulls will
guide you to feeding fish. This is especially true in waters where shad
minnows are present. Black bass and white bass will often drive these
baitfish to the surface, and gulls will be seen diving and wheeling over
them to snatch any disabled baitfish.

A fish has a tiny brain and is usually considered "dumb" when compared to man or land animals. But fish learn from experience, and if they see a certain lure too often, they quickly learn to avoid it—especially if they were hooked on that lure once or twice in the past. That is why many expert freshwater anglers carry a wide assortment of lures when they go fishing. If the old familiar lures fail to work, they can change to a different one. If they try enough lures, they stand an excellent chance of finding one which will interest the fish.

If you catch a big fish from a certain spot, keep that location in your mind. Sooner or later, another big fish will move in to take its place.

The ability to "read" a stream or lake and locate the hot spots separates the men from the boys in freshwater fishing. The best fishermen know where the fish lie or gather in a stream or lake and do not waste time fishing barren areas. It usually takes a long time to become familiar with the waters in order to locate the best spots. The novice or angler fishing strange waters is better off if he hires a guide or fishes with someone who knows the stream or lake and can point out the best spots.

During the hot weather months, it's a good idea to pass up the lakes that are uniformly shallow. Here, fish are sluggish and rarely bite well when the water is warm. Instead, look for lakes which have deeper, cooler water.

Long casts are rarely needed when fishing in fresh water. In fact, they should be avoided unless they are absolutely necessary. You have better control over your lures and will hook a greater percentage of strikes on the short line. Instead of trying for distance, bring your boat closer to the area being fished, or wade closer to the spot. Accuracy is more important than distance when fishing a shoreline or trout stream. The angler who can place his lure or fly exactly where he wants it will catch more fish than the guy who casts far, but several feet off the target.

When retrieving surface lures or pork chunks in lily pads, keep your rod tip high. In fact, if your boat is stable you can stand up so that you can hold your rod still higher and retrieve the lure better.

A good bet in hot weather is an underwater spring that empties into the stream or lake and keeps the water cool. Fish such as trout and bass will often hang around a spring during the summer months.

When fishing big rivers and lakes, use underwater lures and natural baits when it is windy and the surface of the water is rough or rippled. On windless days when the water is flat and calm, a surface lure is often effective. A lake may be calm in the morning, rough during the day, and then calm again in the evening and at night. So you can fish surface lures in the morning and evening and underwater lures or bait during the middle of the day.

When fishing a strange lake or river, trolling is a good way to learn where the fish are. When trolling, vary your speed until you get a strike—then stick to that speed. You can continue trolling in the same area where you are getting strikes, or you can anchor or drift over it and cast lures.

Big fish are scarce in fresh water because they need a lot of food, a lot of room—and big fish often take over certain territory and chase other smaller fish away. To catch them, you have to locate this hangout and present a lure or bait when they're in a feeding or striking mood.

During the hot weather, fish do not feed for long periods like they do in the spring and fall. The feeding spree is usually short, and the angler has to be there when it occurs. For trout, this usually happens in the evening just before dark during the summer months. Bass may also decide to feed either early in the morning, in the evening, or during the night.

A fishing thermometer used to read water temperatures can be useful when ice fishing. It can be used to locate warm spots where fish tend to gather and are more active and apt to feed. Such spots are often created by underground springs which flow into the lake.

When fishing lakes or small ponds in shallow water, a light breeze which ruffles the water is usually better than no wind. The ruffled water permits you to approach the fish without alarming them, as often happens when the water is calm and flat.

A bobber or float can be used to carry your bait out to cover more fishing area. If there's a wind, drop the bobber into the water and let the wind take it away as you let out slack line. In a river, you can let the current take the bobber and bait out a good distance. Besides covering more territory, the moving bait will also attract more fish.

When a slow or moderate retrieve fails to bring a strike, try skipping a streamer or bucktail across the surface, fast. This imitates a frightened minnow or small fish trying to escape a larger one.

In shallow or warm waters during the summer, fish will seek such cooler spots in lakes as spring holes, channels, and brooks, or streams entering into the lake.

One good way to locate fish in a lake is to start trolling close to shore, then on the way back go out a little farther in deeper water. On the next troll, run the boat still farther out from shore. This way, you cover different depths and areas.

A lake or reservoir which has fluctuating water levels is tougher to fish than a body of water which remains the same. In a rising or falling water level, fish have to move often to find the most comfortable depth and new feeding areas. In a lake or reservoir with a stable water level, you can usually find the fish in the same spots month after month.

The best freshwater fishing spots are usually found where the fish find both food and cover or protection. Rocks, boulders, stumps, weeds, sunken trees, logs, debris, overhanging banks, bushes, or trees all provide these necessities and attract fish.

When ice fishing, look for spots where springs, brooks, streams, or rivers enter a lake. Moving water brings more oxygen and is often warmer, thus bringing fish to the area.

Fishing a shallow shoreline requires a quiet approach. Fish in such waters are spooky, and an outboard roaring into the area will frighten them. Instead, cut your motor at least 150 or 200 ft. from shore, and row or paddle quietly toward the spot to be fished. Or, if there is a fairly strong wind blowing, you can use it to drift toward the fishing spot.

One of the best ways to use a spinner in fast water is to cast quartering upstream, raise your rod high, and start the retrieve. Let the current carry the spinner downstream, and let it be pulled by the drag in the line, and hesitate, rise, and swing with the current. When it is downstream below you, reel the spinner back slowly with pauses in the pockets and occasional drop-backs to imitate a small minnow struggling against the swift water.

SHORE

When casting from shore doesn't produce, or casting from a boat toward shore doesn't work, try holding the boat a few feet from shore, and cast your lure so that it swims parallel to the land. This way, you cover many good spots during the retrieve.

When casting plugs, spoons, or other heavy lures in clear, shallow water, try to make them land without too much of a splash. It is a good idea to cast your lure beyond or to one side of where you know a fish is lying rather than right on top of him; then work your lure toward or past the fish. Most fish such as trout, bass, pike, and pickerel are extremely wary and easily spooked in shallow water. A lure landing with a big splash right on top of them will cause them to take off in a hurry.

While fishing, always examine your lure to make sure that it is free from weeds or other debris. This is especially important when you are trolling in weedy areas or down deep where your lure scrapes bottom often. Reel in your lure at regular intervals and look it over; a fish won't hit a lure which has any weeds fouled around it.

If on a lake on a windy day, fish the shore from which the wind is blowing. Strong winds blow insects into the water or make minnows seek shelter along the shoreline, thus attracting gamefish.

Carry two anchors in your boat when fishing a lake or river. Once you locate a productive spot, drop both anchors to hold the boat in the exact position.

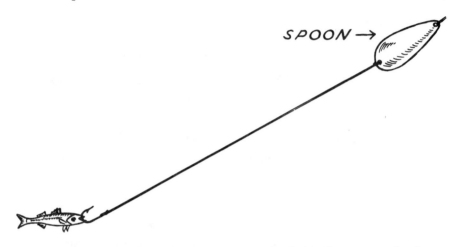

SPOON →

Ice fishermen usually fish with minnows down deep near the bottom. It is dark there, especially if the ice is thick or there is snow on top of the ice. So, one trick is to add an attractor such as a spoon or spinner above the minnow. The hooks should be removed from these lures, and they should be tied a couple of feet above the hook with minnow. Jig them once in a while to make them flash in the depths.

When using a sinking lure such as a spoon, spinner, plug, or jig, you can tell how far down it should go by slowly counting as it sinks. When you get a strike remember the count, and on the next cast you know just how far the lure should sink before you start to reel it back.

Fresh water fish can often be teased into striking a lure even if they may not be hungry. The big fish usually have certain feeding or resting spots which they guard against intrusion by other fish. If you can locate such a fish, try casting and reeling a plug, spoon, spinner, or large streamer or bucktail fly past him. Keep doing this, and chances are good that eventually the fish will get excited or angry and grab your lure.

In a hard-fished lake, it often doesn't pay to fish the obvious spots alongshore that everyone tries. The fish you'll catch here are usually small. Instead, look for deeper locations underwater—where the big ones hang out.

Do fish depend on sight or smell when feeding? It depends on the species. Some, such as catfish and carp in fresh water, mainly use their sense of smell to locate food. Other fish, such as trout and muskies, pike and pickerel, depend mostly on sight to locate food.

Fish catch on quickly after a few have been caught. You'll notice that when you first locate some fish the bites or strikes come often. Then after you catch a few of the fish, they are not as likely to take the bait or lure. That is the time to change baits, lures, or techniques of using them. Or you can leave that area and look for a new school of fish that haven't been worked yet.

Fishing surface lures requires a constant alertness to be ready to set the hook. And try to prevent slack line. It is difficult if not impossible to set the hook if the line is slack when a fish strikes. And the angler who is not alert or is taken by surprise when a fish strikes misses a lot of fish.

When fishing a lake, one of the best spots is a drop-off where the water suddenly deepens. In small lakes, the drop-off will often be the same distance from shore all the way around the lake.

During hot weather, fish do not move around as much, or feed as often, or as actively, as during the cooler periods in the spring or fall. So to get a strike or bite, it is vital that a lure or bait be placed as close as possible to the fish's snout.

One of the few times when surface fishing is productive in deep water in the middle of a lake or reservoir is when black bass or white bass chase small shad minnows on top.

A highly effective way to fish a floating plug of the wobbler type is to cast out, let the plug float a while, then jerk it or reel it fast to make it dive a foot or two. Then let it pop to the surface and let it lie on top again, then pull it under once more. Keep repeating this during the entire retrieve.

If you have only a day or two for fishing, always choose the closer, more familiar waters rather than strange, distant lakes or rivers which you have never fished. It usually takes a day or two to learn the most productive spots in a strange body of water. So unless you have several days to fish or plan to hire a guide, stick to the closer waters.

When fishing a rocky or snag-filled bottom with a deep-running or sinking lure, you have to develop a sense of "feel" which enables you to lift the lure over the snag almost before or just as it barely touches it.

Anglers who lose or forget to bring along a ruler can still measure any small fish they have caught. One method is to measure the span of your hand from tip of the thumb to the tip of your smallest finger. Then remember how many inches this span represents. Another way is to use a dollar bill as a ruler. Since it is 6 in. long, it can easily be used to measure the length of a fish or anything else.

CHAPTER 11

Saltwater Fishing Tackle

RODS

MANY freshwater fishermen who have a freshwater spinning rod and reel wonder if they can use such an outfit in salt water. Although such an outfit may be on the light side for day-in and day-out saltwater angling, there are many saltwater spots where you can use a freshwater spinning outfit. This outfit is best for casting lures such as spoons, plugs, and jigs in bays, inlets, and ocean. Using 6- or 8-lb.-test line you can handle such fish as small bluefish, small stripers, and most weakfish. You can also use it for jigging for such bottom fish as porgies, sea bass, flounder, or fluke, and many other species.

Which outfit is better for surf fishing, the conventional rod and reel or spinning tackle? Both are good, depending on conditions, personal requirements, and preferences. The conventional rod and reel is ideal for casting heavy lures, baits, and sinkers. It is best for fishing in a heavy surf and when big fish are expected. A surf spinning outfit is better for casting the smaller lures for smaller and medium-sized fish. Casting with a conventional surf rod and reel is more difficult and requires more practice; if you don't fish very often, stick to spinning surf tackle.

If you are casting from shore or a boat for small or medium sized fish such as striped bass, bluefish, weakfish or sea trout, snook, etc., use a one-handed spinning rod from 6½ to 7½ ft. long and a small, but strong spinning reel filled with 8- or 10-lb.-test line. With such an outfit you can "work" or manipulate such lures as plugs, spoons, and jigs better than with a long, clumsy, heavy, two-handed rod. You can also cast the lighter lures farther and more efficiently.

Ordinary ring guides on a rod are best for casting and light trolling, with lines up to 40 or 50 lb. For heavier fishing and trolling, a rod should be equipped with roller guides. A roller tip-top guide is best for use with wire lines.

Many saltwater anglers make the mistake of leaving their rods joined for days or even weeks at a time. The ferrules corrode, and then the rod cannot be pulled apart. If this happens, pour some penetrating oil or carbon tetrachloride on the joint, and wait a half hour before trying to separate the rod. Another trick which often works is to heat the outside or female ferrule quickly so that it expands. But the best thing to do is separate the rod after each fishing trip, and wash the ferrule with fresh water. Adding a thin coat of grease or oil on the male ferrule helps to keep it from corroding.

In areas where gamefish are apt to surface and show on top, it's a good idea to rig up a one-handed spinning rod outfit in advance and have it ready in the boat. Then you can cast into the fish as soon as you sight them.

REELS

When surf fishing, set your drag on your reel according to the lure you are using. When using metal squids, spoons, jigs, underwater plugs, and rigged eels, your drag should be tighter than when you are using a surface plug. When bait fishing with a sinker and rig, your drag should be set tighter than when fishing with lures.

And when fishing for big fish with big lures, set your drag tighter than when you are fishing for smaller fish with small lures.

When fishing with light tackle, it is very important to use a light drag setting. And before you try to boat or land a fish, it should be played out completely. Trying to land a fish that is still green or active will pop a light line.

When you are through fishing for the day or are storing your fishing tackle, loosen the drags on the reels.

LINES

Always check the first few feet of your line when fishing. The constant wear and tear on the first few feet of line while casting or bottom fishing weakens the line considerably. Check your line before starting to fish and also while fishing. If it looks nicked or frayed, cut off a few feet.

For offshore trolling and fishing, monofilament line is fine in tests up to 50 lbs. Over that strength, you'll find braided Dacron line easier to handle and to use.

Wire line can be handled better and easier if you leave the click on the reel as you let the line out. First you may have to pull the line off the reel, but as the boat moves and 100 ft. of line is out, it will usually come off the reel by itself and, only a slight pressure with your thumb on the revolving spool will keep it moving smoothly.

To mark your line quickly when trolling, carry along some ordinary plastic Band Aids used for cuts. Then wrap the plastic around your line where you want to mark the length to let out.

The line you use in trolling will depend on how deep you want to go. Monofilament and braided lines are good for trolling on or near the surface. To get them down deeper you must add a trolling weight. Lead core lines get down fairly deep and are good when used close to shore in shallow water. Solid wire lines are best when you want to get down still deeper.

Two types of line are best suited for deep-water bottom fishing. One is the braided Dacron which has the advantage of little stretch and this is very good when fishing in great depths. But it is expensive and doesn't last too long. Most anglers fishing for bottom fish use monofilament in tests from 30 to 60 lbs.

LEADERS

When putting a wire leader on a plug, spoon, or metal squid, make sure you form a large loop that doesn't slip at the eye of the lure. A small, narrow loop, or one that slips and tightens will prevent the lure from working right or will kill the action.

When drifting on the bottom, use a weaker leader or dropper to hold your sinker than the one which holds the hook or your main fishing line. Then if the sinker hangs up, you will break off and save the rest of the rig and your line.

Avoid the bright shiny leaders for daytime fishing. They are okay for night fishing, but are too easily seen on bright, sunny days. Use the dull-finish brown, gray, or blue wire leaders for daytime fishing. A monofilament leader is even better when fishing for fish which don't have sharp teeth.

When fly fishing for tarpon or snook, add a short 12 in. tippet of wire or heavy monofilament on the end of the leader. Wire, of course, is a must if you want to land any bluefish or barracuda you hook.

Hooks

Hooks play an important part in saltwater fishing, and it pays to buy the best ones you can find. They have sharper points, better temper and finishes. Those that are tinned, gold-plated, or cadmium-plated stand up best in salt water. The new stainless steel hooks are fine, especially for lures which have hair or feathers that discolor from rust.

Every saltwater tackle box should contain a piece of emery cloth in it. It comes in very handy for touching up the point of a hook which has become dulled. It can also be used to remove rust from hooks, lures, knives, pliers, and other tools.

Some of the lures used for saltwater fishing have weak single or treble hooks attached. One way to test a single hook is to put a rag against the barb and point, and then try to straighten out the hook; another way is to sink the point of the hook into a block of wood, and then try to straighten it out. A good hook will resist straightening and will spring back into shape when pressure is released. If the hook straightens out too easily or snaps off, replace it with a stronger hook.

Other Tackle

Too many bottom fishermen make the mistake of using one weight of sinker all day long. You will catch more fish if you carry several different weights and change according to the depth of the water and strength of the tide. If the water is shallow or the tide is weak or slack, use a light sinker. In deep water and fast tides or currents, change to a heavier one.

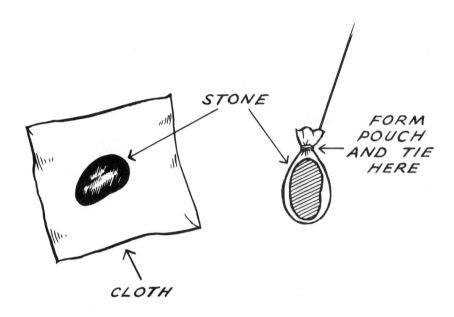

If you are fishing a rocky area where a lot of sinkers get lost, you can make a cheap, disposable sinker by cutting off a square of cloth and wrapping a stone in it. If it gets hung up on the rocks and gets lost, you can easily make up another one. To save fishing time, make up several of these sinkers in advance.

Many anglers in small boats attempt to fish for such big fish as swordfish, giant tuna, and sharks without a harness or a fighting chair. This is asking for trouble, and you can injure yourself if you hook a big fish without such equipment. If you lack the proper equipment, use your boat for the smaller species. When you tackle the "monsters of the deep," fish from an offshore sportfisherman which has all the gear and equipment necessary to hook, fight, and boat big fish.

Metal lures such as spoons, spinners, or metal squids have to be cleaned every so often to remove the tarnish or corrosion. An ordinary metal polish will do a good job. Then you can wipe the metal lure with an oil-soaked rag, and it will stay bright and shiny until the next fishing trip.

Pipe cleaners can be used to keep coils of monofilament leaders, snelled hooks, and rigs from becoming loose or tangled. Just twist a short length of the pipe cleaner around the coils of leaders or rigs.

Most fish are lost after they are hooked because the tackle is faulty or weak, or because the angler made a mistake or was too impatient. Always use lines, swivels, snaps and hooks, and lures that are in good condition. And take plenty of time to fight and land a fish without straining the rod, line, or other gear.

Carry a few of the lighter trolling weights, around 2 or 3 oz., even when you intend to cast only. They provide a good casting weight with various lures. Merely add a 20 or 24 in. mono leader to the snap on the trolling weight, and attach your lure to the end of this leader.

The two types of trolling weights shown on top of p. 122 are handy to use when you want to get down a bit deeper than with an un-weighted line. They come in various sizes from a fraction of an ounce to several ounces. The first has a keel, and this, together with the bead swivels, helps to prevent line twist when using lures that spin. The second is a plain cigar shape which offers little resistance to the water. When using either, the usual method of rigging is shown in (C). First the weight is tied to the fishing line, then a leader of any length you prefer is attached to the weight; finally the lure is attached to the end of this leader.

It pays to invest a bit more and get the ball-bearing type swivels for most trolling rigs. The barrel-type swivels may serve the purpose

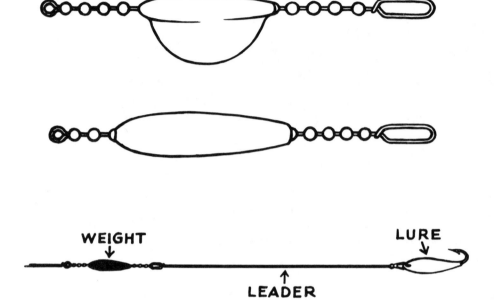

for light-tackle fishing, but for heavy work the ball-bearing swivels are much better.

To make a quick, simple snagging rig, simply attach a treble hook to a trolling weight. This can then be cast into a school of baitfish, to snag them for use as bait.

The wise fisherman always carries spares whenever he goes fishing. Always have a spare rod, reel, line, and duplicate lures on board a boat; or when fishing from shore or surf, carry the spares in your car. You can never tell when you may lose or break your rod; your reel may not work; the line may be cut off or frayed—or you may lose your favorite lure. If you have duplicates, you can continue fishing.

CHAPTER 12

Saltwater Lures

PLUGS

WHAT color plug is best for saltwater fishing? Most of the time the best ones to use are those with plenty of silver or natural scale finishes because this resembles such baitfish as mullet, menhadens, herring, anchovies, and spearing. But plugs with white or yellow bodies are also good producers.

A general rule to follow when using surface plugs, such as poppers or swimmers for striped bass and many other fish, is to reel slowly at night—just fast enough to bring out the action with occasional pauses and short jerks. During the daytime, however, work your surface plugs faster with more vigorous jerks, making the plug throw a big splash.

When mullet appear in the surf, the surface types such as poppers and swimmers are best to use, especially when the water is calm or moderate. However, if the surf gets very rough, you can try underwater plugs, metal squids, and hammered stainless steel spoons to take striped bass, bluefish, and channel bass.

Adding feathers or bucktail to the tail hook of a plug will cause it to have a slower, lazy swimming action. You can add the feathers or bucktail to both the underwater and surface plugs.

Most underwater plugs come with the metal lip bent as shown at (A). This causes the plug to dive and wriggle fairly deep. To make the plug travel closer to the surface, bend it as shown at (B); to cause the plug to swim on the surface, bend it back to the position shown at (C). In this position, reeling the plug slowly will make it wriggle across the top of the water. Reeling fast and jerking at regular intervals will make the plug throw a splash like a popper. Most of the plugs in the smaller sizes can be bent by hand, since the metal lips are thin; but on the larger models, or those with thick metal lips, a pair of pliers may be needed to do the job.

Surface plugs are usually more effective in surf fishing during the daytime, daybreak, and dusk. They will take fish at night, at times. Underwater plugs can be used during the day and are also very good at night; jigs with pork rind can also be used at night. Metal lures such as metal squids and spoons are best during the daytime.

When fishing with underwater plugs, reel fast if you want to have the lure travel deep; reel slower to make it travel closer to the surface.

Jigs

Nowadays, no saltwater fishing box is complete without an assortment of jigs in different sizes and weights. You should have some with bucktail, feather and nylon, or plastic skirts. The best colors are all-white, all-yellow, white and red, and blue and white. Most of the heads are painted to match these colors, but silver or chrome heads are also good. Jigs can be trolled or cast, in bays, inlets, and tidal rivers for many small gamefish. They can also be trolled and cast along the surf off the beaches. Offshore, the larger sizes can be trolled for school tuna, bluefish, albacore, and bonito. And you can use them almost anywhere for jigging near the bottom to catch gamefish and bottom fishes.

When fishing for sharp-toothed fish such as bluefish, barracuda, Spanish mackerel, and king mackerel, use nylon jigs instead of bucktail types. They will last longer and catch just as many fish.

Jigs or bucktails are highly effective lures in many types of waters. But they are especially deadly in fast currents and strong tides. Here they can be cast up-current or up-tide and allowed to sink to the bottom to reach fish lying deep.

In waters where there are shrimp, one of the top lures is a small jig. You can imitate the shrimp in size and action by working it in a stop-and-go swimming motion used by the natural shrimp.

When fishing over a sandy or mud bottom in salt water and using a jig, the bottom bouncing technique is very effective. Here you let the jig sink until it hits bottom, then reel in slowly, raising and lowering the rod tip so that the jig skips along the bottom. The jig raises puffs of sand or mud which will attract fish.

When using a jig over a grassy or weedy bottom or rock bottom, the retrieve should be just fast enough to barely clear or brush against the weeds or rocks. In such places a light jig is better than a heavy one.

A jig used in fast or deep water can be cast up-tide or up-current; and let the line run freely from the reel spool to allow plenty of slack. Using a light line will also help to get the jig down to the bottom in a fast tide or deep water.

Bottom-feeding species can often be caught on jigs. One method is to lower the jig under a boat and "jig" the lure up and down. Another method is to cast out the jig, and reel it slowly, dragging or bouncing the bottom.

METAL SQUIDS

Metal lures are excellent lures for casting, trolling, and jigging from surf, shore, or boat. In recent years the flat, stainless steel, hammered types have been killers. They are now available with single feather of bucktail instead of treble hooks, although the treble hook types are still being used. The oldtime metal squids made from block tin or other metal are also good. Chromed squids are popular now but cannot be bent like the block tin ones. They also chip and flake when banged around rocks.

When using a metal squid in the surf, work different depths. First make a cast, and reel fast so that the lure travels just below the surface. On the next cast, let the lure sink a couple of feet and reel slower so that it stays down at about that level. Finally cast out, and let the lure sink almost to the bottom, and reel slowly so that the lure moves close to the bottom.

The action of metal squids can usually be improved by bending them. In top one, a single bend was made in the middle of the lure. In bottom one, a second bend was made. The best way to bend metal squids is near a body of water where you can try their action immediately. A little experimenting will show you just how much of a bend you should make. Naturally you can only bend metal squids made from soft metals such as lead or block tin. Those made from harder metals can't be bent or they would break in the process. Even thick lead or block tin squids often prove difficult to bend. The edge of a table, bench, or a vise can be used to bend squids too thick to bend by hand alone.

If you surf fish with a block tin metal squid and you find that it is tarnished, you can polish it quickly right at your feet: merely rub the metal squid in the damp sand until the tarnish is removed.

DIAMOND JIGS

Diamond jigs are the most versatile and dependable lures you can use in salt water. They can be cast from shore or a boat and reeled fast to take many top feeders. They can be trolled fast for these same fish or down deep. But as the name implies, it does the best job when used "jigging" at various depths. Usually, working it just off the bottom is most productive. Use small diamonds from 1 to 3 oz. for small fish, light tackle, and shallow water, and larger ones from 3 to 12 oz. for bigger fish, heavier tackle, and deeper water.

When using a diamond jig, it's often a good idea to sweeten the lure with a small piece of bait such as a seaworm, clam, squid, or strip of fish. The toughest addition of all is a small strip of white or yellow pork rind. This will stay on longer than any natural bait, and the flutter of the rind will draw more strikes. (See illustration, p. 129.)

A lead mackerel jig was used as early as 1816 by commercial fishermen in this country. By 1870, it was replaced by the purse-seine. Today, of course, commercial men use seines, and anglers use the mackerel jig. Only, it has been improved by chrome plating and is made in many sizes and weights. A recent innovation is to add 4 or 5 tiny plastic tube lures above the jig.

EELSKIN LURES

Eelskins and eelskin lures are highly valued and productive lures—especially in New England, for striped bass and bluefish.

Long eelskin lures can be used trolling. Shorter ones with rigid hook connectors are used for casting and probing the bottom in fast water tides, rips, and narrow raceways, such as canals and inlets.

TIE HERE

An effective eelskin lure can be made quickly by using a metal squid or heavy spoon. You slip the eelskin on the lure, and tie it at the head so that it doesn't come off. The hook should protrude through the skin as shown.

Various Lures

Striped-bass anglers, using large spoons such as the bunker type for trolling, often find that painting all or part of the lures with yellow or white produces more strikes than the silver or chrome finish.

Take a large 2 or 3 oz. bucktail jig, and add a second hook to the first one by bending the barb of the jig hook and slipping the eye of the second hook over it. Then impale a baitfish, such as a small menhaden, sardine, mullet, or balao on the two hooks as shown. With a soft flesh fish such as the menhaden or balao, the second hook can be left imbedded inside. With tougher fish such as mullet, leave the point and barb of the second hook exposed. This rig is very good in southern waters when drifting for king mackerel, amberjack, dolphin, barracuda, grouper, and red snapper.

When fishing during a windy day from a boat or shore, keep your rod tip low when reeling in a lure. This will prevent a belly from forming in the line, and you'll feel a strike. You'll also get more strikes because the action of the lure will be better.

Saltwater anglers casting or trolling for small gamefish often have trouble with short strikers. The fish nip at the tail, bucktail, feathers, or pork rind, but fail to get hooked. You can remedy this to some extent by using the tail-hook combinations above. Figure A shows a metal squid with a long strip or pork rind (5 to 6 in.) and a small treble hook attached. You merely slip the end of the pork rind through the eye of the treble, and push the point and barb through the rind. This is a killer for small stripers and weakfish in the surf. To get the most action, use a thin, light, metal squid. The strip of pork rind should be narrow, thin, but strong. Drawing B shows a smaller swinging hook attached to the larger main hook on the metal squid. C shows a strip of pork rind with a single hook attached. This pork rind can also be used on metal squids and spoons. Most tackle stores sell such pork rind strips in jars.

If you forget to bring along a jar of pork rind, there are several substitutes you can use. A strip of white cloth can be added to a lure, or cut a strip from a rubber or plastic sheet. A strip of squid can also be used; and if you have caught any fish, you can cut long strips from the bellies of such fish to use instead of the pork rind.

The "turkey-bone" lure, which originally was used for bluefish in North Carolina waters, was called by this name because a real leg bone of a turkey was used to make the lure. Now a 3-in. white plastic tube is used. For bluefish it is trolled with a single hook; when used for striped bass a tandem or double hook is used, and two or three sandworms are impaled on the hooks. The lure is trolled at very slow speed. This keeps it down about 2 or 3 ft. below the surface. It is most effective in shallow water areas where there are rocks, boulders, or weeds which will catch deeper-running lures.

When using lures which are reeled slowly such as jigs, rigged eels, plastic worms, or eels, try rubbing some cod-liver oil or sardine oil on such lures, especially if you use them at night or in roily water.

The tandem rig here has a 12-in. leader tied to the hook of a jig, and on the end of the leader a small silver or chrome spoon is attached. The leader can be a light, coffee-colored stainless steel wire for fish with sharp teeth, or monofilament for those that lack teeth and are leader shy. This rig can be used down South by trolling to locate such fish as Spanish mackerel, bluefish, and blue runners. But it can also be used trolling or casting for many other saltwater species.

Flies used for bonefish should vary in size according to the depth being fished. Use small flies in shallow water where a light landing, slow-sinking fly is needed; use larger patterns in deeper water.

Many saltwater lures now have the hooks attached to the body by means of split-rings. These rings should be big and heavy if used for good-sized fish. Those that are made of brass can be strengthened by dropping some solder on the ring. Steel split-rings will rust and weaken. They should be replaced with new ones at regular intervals. Stainless steel split-rings have recently appeared, and these, of course, are strong and rustproof.

Don't throw away the old Japanese feather metal heads when the feathers get discolored or thin out. Save the metal heads and make some quick, effective lures. One such lure can be made by obtaining some plastic skirts from a fishing tackle store or mail-order house. These can be tied around the head to make an effective trolling or casting lure. Another lure can be made by attaching an eelskin to the metal head.

Currents, tides, and waves often govern lure speeds. Lures moving with the current have to be reeled or trolled faster than those moving against the current. The same goes for those moving in waves or

Saltwater Lures

Saltwater Lures 135

swells. As a wave reaches the lure, more speed is required to bring out the best action. When a wave has passed, a slower speed is needed. In a strong undertow or backwash in the surf, merely holding the lure in one spot is enough to make it work.

Surgical tube lures have become killers for blues and stripers in recent years, when trolled. To have the right action, a surgical tube should have a bend or curve in it. The smaller single-hook surgical has a long-shanked hook inside which can be bent. The longer 12 or 15 in. surgical with two hooks should be curled around a round can, bottle, or similar object, and tied in place so that it takes a set in the form of a curve.

When using underwater lures while casting, you must acquire a certain "feel" which travels up the line and indicates that the lure is working right. When using heavy spoons, metal squids, and wriggling plugs, it is fairly easy to feel them working. But rigged eels, mirror-type plugs, and jigs have no built-in action, and here you must supply fish-appeal by working your rod tip in short, sharp jerks.

CHAPTER 13

Saltwater Rigs

THE "live line," or "free line" rigs, as they are called, are used when fishing near the surface or at medium depths for various saltwater gamefish. Here, instead of using a heavy sinker as in bottom fishing, little or no weight is used. The first rig (A) is merely a hook tied to the end of a leader. If you are using monofilament line, you can tie the hook directly to the line. But when using braided nylon or Dacron line you can attach a monofilament leader to the end. The barrel swivel is optional but is often used in a fast current where the bait may spin. The second rig (B) is similar to the first except that a float is added above the hook. The distance between the hook and float will vary and should be changed to find the depth at which the fish are feeding. A clincher sinker is often added to keep the baited hook down in a fast tide. Both rigs are used with various natural baits such as seaworms, clams, crabs, shrimp, and baitfish, or pieces of fish. These are drifted as naturally as possible in the tide or current.

A good Pacific salmon rig for slow trolling or drifting is shown here. A whole or plug-cut herring is used on a two-hook rig and is attached on a leader about 3 ft. below a crescent sinker of from 2 to 6 oz., depending on the current and depth. To find the depth at which the salmon are feeding, let the rig down to the bottom then reel it back slowly. Once you get a hit or a fish, mark your line and let the rig down to the same depth.

There are many kinds of spreaders on the market which can be used for flounder fishing. These are usually rather heavy wire or plastic rigs which enable you to use 2 hooks right on the bottom. They work, but a simpler, less bulky flounder rig can be made by simply tying a hook on a 16 or 18 in. leader just above the sinker; then you can tie a second hook at the middle of the leader or snell of the first hook.

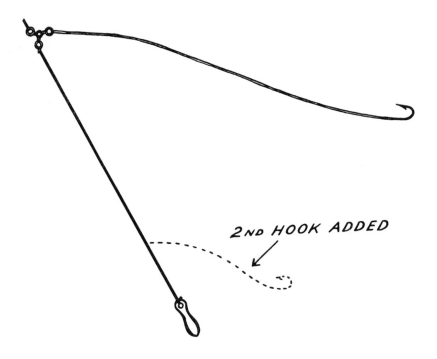

2ND HOOK ADDED

The "high-leader" rig is good for weakfish, striped bass, blue-fish, and other species which swim off the bottom. In this rig, the leader may be anywhere from 4 to 6 ft. long. And it is tied on the line the same distance above the sinker. But for ease of handling, it can be from 3 to 4 ft. long and tied the same distance above the sinker. The sinker should be heavy enough to hold bottom in the current, but light enough to move when lifted. You can bait this rig with seaworms, a strip of squid, shrimp, shedder crab, or a small baitfish and let it out with the tide, bouncing bottom. Then reel it back slowly and repeat the process. You can also add another hook on a short snell near the sinker to catch bottom species while waiting for action from the high-level feeders.

A rig used to boat hickory shad 2 and 3 at a time can be made of 2 shad darts on droppers and a small ¼ oz. stainless steel spoon-type lure on the end. It is most effective when cast from a boat. This rig should also work on other small fish of the herring family and for mackerel.

Whiting or silver hake fishermen of New England, New York, and New Jersey favor the multiple hook rig during the winter months. Carlisle hooks in sizes 4/0 or 5/0 are usually preferred and are baited with silversides or spearing, sand eels or strips of fish. The same basic rig, with hooks in sizes to suit the fish sought, is effective on ling, hake, smelt, herring, and many other fish which tend to travel in schools and feed on or near the bottom. Although light, 3-way swivels or spreaders can be used to attach the hooks to the main line, many anglers prefer to tie the leaders or snell directly to the line to avoid unnecessary hardware. (See illustration, p. 139.)

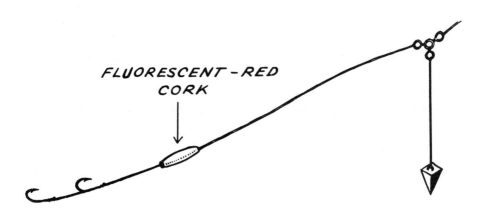

FLUORESCENT - RED
CORK

One problem when fishing a bottom bait in the surf is casting it so that it doesn't fly off the hook. Also, to hook the bait so that it lays neatly on the hook. The rig shown here helps to solve this by providing 2 hooks on the end of the leader to hold the bait better. It also has a florescent-red cork which keeps the bait off the bottom and attracts fish. The rig is especially effective when using sandworms or bloodworms for striped bass, but can also be used with clams, strips of squid, or with small, dead baitfish for any other fish found in the surf.

This double-hook fluke rig is made by tying a 20-in. leader testing about 30 lbs. on the end of the main fishing line. Then a second similar-length leader is tied at about the middle of the first leader. Use No. 4/0 light-wire Aberdeen Eagle Claw hooks. The hooks should be baited with the largest killifish you can get. Use it with a conventional rod and reel, and let out about 100 ft. of line so that the boat and rig will drift over shallow flats in water from 3 to 6 ft. deep.

The surf rig shown on p. 142 is a good one for fishing for high-swimmers when you want to keep your bait off the bottom to avoid crabs, blowfish, skates, and other pests. You use an extra long 4 ft. long

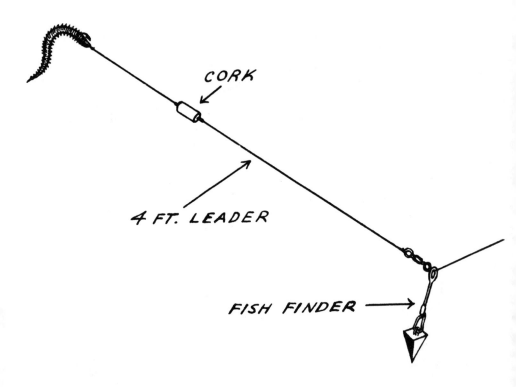

CORK

4 FT. LEADER

FISH FINDER ⟶

leader and add a bottle stopper cork about 10 or 12 in. from the hook. You also use a fish finder to hold the sinker. This rig helps keep the bait off the bottom when using a light bait, but is particularly effective when a single large sandworm is used.

Most anglers use the plain, diamond jig when jigging for various saltwater fishes. For fun and fast action, try the combination diamond jig and bait rig. (See illustration, p. 143.) Tie 2 hooks on short nylon leaders above the diamond jig. The size of the hooks and jig will depend on the size and species of fish, the depth of the water, and strength of the tide. The leaders should be short so that they don't tangle around the line or with each other. The hooks can be baited with any kind of bait. If you hook a fish on the diamond jig, chances of hooking another one on the bait are excellent. Most school fish tend to follow a hooked fish and will strike at another bait or lure.

A good rig for pier or bridge fishing for Spanish mackerel and blue-fish is made by using a 3-ft. wire leader to hold the double hook; then a barrel swivel is tied, and a 3-ft. monofilament leader is added. Slip a 1 oz. egg sinker onto the mono leader, then add a float. The double hook is baited with a strip of mullet or other fish, and the whole works is drifted out in the tide or current. (See top illustration, p. 144.)

Combination rigs used when casting from shore or boats are the "splasher" rig (top), which makes use of a round, wooden piece with an eye on each end. A nylon or flexible-cable wire leader is

attached to one end, and the line is tied to the other. On the end
of the leader a small bucktail jig or tiny spoon is attached. The size
and weight of the wood splasher provides casting weight and makes
a commotion. This attracts fish such as striped bass, bluefish, mackerel, bonito, and weakfish.

The other rig (bottom) makes use of a metal squid from which
the hook has been removed. The leader is tied to the eye which held
the hook. On the end of the leader, a small bucktail jig is tied—or
it can be a tiny spoon. The metal squid acts as an attractor and
provides casting weight for small lures.

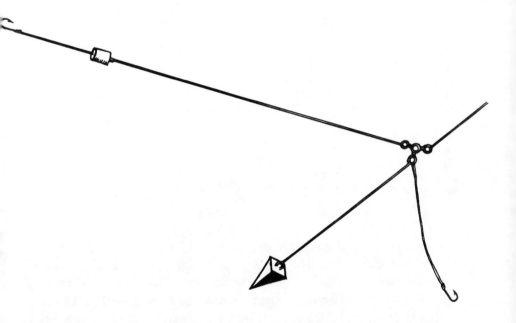

Combination surf rigs enable you to fish from the beach for more
than one species at the same time. A 3-ft. leader and hook with cork
added is attached to one eye of the 3-way swivel. A shorter leader
or snell with hook is attached to the other eye, also to which the
sinker is tied. The longer leader with cork can have a larger hook
and can be baited to attract striped bass, bluefish, or weakfish. The
shorter leader can have a smaller hook to catch kingfish or whiting,
croakers, flounders, or any other small fish.

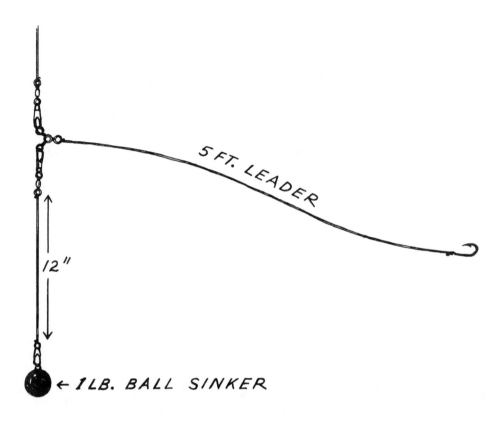

5 FT. LEADER

12"

← 1 LB. BALL SINKER

This rig is used to catch striped bass in the fast currents of San Francisco Bay Channel between the Golden Gate Bridge and Alcatraz Island. For bait, you use an anchovy that is hooked through the lips or nose. The rig is mainly employed from a drifting boat and is tried at different depths, but best results are usually obtained near the bottom. The 1-lb. sinker is required because of the strong currents near Alcatraz, but lighter weights can be used in other waters where the tides are weaker.

Two effective pollock rigs are shown on p. 147. The top one is the wooden float and small bucktail—also used for school stripers. The wood float can be short and light for spinning rods, or long and heavy for conventional surf rods. The nylon leader from float to jig can be about 20 in. long. This rig is best when the pollock are in shallow water near shore. The second rig is a diamond jig with a feather teaser about 2 feet ahead of it. This rig is used in jigging or dropping down and reeling in deep water, usually around sunken wrecks.

To make the "no hardware" rig, start with a piece of monofilament about 40 in. long (see illustration, p. 148). Tie a small loop on one end, to which the line is attached; on the other end, tie a large loop for holding the sinker. In between, tie 2 dropper loops, to which the hooks are attached. Dull or rusty hooks can be quickly replaced on this rig and sinkers can be changed in a hurry to suit fishing conditions. Such a rig is inexpensive and is especially suited to fishing in rocky areas or around obstructions where one gets hung up often and loses rigs.

Most anglers use only 1 jig when fishing for gamefish or bottom fish, but there are occasions when 2 jigs fished at the same time will prove more effective (see illustration, p. 149). Use a barrel swivel on the end of your line, then attach a short leader of about 8 or 9 in. to this swivel, and tie one jig to the end. Then take a leader twice as long (16 to 18 in.) and tie a snap to one end and another jig to the other end. Then attach the snap to the lower eye of the barrel swivel.

When using 2 jigs, you not only have added attraction but can use 2 different types of jigs. One can be bucktail and the other nylon or plastic. You'll also get "doubles" or 2 fish at a time when fishing in a school of fish.

Since it is impossible, or at least difficult, to cast lures which weigh a fraction of an oz. on the average saltwater spinning or casting outfit, a rig such as the one shown on p. 150 is valuable to have in your kit. You merely take some nylon-covered wire, slip on an egg sinker and a barrel swivel, and make a loop which is then crimped behind the sinker. Finally, tie or crimp on a snap where the lure will be attached.

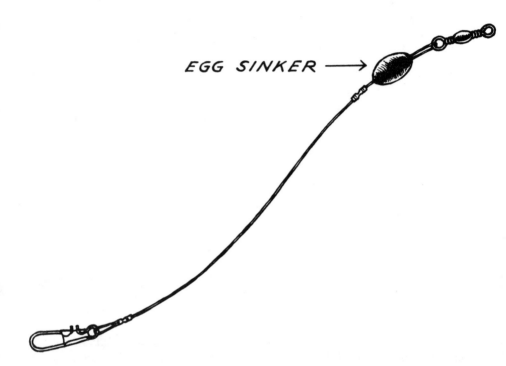

EGG SINKER ⟶

CHAPTER 14

Saltwater Natural Baits

Clams

THE bait usually used for cod is the "skimmer," or sea clam. Most anglers use the whole insides of one big clam on the hook. Some bury the hook point and barb, but you'll hook more fish if you leave the point and barb exposed. If bergalls are stealing the clam bait, you can add a chunk of whelk or "conch" or a strip of squid to the hook. Then if the clam is stolen, the tougher conch and squid remains to attract a cod.

Clams or mussels can be kept fresh for long periods by simply placing them in a plastic bag and putting them in a freezer. To save space, you can open the mussels or clams and just freeze the meat. They can be used at any time later by thawing them out.

Soft clams make a good chum for striped bass in bays. Here, you mash up the clams and dribble them overboard to form a slick. Chumming is best in rips and strong tides. Then bait a hook with a whole soft clam and drift it out in the tide.

Skimmer clams not only make good bait, but they can also be used as chum for porgies, sea bass, flounders, blackfish, croakers,

151

black drum, and cod. Big stripers can also be attracted by the clam chum when used in sloughs in inlets and under bridges. Put the chopped up clam meat into a chum pot or bag and lower it under the boat. You can also scatter some clam shells and clam meat around the boat.

CRABS

Shedder crabs and soft-shelled crabs are plentiful during the summer and early fall, and can be caught in bays. Use a long-handled net and wade the shallows where there is a heavy growth of eelgrass. Save the hard-shelled crabs for eating, but use the shedder crabs and soft-shells for bait. They will take striped bass when drifted in the tide in bays, and stripers and blues will also go for them in the surf. You can also use small pieces of shedder crabs for kingfish, weakfish, and croakers.

Fiddler crabs make good bait for blackfish or tautog and are sold by many tackle stores and bait dealers. If you want to catch your own, try the sand or mud flats and marshes of bays. The "mud" fiddler is dark, dirty green, and prefers the mud flats. This one isn't as good for bait as the lighter cream or tan colored "chinaback" fiddler which lives in burrows in sandy sections of bays. You have to catch fiddlers at low tide before they scoot into their holes, by making a trap from two long boards nailed together to form a corner. This is placed on the ground along the routes used by the crabs, and the fiddlers are chased into it where they get trapped in the corner.

A choice bait for striped bass in bays, rivers, and other inland tidal waters is a soft-shelled or shedder crab. It should be used whole and tied on to the hook. For best results, use it at night and drift it naturally out with the tide into likely spots.

When using large crabs for blackfish, remove the top shell and the two big claws. Break the other legs off at the joint; then cut the crab in half or in quarters, depending on the size. Insert your hook into one of the leg joints and into the body of the crab.

You can't beat a hermit crab as bait for sheepshead. These crabs which drag shells around are fairly plentiful in shallow water and can be gathered in large numbers. Crack the shell to remove the crab with its soft tail. Use the whole crab if it is small; if big, use only the tail portion.

You can often parlay a few calico or lady crabs into more bait when fishing for stripers during the summer months. After you catch the first fish or two, cut open their stomachs. You'll often find more calico crabs or other bait inside, which can then be used on the hook.

BAITFISH

When using a live killie for fluke or summer flounders, hook it through both lips. A dead baitfish such as a spearing, sand eel, or shiner can be hooked through the eye and then through the body. Live killies can be fished at anchor or while drifting and will swim and attract fish. Dead ones are best if drifted so that they have some motion.

Two great baits for drift fishing in Pacific waters for striped bass are a live shiner perch or a live anchovy. The perch are tougher and stay alive longer on the hook. Hook the live ones through one or both lips. A dead anchovy should be hooked with 2 hooks—one going through the lips and the other into the vent and out of the side.

The most effective methods of hooking dead baitfish such as spearing or silversides, sand eels, sardines, anchovies, small herring, menhaden, or mullet, are shown on p. 154. The top drawing shows the hook being run through the mouth and out through the belly.

In the bottom drawing, the hook and leader run through the mouth and out through the gill opening and then also hook through the body near the tail.

To catch big tarpon use a pinfish, squirrel fish, mullet, or crab on a hook. Live baits are best, but tarpon will also take a dead one at times.

The real secret in using live baitfish is to choose lively active fish, and hook them carefully so that they live a long time. As soon as the baitfish gets "tired" or is mauled or injured, it should be removed and a new one should be substituted.

Herring-mooching rigs used by West Coast anglers when fishing for salmon, while trolling or drifting in a boat, are rigged as shown on p. 155. Rig (A) uses a whole herring and 2 hooks which are tied on the end of the leader about 2 or 3 in. apart. The end hook is first inserted through both jaws of the herring, followed by the second hook. One hook is then inserted through one side of the herring, and the other hook is then run through the opposite side, as shown. The plug-cut

herring (B) is made by cutting the head of the herring at a 45°
angle and removing the entrails. Both hooks are then pulled through
the hole made at the cut head of the herring and impaled as shown.
Rig (C) is a cut spinner, made by cutting a pennant shaped fillet
from the side of a herring. It can be hooked with 1 hook as shown
or with 2 hooks.

You can easily catch your own spearing or silversides, to use as bait. These small baitfish usually hang around under piers or bridges. Crush some mussels or clams in an umbrella-type net, and lower it into the water a couple of feet below the surface. When the spearing gather over the net, pull it up quickly to catch the small baitfish.

You can hook a small lead baitfish by merely running the hook through the eye. However, a more secure way, and better if the fish are chopping off the tails of the bait, is to run the hook into both eyes and then into the body. (See illustration, p. 155.)

Two methods are best for hooking live baitfish. In the first, the fish is hooked through the back just ahead of the dorsal fin. Be care-

ful not to run the hook so deeply that it strikes the backbone. This
will kill the baitfish in a short time. This method is best when
still-fishing in one spot from shore, or in an anchored or slowly
drifting boat. The second way of hooking is through both lips. This
method is better when the baitfish is cast any distance, or when
fishing from a fast drifting or trolling boat.

A small whole bunker makes a good bait for cobia. Best results
are obtained if you bury most of the hook inside the baitfish.

For a change of pace or when the baitfish you are using are
small, try putting 2 or 3 of them on a single hook (see p. 157). Along
the Atlantic coast this can be done with sand eels, spearing, and
shiners. On the Pacific coast, you can try it with smelt, anchovies,
and sardines.

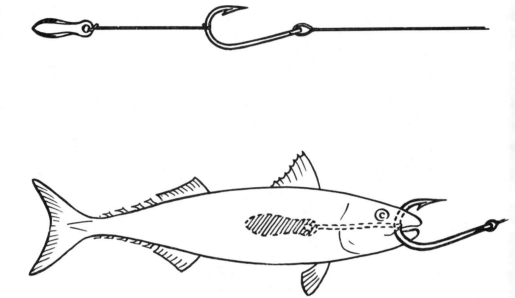

One problem often encountered when fishing with a large whole dead baitfish is how to get down deep in a tide or current. This can be done by the method illustrated here. Attach the hook to the line or leader, and then tie a short length of weak cord to the bend of the hook. To this, tie a sinker. Then shove this sinker through the mouth and into the throat of the baitfish, and insert the hook into the jaw of the fish. This way, the sinker is buried inside the baitfish, providing weight without hindering the presentation of the bait in any way. Such a weighted bait can be used for jewfish, black sea bass, grouper, tarpon, sharks, and any other large saltwater fish.

A fresh, lively anchovy will get more strikes from an albacore than a tired, sluggish one. One trick you can use is to give the reel hand a quick turn every few seconds to keep the baitfish moving.

Best bait for big stripers? Up Rhode Island way you can't beat a live eel used either from a boat or from shore. Live eels work from June to November and will take stripers during the day, but evening and night hours are best.

Live eels that are to be rigged are difficult to handle. You can kill them in about 15 or 20 min. by placing them in a container of salt; or, you can put the eels in the freezer compartment of your refrigerator. After a couple of hours take them out. They will be chilled and stiff and easier to handle.

If you plan to use a live eel for stripers, use a snap-swivel to hold the hook. Using such a device helps to prevent some of the tangles which result when an eel doubles back on the leader and twists himself around it.

Although live eels are usually fished from an anchored or drifting boat, there are times when slow-trolling with them deep produces good results.

LEAD HEAD

Two eel-tail lures which can be easily made are shown above. The first one is made by cutting an eel in half, pulling back the skin for a couple of inches, and then inserting the hook and the lead weight in front. Then the skin is tied tightly ahead of the lead. In the second lure, a larger section of meat is removed from the tail and a metal squid is inserted in the skin. Then the skin is tied around the front of the squid where a groove or notch has been filed. In both lures, the solid meat at the end of the tail is left to provide casting weight and durability.

Rigged eels and eelskin lures will take fish in the daytime, but are most effective around daybreak, dusk, and during the night. Some of the biggest stripers are caught on them when reeled or trolled slow after dark.

Millions of baby eels move into the Chesapeake Bay during the spring months after migrating from their birthplace in the vicinity of the Sargasso Sea. They enter the rivers or live in the saltwater bays and marshes. Striped bass and cobia feed on them, and small live-eels make a good bait for the fish in these waters.

Rigged eels, if they are small (between 8 and 15 in.), can be rigged with two hooks. But if they run up to 18 or 20 in., you can use 3 or 4 hooks.

OTHER BAITS

The jumbo edible shrimp found in the fish markets makes a good bait in salt water. Such shrimp and smaller ones are commonly used in Florida and Southern waters. But even up north, you can use dead shrimp for kingfish and weakfish in the surf, and for blackfish, porgies, and sea bass in the bays.

The natural squid is one of the most versatile baits an angler can use in salt water. A whole squid rigged with 1 or 2 hooks can be used offshore for swordfish and marlin. A whole small squid is good for big striped bass when surf fishing. Smaller pieces of squid can be used for school stripers, bluefish, and weakfish. Small pieces and strips can be used for fluke, sea bass, porgies, and silver hake or whiting. Strips of squip can also be added to artificial lures.

Although the plain jig or bucktail takes fish, it can often be made even more effective by adding additional attractors such as various natural baits to the hook. A half of a bloodworm or sandworm, a strip of squid, piece of shrimp, clam, or strip cut from a small fish are all good.

A quick way to obtain pileworms in rocky Pacific coast areas, where there are a lot of mussel covered rocks, is to pour some bleach such as Clorox over the mussels. This drives the worms out where they can be grabbed.

Strips cut from the sides and bellies of various fishes such as bonito, albacore, dolphin, and mackerel are used for offshore fishing, when trolling. Most of these strips run from about 8 to 14 in. in length and taper to a point at both ends. Some of the more popular shapes used for strip baits are shown here. The strips vary in thickness from ⅛ to ½ in. at the center, but are thinned or beveled along the edges. There are various ways of attaching these strips to a hook. One of these is shown here, making use of a safety pin catch which is formed from the stainless steel wire used as a leader. This holds the strip in place so that it rides straight when trolled through the water. Strip baits are used for sailfish, marlin, dolphin, barracuda, and many other offshore fish.

A good bait for sheepshead, blackfish, striped bass, and pompano along sandy beaches is the sand bug. These are the egg-shaped crustaceans which burrow into the wet sand where the waves break. You can probe for them with your fingers in the sand and grab them when you feel them. They can also be caught in wire basket scoop traps with long handles. These are placed flush against the sand where the receding wave can wash the bugs into the basket.

In hot weather, it is important to keep offshore baits and strips fresh. Keep them in plastic bags on ice until you are ready to use them.

The bergall, or cunner, is considered a pest and bait-stealer, but it can also be used for bait. The small ones can be hooked through the back and lowered to the bottom for cod. Larger ones can be cut into fillets and used for whiting or cod.

To drop chum under a boat, fill a paper bag with cracked mussels or clams and tie a cord around the mouth of the bag. Then lower it to the bottom and jerk hard to break open the bag, and drop the contents on the bottom.

California yellowtail can be caught on a strip bait which is cut from the side or belly of a bonito. The strip can vary from 4 to 6 in. in length and about an inch wide at the front end, then tapering to a point. Hooks in sizes 1/0 to 4/0 are used to hold the strip, as shown. A lead-core sinker weighing about ⅜ oz. is added to the leader about 3 ft. above the strip. To use the strip, cast out near a kelp bed or where yellowtail are present, let the rig sink a few feet, then reel it back with rod action to make the strip look alive.

If your bait is being stolen by crabs or bergalls, there are a couple of things you can do. In the surf, you can add a cork to your leader to keep the bait off the bottom. And then move the bait with a sharp yank every minute or so to frighten crabs away. When bottom fishing you can try changing to a tougher bait. Use squid, conch, crabs, or strips of fish. Such baits may also be stolen, but it will take a long time to chew them off.

A quick, handy strip bait rig can be made using 2 hooks and bending the barb down on 1, then sliding the eye over it and bending the barb back. Then you place a strip cut from bonito, albacore, mackerel, or mullet on the 2 hooks. It can be used for trolling offshore for various species. Such a rig used with a mullet strip is a killer for barracuda in Florida.

When fish are chopping off the tail part of a live or dead baitfish without getting hooked, the two-hook rig can be used (see illustration on p. 165). A short length of nylon or wire and a second hook is added to the first hook (A). The first hook is run through the fish's lips, while the second hook is impaled through the tail with the point facing down (B). When a live baitfish is used, the hooks should be small and of fine wire, in order not to kill the baitfish or to hamper its movements. This rig is used on the Pacific coast for barracuda when these fish are striking short. But it can be used for any saltwater gamefish that has a habit of chopping off the tail of the baitfish.

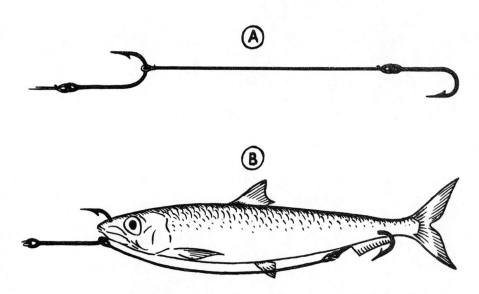

It is usually a waste of time to chum during slack tide since the chum sinks to the bottom directly under the boat, and this is also a poor time to fish anyway. Wait until the tide starts running before you resume chumming and fishing.

CHAPTER **15**

Striped Bass, Channel Bass, Bluefish, and Weakfish

STRIPED BASS

THE first stripers in the spring are usually caught in the tidal rivers and bays. In the beginning, they are sluggish and are taken on the bottom with sandworms or bloodworms for bait. Later on, they hit trolled spinners and worms, jigs, and small plugs. Most of these artificials should be worked slowly and deep early in the year. Later when baitfish appear; they can be worked near the surface or on top and reeled at faster speeds.

When fishing with bloodworms or sandworms for striped bass in the surf, cast out your baited rig, reel in your slack, and let the bait lie on the bottom for a few minutes. Then lift your rod to raise the sinker off the bottom, and reel in a couple of feet; wait a few minutes and reel in again. Keep doing this until the rig and bait is almost on the beach before you reel in for the next cast. This way you cover more territory and give the bait some movement.

The biggest stripers are usually found lying or feeding around boulders, deep-water reefs, or bars and rips, some distance from shore.

166

Here, they feed on menhaden, herring, whiting, small blackfish, bergalls, eels, and crabs which are found in such spots.

What lures does a surf angler need for stripers along the Atlantic coast? Well, there are 5 basic types of lures which will handle most striper surf fishing situations: First, there are the *metal squids* of flat, hammered stainless steel type lures. These are good for school bass, for long casts, and when the water is rough. Then there are the *jigs*, which are used with pork rind most of the time to take school bass from jetties and the beach if they are close in the wash. Next we have the *underwater plugs*, such as those with metal lips, or the straight mirror type plugs which travel at various depths. They are good day or night for both small and big fish. Other plugs which should be carried are the *surface plugs*, such as the swimmers and poppers. They are good day or night and are most effective when fish are breaking or chasing baitfish on the surface. Finally we have the *rigged eels* which are tops for big fish at night, daybreak, and dusk.

When trolling for striped bass, it is important to run the boat at the right speed and have the lure travel at the correct depth. As a general rule, troll slowly for striped bass. If there are charter boats trolling in the area, you can match their speed. How much line you let out will depend on where the stripers are feeding and the depth of the water. When fish are breaking on top and in shallow water, you let out less line than when the fish are lying near the bottom in deep water. Most experienced anglers mark their lines every 50 or 100 ft. so that they know how much line to let out each time.

Anglers seeking stripers in tidal rivers or creeks must know their tides. On the incoming tide you can move and change your location from one spot to another, following the tide as it increases in strength and creates eddies and rips at different places. Then on the outgoing tide, you can work your way back, trying the different spots along the way.

If the surf has been flat for several days and the water clear, wait for the day when an onshore wind kicks up and creates some white water. Surf fish, especially stripers which have been fasting during the calm period, will be hungry and prowling around for food when the water gets rough.

When stripers are seen breaking on top, you can take them by trolling or by casting. Casting from a drifting boat will not put the fish down like trolling through the middle of the school often will. If you do troll—troll along the edges of the school and do not speed up the boat. If you do open her up to reach another school of fish, slow down at least 100 ft. from the surfacing fish.

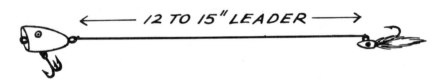

A good combination for the smaller striped bass in bays, sounds, and rivers is a small popping plug in front, and a light tiny jig on a 12 to 15 in. trailer behind it. This is popped to attract the stripers which usually hit the small jig.

More and more striped bass (and bluefish) are being caught on the new plastic eels. They can be used from boats for casting and trolling, and also from the surf. You may have to add a metal lip or other weight to give them action and casting weight.

When trolling for stripers in a shallow water from 4 to 10 ft. deep, let out a lot of line, especially if the water is clear. A boat will usually scatter a school of bass, but then they return behind the boat. With a long line out, they'll see your lure come by just as they are regrouping.

Striped bass in bays and rivers usually move up on the flats and into the shallow areas on the flood tide, then drop back on the ebb tide; therefore, the best procedure is to fish the shallow areas around high water and the deeper holes and channels during low water.

Your best chances of fooling a striped bass in the surf with a lure is when the water is slightly roiled or when it is rough and white. Other good times to fish are in the period around daybreak, dusk, and during the night. Under all these conditions, the wary striper has less opportunity to see or examine the lure carefully.

When fishing around bridges for striped bass, try to get there on the outgoing tide, especially at daybreak, dusk, or during the night. Stripers feed most heavily when the last of the outgoing tide occurs at these times.

The tiny grass shrimp usually used for weakfish as chum also attract striped bass in bays, creeks, rivers, and inlets. Two or three of these tiny shrimp can also be used on a small hook for bait.

If you want school stripers, fish from the surf. If you are mainly interested in catching big bass or "cows," fish from a boat. Of course, big bass are also taken from the surf, especially from deep-sloping beaches and jetties, but most of the fish that come close to shore are the schoolies. The big cows do most of their feeding and resting in the deeper holes, currents, and rips.

Striped bass feed on mackerel when they come close to shore. You can try plugs about the size of the mackerel; if that fails, use a tiny mackerel jig, or spoon, or metal squid, and try to catch some mackerel. Then hook it through the back and cast it out for stripers.

Stripers have been caught with big fish such as bunkers, whiting, long eels—even flounders—in their bellies. One angler caught a 50 lb. striper which had a smaller striper in its stomach. Maybe you can't use small stripers as bait, but it proves that BIG stripers like a BIG mouthful. Big lures may frighten or chase away small fish, but it attracts the big ones.

When you are fishing the surf from a beach or jetty at night, avoid using a light if you can. Most expert striped bass anglers claim that a flashing or moving light shined directly into the water will spook or alert a fish and it will not bite. If you must use a light, always face the beam toward the rocks or land instead of into the water. Of course, this doesn't mean you shouldn't use a light to gaff or land a fish in the final stages of the battle.

Anglers fishing the bridges on Long Island, N.Y., have been catching large striped bass by using live blackfish for bait. Best results are obtained with small blackfish about 5 to 6 in. long. The blacks are hooked through the lower lip and allowed to swim toward the bottom from a drifting boat. The fishing is usually best when the tide is not too strong at the start of the ebb.

The sandworm is a highly effective bait for striped bass and can be used in many ways. You can use a large, whole worm in the surf, on the bottom. Or, you can fish the worm with a sinker and a 3 or 4 ft. leader, while anchored or drifting in a river or inlet. You can also drift in a boat over a tidal flat or along shallow shores, letting the worm trail without any weight; or you can troll 1 or 2 sandworms behind a Cape Cod or willow-leaf spinner.

Some striper anglers believe that when striped bass hit lures or rigged eels, they first slap the lure with their tails before turning to grab them in their mouths. If this were true then there would be many stripers foul-hooked near the tail. But this rarely occurs. What probably happens is that a striper makes a pass at the lure and either misses or changes its mind in the last second. That is why you see so many swirls at surface lures.

When using lures for striped bass, reel them fairly fast if the water is clear or calm. If the water is rough and white or a bit dirty, reel the lures slower. Reel lures faster in the daytime than at night.

If you are fishing with a bottom rig for stripers, it's a good idea to add a smaller No. 1/0 hook on a short 12 or 14 in. leader just above your sinker, and the longer leader with a 4/0 or 5/0 hook just above it. Bait the larger hook with a whole sandworm for stripers, and the smaller hook with a 2 in. length of bloodworm for kingfish or northern whiting.

Boat anglers can make good catches of striped bass, even during the middle of the day. But surf anglers will do better if they stick to the daybreak, dusk, and night routine. However, if the day is cloudy or there is a storm or heavy surf, daytime fishing can often be productive, even from the beach or jetty.

Striped bass like to lie just inside the shadow caused by a lighted bridge at night. Here they wait for baitfish moving with the tide. As soon as the baitfish enter the shadow, the stripers charge them. To get these fish, the best procedure is to cast your lure anywhere from 10 to 30 ft. outside the shadow line and let the tide sweep it into the shadow area. If the stripers are near the surface, your casts can be close to the shadow line; but if they are down deep, cast well up-tide.

Striped bass will often hang out below boats, docks, piers, fish-houses where clams, crabs, or fish are being shucked or cleaned, and where the remains are thrown into the water. This is chumming on a large scale and the bass stay around for the free hand-out. So these places are also good to fish with similar baits.

Locating striped bass along rocky coastlines, such as those found in Rhode Island, is easier than along open sand beaches. Stripers lurk in certain spots along a rocky coast, and these usually remain the same year after year. So once you learn their locations you can take fish from them regularly. Even if you catch a fish from such a spot, another one will take its place in a short time.

When surf fishing for striped bass and using worms, bring along plenty of bait. Use a whole large sandworm on the hook or 2 or 3 bloodworms. The stingy angler who cuts his worms and uses small pieces rarely catches any stripers.

If you are casting to a school of stripers and hook a fish, wait until you have the fish under control, then have another angler cast just behind the hooked fish. Often several stripers will follow a hooked bass and will go for another lure cast into them.

Striped bass in bays, tidal rivers, and inlets like to lie around obstructions such as bridges, piles, rocks, and rocky points where a strong tide prevails. Bridges are prime fishing spots. One of the best ways to fish these is to anchor the boat about 50 ft. above the bridge and work your lures or baits under the bridge. When the tide changes, you move the boat to the other side of the bridge.

If you want big stripers, you have to specialize and concentrate all your efforts on them. The reason many surf and boat anglers don't catch more big stripers is because they get sidetracked and fish for the smaller ones. There are more small stripers around than big ones and they are easier to catch. But you can be wasting your time with the small fish when the time is ripe for the big ones.

Look for striped bass in the tidal marshes in the deeper holes in creeks, or where these creeks join the main channels in the bay.

In areas where slow trolling or drifting is done with sandworms or bloodworms, you often have trouble with bergalls or cunners, or blowfish or sea robins hitting the worm. Then, it's a good idea to wait until dark and troll or drift after the sun goes down. Striped bass usually bite better then, anyway, and you don't have to worry about the bait-stealers.

Chasing the birds is a common practice when striper fishing—especially in the fall of the year. With huge schools of bass feeding, gulls are attracted and pinpoint the action. If you see birds "working." you can run up to the edge of the school and cast or troll. However, if there are too many boats around, you'll probably catch more fish if you stay away from the rest of the fleet and try to locate a different school of fish. Or you can try steady trolling in the immediate area and let the others chase the fish. You'll probably catch more fish in the long run, although casting does provide more fun and sport.

One reason why striped bass fishing is better at dusk, or sundown, and at night is that baitfish head inshore as it gets dark. They hug the shoreline or move up the sand and rock bars, coves, and river mouths, or even into the breaking surf to escape the bass. But the striper which isn't afraid of rough, white water, or sand in its gills, or shallow water, moves in right after the baitfish.

As a rule, striped bass do most of their fighting below the surface and rarely break water. Small or medium sized fish will often put up a fuss on top if hooked near the boat or shore. Even a big striper may roll or thrash around on top if hooked on a surface plug or rigged eel. When this happens, lower your rod tip quickly and loosen up on the drag. Let the fish run and sink below the surface, and you're less likely to lose him. A good-sized striper can straighten out the hooks or break the line when he rolls and twists on top on a short line.

When you catch your first striper, cut a strip from its belly and add it to a jig, spoon, or metal squid. The white belly serves the same purpose as pork rind as an attractor, but also gives off a fish scent which the rind lacks.

CHANNEL BASS

Big channel bass may be found along the surf, in an inlet, or in a bay. In most cases if they can be seen, they can usually be caught. Trolling big spoons takes them, and is best in deeper water or roiled water. In clear or shallow water, casting metal squids or heavy, stainless steel type lures is better.

Channel bass are caught in the surf mostly on natural baits. It is believed that they locate such baits by their keen sense of smell more than by sight, so a fresh bait is important in this fishing. Keep changing baits often and cast them into spots where the scent or odor from the bait will be carried out into deeper water, or toward a break in a bar or entrance to a slough.

One of the top lures used in trolling for big channel bass is the spoon. Use big spoons up to 7 or 8 in. long in Virginia and North Carolina. Use smaller 2½ or 3 in. spoons for the smaller redfish or "reds" found in Florida and the Gulf of Mexico.

Channel bass fishing in the surf is best in a slough. This is the deeper water inside the outer sand bar. The most productive sloughs have a break or cut in the outer bar, or are near an entrance or exit to deeper water.

Artificial lures are best for channel bass when you can see them in a large school near the surface. Then, a metal squid or stainless steel hammered type lure cast into them will usually bring a strike.

Channel bass in the surf will take such baits as shedder crab, bunker, mullet, spot, whiting, and other small fish. Strips or fillets cut from these fish will work, but do not last as long as the head and part of the body on the hook.

A moving bait covers more territory and gets more bites from channel bass in the surf than one which stays in one place. The sinker should be heavy enough to make a good cast, but light enough to move with the current in a slough. As the bait moves along the beach, the angler should follow it.

Big channel bass are spooky in clear, shallow water, and trolling boats will scatter them quickly. In such waters, trolling 200 or 300 ft. behind the boat is best.

When trolling for big channel bass and you hook a fish, reel in the other lines and jerk the spoons on them. You'll often hook other fish which are following the hooked drum.

Small channel bass or redfish come into shallow water to feed over shellfish beds, grass flats, and to lie in the potholes waiting for an unsuspecting baitfish, shrimp, or crab to wander by. Often you can see the reds cruising or lying near the bottom. In real shallow water, you can spot their tails breaking the surface.

The smaller channel bass found in southern waters will often hit lures such as plugs, spoons, and jigs. But all these lures should be worked as slowly as possible to obtain strikes. And wait a second or two before setting the hook, to give the redfish a chance to mouth the lure.

Look for redfish in Florida along mangrove-lined shorelines or over oysters bars. The best tide to fish is from high water down to about half-out.

When wading the flats for channel bass or redfish, quiet stalking is necessary. The water is usually shallow and clear, and the fish are spooky. Crouch low when casting and try to place your lure about 2 or 3 ft. ahead of a cruising redfish. If your lure lands too far ahead of the fish, he won't see it; if it lands too close, it will scare him.

Look for small channel bass in a wide variety of spots: flats, holes, in rivers, inlets, or passes and sounds or bays. Because once you locate them, they are usually willing biters and can be made to hit a lure or take a bait.

BLUEFISH

You'll catch more bluefish when chumming if you let your butter-fish bait drift naturally with the tide. Just holding it in the current or reeling it against the tide isn't as effective as a bait drifting with the flow of water. When a bluefish picks up the bait. don't try to set the hook too soon. Let him run with the bait a few feet and sock him.

When chumming for blues and you get a lot of strikes and pick-ups, but fail to hook the fish, try changing to a smaller hook, such as a 4/0 or 5/0, and use a smaller piece of butterfish for bait. When small blues are around, they often have trouble swallowing the larger hooks and baits.

Trolling is a favorite and dependable way to catch bluefish in most waters. If they are on or near the surface, you can use monofilament line, a 3 or 4 oz. trolling weight. Lures such as small spoons, jigs, and feathers can be trolled fairly fast. If the blues are down deep, use surgical tube lures or small spoons on a wire line and troll slower.

When bluefish come into the surf, the best lures to use are metal squids, heavy spoons, and surface plugs. If they don't hit these, try fishing on the bottom with such baits as cut mullet, menhaden or bunker, butterfish, or any other fish.

Avoid shiny swivels, snaps, or other hardware when fishing for bluefish. These fish snap at anything shiny and also follow a hooked fish; and they often bite at shiny snaps or swivels on a leader or line. If you must use such connectors, use dull brass swivels or those finished in black.

Bluefish usually show on the surface early in the morning right after daybreak and in the evening.

Bluefish can often be caught in the surf in the same place and time as striped bass. And, like striped bass, they'll often hit best when the surf is on the rough side and the tides and rips are strong.

When bluefish are following your lure without hitting, try speeding up your retrieve. If that doesn't work, change lures and keep changing until you find one they want.

Blues can often be caught with a diamond jig. One method is to cast and let the lure sink a few feet, then retrieve it fast. Or you can let the lure settle to the bottom under the boat, then jig it up and down near the bottom.

For big bluefish, the Azores in the Atlantic Ocean are the place to fish. The world's record rod-and-reel bluefish was taken at San Miguel in August 1953 and weighed 24 lbs. 3 ozs. Commercial fishermen have taken them on handlines here weighing up to 39 lbs.

Weakfish

Best lures for northern or gray weakfish in the surf are small spoons, metal squids, jigs, and underwater plugs. Best natural baits for these fish are sandworms, jumbo shrimp, strips of squid, strips of fish, and shedder crabs.

Fishing for northern weakfish, or sea trout too, is often good from a pier, bridge, or dock with bright lights. Some anglers hang lamps or lanterns over the water to attract the weaks. Actually what happens is that the light attracts small baitfish and shrimp—which in turn draws the weakfish.

Jetties and breakwaters are better fishing spots for northern weakfish than the beach itself. These fish usually prefer deeper water than other surf fish. At low tide, or the change when it starts to come in, is a good time to fish for weaks. By fishing from a jetty or breakwater, you'll have plenty of deep water near the end at low tide.

Spotted weakfish, or sea trout, are most numerous over grassy flats which harbor baitfish, shrimp, and crabs on which they feed. The best flats to fish are those which have a good current or tide and plenty of grass beds with deeper, sandy holes among the weeds.

For drifting the grass flats for sea trout, a light wind is best. It ripples the water and also moves the boat at the right speed. A dead, flat calm is poor for this fishing.

A dependable way of catching sea trout is to use a live baitfish such as a small pigfish under a popping cork. The leader below the cork can be about 10 or 12 in.

If you want to catch the big "gator" sea trout in Florida, fish around the full moon and new moon. The best tide is usually just before and after high water. Early in the morning and in the evening are two good fishing periods.

Sea trout or southern weakfish usually leave the grass flats or shallow areas during a cold spell. They move into the deeper holes and channels where they can still be caught on bait or deep-working lures.

CHAPTER 16

Tuna, Swordfish, Marlin, Sailfish, Dolphin, Wahoo, Albacore and Bonito

TUNA

GIANT tuna aren't easy to hook in a chum line, and it's a good idea to have along different kinds of bait. The big tuna have been caught on bunker, mackerel, butterfish, whiting, ling, and herring. Live baits are very good, but are difficult to keep and catch when needed.

WHOLE SQUID

HERRING

When giant tuna refuse to take a single trolled bait, it's a good idea to try a gang of baits. This can be several squid, herring, mackerel—or a combination. Usually the end bait is a whole squid rigged with a single hook. The others above are teasers without hooks, and rigged so that they fall off when a tuna grabs the end bait.

School tuna are partial to such lures as Jap feathers, nylon jigs, and spoons or metal lures. Some days they'll show a preference for one color or another. Thus its a good idea to carry feathers and jigs in white, yellow, red and white, black and white, orange and blue. You can troll a different color on each line and find out which one they go for.

School tuna in the larger sizes often strike rubber and plastic lures such as imitations of eels, squid, balao, and various other baitfish.

When trolling for school tuna, best results are usually obtained with lures trolled anywhere from 15 to 40 ft. astern. However, there are times, such as when the water is calm, when they'll hit better if the lures are dropped back 50 to 80 ft. behind the boat. Once the correct distance is determined, all the lures can be trolled in a line parallel to each other.

What's the best trolling speed for school tuna? Generally speaking, most school tuna trolling is done at speeds from 6 to 10 knots. The exact speed will depend on the particular boat used, the lures used, and what the tuna want that day. Each boat owner must experiment until he finds the correct speed for his boat.

When the water is flat and glassy offshore, school tuna are often shy and refuse to hit lures. Then it's a good idea to wait until a breeze picks up and the water becomes ripped or choppy. Try trolling again, and chances are good that the tuna will begin hitting.

If you are venturing offshore into school tuna territory, carry some rigged eels with a single hook at the head, and troll them on top. They'll act as a teaser and will often attract the larger school tuna which will grab the eel. And you may even raise a white marlin with the eel.

When you are trolling with 3 or 4 lures and hook a small tuna, keep the other lures in the water, and have the anglers jig them quickly back and forth. This will usually result in more strikes and more hooked fish.

If you know there are school tuna around and they refuse to strike, try speeding up the boat and circling around in the area. This turmoil and white water may excite the fish and cause them to investigate the disturbance.

While trolling for school tuna, do not set the drag on your reels too tight. Set it just tight enough to hook the tuna, but light enough to allow line to peel off the reel freely. At the fast trolling speeds required for the smaller tuna, a hard strike can break the line, rod, or pull the whole outfit overboard—if the drag is too tight. Once the tuna is hooked, you can slow down the boat and tighten the drag.

Look for draggers or commercial fishermen pulling their nets and sorting their catch at sea. This acts as huge chum when fish escape or trash fish are thrown overboard. Giant tuna often gather around such commercial boats.

The usual method of catching school tuna is by trolling various lures. Some of the larger school tuna shy away from the lures; then, one method which often brings results is to use a live whiting or ling. These can be caught by jigging near the bottom with a diamond jig or by bait fishing. Then you hook the whiting or ling through the back, and let it out behind the boat about 70 or 80 ft., and pull it very slowly through a school of tuna.

Once you hook a school tuna, keep it in the water until another angler on the boat hooks another fish. These fish tend to swim together and follow a hooked fish. By always keeping at least one hooked fish in the water, you can hold the school near the boat.

When fishing for giant tuna, and you want to get a live bait down deeper in a strong tide or current, use the rig above. Here, a light sinker is tied to the swivel between the line and leader. This should be tied with weak cord so that it breaks off during the fight.

When school tuna first arrive in northern waters, they are usually far offshore. As summer progresses, the tuna move in closer to shore, but they like to stay in the bright blue water which eddies from the

Gulf Stream. Such eddies often have bits of sargassum weed, sea turtles, and other tropical sea life in them. This is the best place to troll your lures.

When fishing for tuna at the Mud Hole or 17 Fathoms off the New Jersey coast, carry some hairnets with you. Fill these with some bunker chum and tie it around a hook. Then drift it out in the current in your chum slick. This used to work on these grounds many years ago and could work again when tuna refuse to take the regular baits.

Trolling for big tuna should be done slowly with the bait skipping occasionally, and then riding below the surface. In a strong current or tide, the boat will barely move, but the baits will have plenty of action.

When giant tuna refuse to take baits on the regular stainless or cable wire leaders, try a heavy nylon monofilament leader testing from 150 to 200 lbs. Use at least 15 ft. of the mono material ahead of your regular Dacron line.

When searching for giant tuna, first try to locate schools of mackerel, herring, or whiting, especially on or near the surface. Big tuna feed on these and are more apt to be present where concentrations of these fish are heavy.

If school tuna are on the surface but do not hit the regular lures, try using a spoon. Any spoon about 4 or 5 in. long with a strong hook can be used. Drop it back about 150 ft., then run the boat in front of the school of tuna so that the spoon moves through the fish. To give the spoon more action, jerk the rod at regular intervals; the spoon should ride below the surface and not skip or skate on top of the water.

When fishing for school tuna, have one rod rigged with a butterfish jig or metal squid. When a tuna is hooked, it should be brought up to the boat and held in the water. Then another angler can grab the spare rod and drop the butterfish jig back toward the hooked tuna in case other tuna are hanging around. Other times, casting the jigs or metal squids ahead of a school of splashing tuna will bring strikes, when trolling will only scare the fish away.

SWORDFISH

Swordfish may show up on the surface with their dorsal and tail sticking high out of the water; other times, you'll see only the tips of the fins cleaving the surface; and still other times, they will be seen underwater just below the surface. At such times, a lookout mast or tuna tower is a big help in locating the swordfish and keeping track of the direction in which they are moving.

The best time for swordfish in Atlantic waters is during June and early July. That is when the first fish appear and are more inclined to take a bait. Later on they seem to spread out more, and are more reluctant to strike.

The best days for sighting swordfish are when the ocean isn't too rough. Then you can spot their fins or see the fish below the surface.

If you do see a swordfish on the surface and then lose sight of it, don't give up and move away. Hang around and wait for the fish to re-appear. Also look around for another fish. Swordfish often travel in pairs and sometimes in small packs or schools.

MARLIN

When a blue marlin rises behind your teaser, keep him interested by pulling the teaser away from him, then dropping it back so that he doesn't get it but also doesn't lose sight of it. In the meantime, let out your bait so that the marlin can spot it and hit it.

If you see dolphin leaping out of the water as if trying to get away from something, run your boat over to the spot and troll in the area. Chances are good that there are blue marlin below which are chasing the dolphin. The dolphin referred to is, of course, the fish, and not the mammal.

When a white marlin follows your bait but refuses to strike, reel in all the baits except one. Then when the fish approaches, reel in a few feet of line so he doesn't get the bait. Keep teasing the fish this way until he gets angry and charges the bait, and grabs it without any hesitation.

MAKE HOLE AND
INSERT HOOK

WIRE RUNS THROUGH EYE
OF THE HOOK.

Although the rigged eel is a killer for striped bass and bluefish, it is also a good lure for white marlin when trolled offshore. It can be rigged quickly using a large single 8/o or 9/o hook at the head. To do this, simply make a hole at the eel's throat, insert the hook eye first so that it emerges inside the eel's mouth. Then run a stainless steel wire leader through the eel's nose, into the eye of the hook, and form a loop by twisting the wire. For best results, troll the eel so that it skims the surface with the tail slapping the water.

When searching for white marlin, look for an "edge"—a line where the clean blue offshore water meets the greener, dirtier inshore water. In some areas this may be only about 8 or 10 mi. out, but in other areas you may have to travel 30 or 40 mi. offshore to find the marlin grounds.

A good bait for both white marlin and blue marlin is a small dolphin. For white marlin, a dolphin about 10 in. long is best. For blue marlin, you can use a bigger one up to 15 or 18 in. Rig the bait with the hook protruding from the belly. It can be trolled so that it skips on the surface at times and also submerges a few inches at other times.

When marlin fishing, rig up several baits in advance, and especially a variety of different baits. Then if the fish refuses one kind, you can quickly attach and try a different kind.

On days when white marlin aren't showing on top or following skipped baits, you can try trolling below the surface or drifting a bait deep. If live baits can be obtained, they should be used for drifting. But fresh, dead baits such as mackerel, butterfish, and squid can also be used.

Most anglers fishing for white marlin and sailfish these days release the fish unless it's the first one they caught or a trophy size desired for mounting. A quick release rig-up can be made by using about 10 or 12 ft. of 100-lb.-test monofilament, to the end of which is tied a swivel and then about 3 or 4 ft. of light No. 4 or 5 stainless

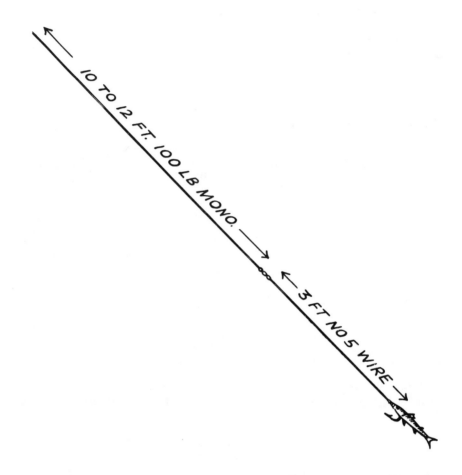

steel wire. To get rid of a fish near the boat, merely jerk on the mono leader to break the wire leader.

If a marlin strikes an artificial lure such as a feather or plastic bait, no drop-back is necessary. Instead, you should set the hook immediately before the fish drops the lure.

On calm, clear, sunny days it is best to troll baits for marlin farther out than on rough, overcast days.

SAILFISH

When sailfish do not take a bait trolled on the surface, you can try a live blue-runner for bait. This small fish is hooked in the head and is trolled very slowly. When a sailfish chases the blue runner and grabs it, you should give it some slack line before setting the hook.

One of the deadliest ways to use a live baitfish such as a blue runner for sailfish is to rig it from a flying kite. This keeps the baitfish on or near the surface where it struggles and splashes to attract the billfish.

Sailfishing off Florida's East Coast is usually most productive when the wind is from the northwest, but not too strong so that the waves are big. A light or moderate breeze is best, and clean water is preferred over "trashy" water filled with weeds and other debris.

If a sailfish is following a bait on an outrigger but refuses to strike, try snapping it off and letting it fall back toward the fish. This sometimes works, and the reluctant fish will grab the bait.

Sailfish have been caught on artificial lures occasionally, usually while trolling for other fish. But some anglers have discovered that they will take certain plugs, and quite a few have been caught deliberately with these lures.

DOLPHIN

If you are trolling well offshore in southern waters or during the summer months in northern waters and spot some floating sea weed, driftwood, boxes, or similar flotsam, swing your boat so that your lures pass close to such objects. Dolphin often lurk beneath such cover and will strike a lure passing near by.

Dolphin found in the Gulf Stream are most plentiful along sargassum weed lines. You can troll your lures along such lines of weeds, and sooner or later you should run into the dolphin.

Small dolphin travel in schools and when you catch one, look for more. Keep the fish in the water until you hook another, and by repeating this process you can often clean out an entire school. Big dolphin, on the other hand, tend to shun company and travel alone or in pairs.

Besides trolling for dolphin, try casting with a light one-handed spinning rod for these colorful fish. They'll hit plugs, spoons, or jigs and put up a long, spectacular fight on the light tackle.

WAHOO

Troll baits or lures for wahoo about 70 or 80 ft. behind a boat. The bait or lure should run on the surface or just below it. Top baits for wahoo are small fish, such as balao or mullet. They'll also hit strips cut from bonito, albacore, and Spanish mackerel. Lures such as feather, jigs, spoons, and plugs also draw hits from these fast, streamlined fish.

Wahoo are most plentiful along the edges of reefs and dropoffs in depths from 100 to 300 ft. Such waters are found in Bermuda and the Bahamas.

A favorite trick a wahoo tries when on the end of a line is to make a long run, then come back toward the boat, resulting in slack line. The alert angler lets the fish run with a light drag, then reels fast to regain the slack line.

ALBACORE AND BONITO

Both false albacore and bonito are leader shy and when they come into a chum slick, you'll get more pick-ups if using small hooks and fine lines. Take off all wire leaders and snaps or swivels; use the lightest monofilament leader you can. On private boats with one or two men fishing you can hook more fish with a spinning outfit and 10- or 12-lb.-test line. On crowded party boats, of course, you'll need 30 lb. line on a conventional outfit in order to handle and lift the fish out of the water.

During August and September, false albacore and bonito usually start showing up in the catches offshore and on the bluefish grounds. They usually hit a lure such as a feather, jig, spoon, or metal squid trolled fast. They often show up in the chum slicks when fishing for bluefish; they'll take butterfish and bunker bait, but if you want to increase your chances of hooking them, bring along some small bait-fish such as spearing or silversides, sand eels or shiners.

False albacore like a fast moving lure. When casting, reel in as fast as you can turn the handle. A rapid retrieve reel is better than a low ratio one for this work. When trolling, move the boat as fast as when you troll for school tuna. Some days the albacore will hit the lures right in the wash, but other times you have to let out quite a bit of line behind the boat.

If you plan to save some school tuna, false albacore, or bonito for eating purposes, gut and bleed these fish as soon as possible. If you can do it as soon as they are caught, the better. And if the weather is hot, keep them on ice or at least in the shade. They are oily fish which spoil quickly in hot weather and soon turn soft. After the fish have been steaked or filleted, place them in cold, salty water for four or five hours. Then you can prepare them as any other fish.

CHAPTER 17

Tarpon, Snook, and Bonefish

TARPON

IN A strong tide such as is found under bridges, an underwater plug is often effective for tarpon. Here, best results are obtained by reeling the plug very slowly against the current; or cast up-tide and let the lure swim toward the bridge, also reeling at a slow-to-moderate speed.

Tarpon often take a dead bait very slowly and can be mistaken for a small fish. However, give them time to swallow the bait, and once the line starts to move out fast, lean back and set the hook hard.

For tarpon fishing on shallow flats, a light wind which creates a ripple is better than a dead calm. Then you can approach the fish closer without spooking them.

Tarpon are great night-feeders and that is the best time to fool and catch them. The period around the full moon is especially good, and they can then be caught in the inlets, passes, and under bridges.

Usually the best technique for tarpon when using a surface plug is to work it fast with plenty of commotion. This works best in deeper water or discolored water. But in shallow, clear water this same retrieve will often frighten the tarpon. Then a resting plug activated by a slight twitch or two will draw a strike.

When fishing for tarpon from a bridge, it is usually best to cast on the up-tide side where the current is coming toward the bridge. Tarpon like to lie on that side facing the tide and wait for baitfish or crabs to swim toward them.

When you see tarpon rolling or showing on the surface, be careful when you approach them. Cut your motor when you are a couple of hundred feet away and row or paddle closer. Drifting is a good way to approach the fish, but not directly over them; let the boat drift alongside, and cast toward the fish.

To catch a big tarpon on light tackle such as a fly rod or a spinning rod or bait-casting gear, fish for them in shallow water. Flats with water from 4 to 8 ft. deep are best for such fishing. In such waters, tarpon tend to leap instead of making long runs, thus tiring themselves out faster.

Lures used for tarpon must be varied in action according to the mood of the fish. When using a surface plug, they often like a fast, frantic retrieve. But on other days a slow, erratic retrieve with occasional twitches of the rod tip is better.

Tarpon often gulp a lure gently and many strikes are undetected. Other fish are lost because an angler strikes too soon before the tarpon closes its mouth. Better results are obtained by waiting a second or two to give the fish a chance to turn downward before setting the hook.

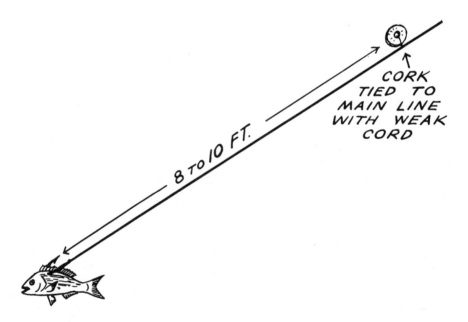

You can fish live crabs and small fish such as pinfish, pigfish, and grunts with a float for tarpon. The float can be cork or any other

cheap kind tied about 8 or 10 ft. above the hook. It should be tied
with weak cord to the main fishing line, so that when a fish is hooked
or leaps the cork or float breaks loose. With this rig, you can either
anchor the boat and let the float and bait move out, or you can
drift in a boat and let the float move along with the tide.

When fishing for tarpon in deep water where a weight is needed,
one problem is how to get rid of the sinker used to get the bait down.
Two rigs which are used for this purpose are illustrated here: The
first one (A) makes use of a regular bank sinker which has a hole in
each end. (You can easily drill such a hole in the bottom end of a
regular sinker). Then a weak thread is used to tie the sinker close
to the barrel swivel and to the leader as shown. In figure (B) the
sinker is attached to the barrel swivel with a weak line for any
distance dropper you want. This also makes a good rig when fishing
over a rocky bottom where the sinker gets fouled quickly. Then the
weak line will break and you'll lose the sinker, but save the rest of
the rig.

When casting to tarpon lying along the mangroves or on the shallow flats, it is important to cast the lure about 2 or 3 ft. in front of their nose. If you cast too close, you may scare the fish; if you cast too far, the fish won't see the lure or will ignore it.

Tarpon have a favorite trick of rolling at or bumping a lure without taking it. When this happens, resist striking, but wait until the line tightens and a solid hit is felt before you try to set the hook.

Live mullet make excellent bait for tarpon fished from a bridge or boat. Hook the mullet through the back and fish it anywhere from 6 to 15 ft. down in the channels and holes.

Surface plugs or popping bugs usually work best on tarpon around daybreak, in the evening, and when the water is roiled or muddy.

The best tackle for catching the baby tarpon found in the canals, creeks, rivers, and mangrove swamps is a fly rod. With this, you can cast the tiny lures such as popping bugs, streamers, and bucktails and wet flies that the small tarpon hit.

When fishing for tarpon with a live or dead bait, it is necessary to give the fish plenty of slack line when he picks up the bait. One way to do this is to cast out your bait and let it sink, then strip off line from your reel and coil it on a seat or bottom of the boat. When you get a bite, let the tarpon take the coiled line and move out until he can swallow the bait; then set the hook hard in its bony mouth.

SNOOK

In the fall of the year when mullet are migrating and northeast storms prevail, snook will be found feeding around inlets and along the beaches. Any lure which imitates these mullet is a good bet. Surface poppers, swimmers, underwater plugs, and mirror-type plugs can all be used.

Snook like to lie close to bridge supports or pier piles. Here a form of walking-trolling often works. You simply lower your lure (usually a jig or plug) and trail it through the water as you walk along the rail. Fairly heavy, stiff rods, strong lines, and strong hooks are required to handle the big snook hooked by this method.

In snook fishing, it pays to wait out the fish. If you know snook are present under a bridge or in some hole but are not striking, keep on fishing. Sooner or later when the tide is right or when baitfish or other marine life appears, the snook may go on a feeding spree.

When snook are in deep water in the Everglades country, a good bait is a needlefish about 10 in. long with a 3 oz. yellow or white jig at the head of the bait. Run the hook of the jig through the head of the needlefish and lash the bill to the body of the jig. This is trolled deep in the holes or channels where snook lie.

A heavy rain which floods the backwaters with fresh water may drive the snook and tarpon away. These fish often come up into brackish water to feed, but a sudden radical change bringing in too much fresh water will drive them away.

Once you have raised a snook or located one, keep casting your lure over the fish; this repeated casting will often get a strike if kept up persistently.

When snook are found in narrow canals or creeks, a fly lure is usually best to use in these confined waters. The small size imitates the tiny shrimp or baitfish snook feed on in such waters, and the light streamer or bucktail lands lightly without frightening the fish.

Snook will often take a strip of rag, cardboard, or even heavy paper that is cut to about 3 or 4 in. long and then is stirred and swished around on top of the water at night from a pier or bridge.

One good way to work a jig for snook from a bridge is to cast against or up into the tide, and let it carry the lure toward you under the bridge. Reel in just fast enough to take up the slack line.

Small snook feeding on tiny minnows or shrimp often refuse to hit the large, conventional spinning or bait-casting lures; at such times a small streamer fly used on a fly rod will often work. If the snook are chasing minnows, work your fly fairly fast in short jerks. If no fish are showing, cast the streamer out, let it sink about a foot, and retrieve it in slow jerks. You can also try surface popping bugs along the shoreline for snook.

Sometimes adding half a shrimp to a bucktail jig will produce better when fishing for snook than the plain jig. Either the front half or head or the tail section of the shrimp can be used.

A darter-type plug is a great lure for snook. For best results cast it near the mangroves. You can pop it a couple of times, then pull it underwater, and reel it at a good speed as you whip the rod.

When snook are lying deep in rivers, canals, and the larger creeks, one of the best ways to catch them is by trolling. For this, use spoons, underwater plugs, and jigs. These should be trolled as slowly as possible and close to the bottom.

Snook get educated fast and after a few are caught from one spot they refuse to strike. Then the best thing to do is to move on to a new spot where the snook haven't been fished hard; another trick that sometimes works is to change lure or colors. Snook are always easier to fool at night, at dusk, or daybreak than in the daytime.

BONEFISH

The best flats for bonefishing in Florida usually have grassy bottoms and clean water with fairly strong tides. Bonefish like warm, clean water, and dirty water chases them or makes it difficult to see them. A cold wind will also chase them into deeper water, but they will return as soon as the water and weather get warm again.

When bonefishing, try to get out early in the morning when there is little or no wind and the water is calm—bonefish are easier to see under such conditions. The sun behind you also helps in spotting the fish. Later on in the afternoon when the wind picks up, the water often becomes too choppy to spot the elusive white ghost.

When a bonefish is seen, the first cast with a lure is the most important. Make it as accurate as possible, because the odds are that you won't get another chance with the same fish.

One of the best bonefish lures is the flat "wiggle" jig worked slowly in water from 2 to 5 ft. deep.

In very shallow water, fly fishing will take more bonefish than heavier lures. Flies drop lightly and sink slowly and work best in thin water. For deeper water, however, where bonefish must be reached on the bottom, heavier lures such as jigs used with a spinning outfit are better.

If a bonefish is swimming toward you, there is an effective way to cast to the fish. Make the lure drop at least 10 or 12 ft. behind the approaching bone, then reel fast to bring the lure up to the fish. Then slow down the retrieve and work your lure to give it the best action as it comes up alongside the fish.

While most casting for bonefish is done directly to the fish, you can sometimes catch them by casting blind along drop-offs. This can be done from a drifting boat or when wading. It's a good idea to cast all around you when wading, since bonefish may be following your path.

The best flies to choose for bonefish are those tied to imitate shrimp or small baitfish. They should also sink slowly in the water since you have to cast well ahead of the fish, and it will take a few seconds before the "bone" reaches and spots the lure.

In some areas such as the Cayman Islands, bonefish are chummed with tiny minnows or "fry." For bait, you can use several of the minnows on a small hook. Jigs with some of the minnows on the hook will also take bonefish in these waters.

If you are using bait for bonefish and the current isn't strong, no sinker is required. Simply lob out the bait to the desired spot. Then let out slack line and back up to shallower water until you are a good distance from the bait.

To hold bonefish in an area while you fish for them, try scattering shrimp or cut conch all around. You can use the conch for bait, or you can cast artificial lures once the bonefish start picking up the chum.

Bonefish sometimes travel in big schools, and here it's a good idea to cast ahead of the school and work your lure slowly as the lead fish approaches it. Usually the biggest fish will be found up in front ahead of the rest.

Bonefish can also be caught at night, especially when there is moonlight. Baits such as conch, shrimp, and crabs are best for this nocturnal fishing.

CHAPTER 18

Saltwater Bottom Fishes

FLOUNDER

A WINTER flounder is not a fluke. The summer flounder, or fluke, will often rise for a bait off the bottom and grab it. But if you want to catch winter flounders you have to keep that bait right on the bottom. In a strong tide, you may need a heavy sinker to hold and keep your baited hook lying on the bottom.

If you can't obtain bloodworms or sandworms to use for flounder, there are other baits you can try. A small piece of clam, oyster, or mussel will often take them; and in some areas and waters you can also catch them on ordinary earthworms or gardenworms.

When fishing for flounders, you can attract more strikes and detect bites better if you lift your bait slowly off the bottom at regular intervals. This often makes a flounder grab the bait or if he has already swallowed it, you will feel the weight of the fish. If you don't get a bite, drop your rig back fast. Then the sinker hits the mud and raises a small cloud. This disturbance often attracts flounders to the scene.

Early in the year, look for flounders in the deeper water from 15 to 40 ft. deep. They are still in the mud and are most plentiful in the holes and channels. Look for such spots with soft, mud bottoms.

If flounder fishing is slow, you can often stir up some action by dragging your anchor along the bottom. In shallow water, a long rake can be used to scrape the bottom. Or you can try chumming with crushed mussels scattered around the boat or lowered in a chum pot or bag to the bottom.

One flounder fishing technique which can be tried to cover more area around your boat is to cast your rig about 50 ft. out. Then when you feel it hit bottom, pull it quickly for a few feet, and let it lie still on the bottom; after a few minutes, pull your rig along the bottom once more for a short distance, and let it lie still again. This dragging of the sinker and rig raises puffs of sand or mud which draws fish to the area.

One way to locate flounders is to drift very slowly while you fish. If the current or wind is strong, let out the anchor on a short line and drag the bottom to slow down the boat. When you catch a flounder, let out more anchor line to hold in that spot, and then you can fish it thoroughly before drifting again.

Look for flounders in the shallow areas around high tide since they tend to spread out on the flat and move inshore then. Toward low water fish the deeper holes, the drop-offs, and channels where fishes congregate at this time.

A new twist has been added to flounder fishing recently. They are now using canned corn kernels or frozen corn kernels as chum for flounders. Proof that it works was shown when many of the flounders that were caught had the corn in their stomachs when cleaned.

FLUKE

When fishing for fluke or summer flounders, look for them around eddies formed by two currents, also along the edges of sand bars and channels. At high water, fish the shallow flats near shore; low tides find them in channels, and big fluke prefer the deeper holes, drop-offs, and rocky bottoms.

In a strong tide or brisk wind, fishing at anchor is usually better than drifting when going after fluke. Here you can try the same rig as when drifting, but use a lighter sinker. The rig should move away from the boat with the tide when the rod is raised. After lowering the rig to the bottom, you let it bounce along until it reaches 100 ft. or more behind the boat. Then you can reel it back slowly as the sinker drags bottom.

Bunker chum attracts big fluke along the beaches and inlets, and a chum pot or mesh bag filled with ground chum can be lowered under the boat, when anchored in one spot. This is a good method to use when the tide or wind is either too strong or too weak for proper drift fishing.

Live killies are good for fluke when fishing in bays, tidal rivers, and inlets, where these baitfish are naturally present. For the larger fluke found along the beaches and over rocky bottoms, a large spearing or sand eel or smelt or other baitfish is better.

Big "doormat" fluke really go for the belly or back cut from a smaller fluke. These should be at least 7 or 8 in. long and cut in a pennant shape. One angler also swears by strips of beef liver cut about 5 in. long and about an inch wide and thick!

When there is no wind and the tide is weak, you can often do better by slow trolling for fluke. Here you can use the same rig as when drifting, but use a smaller hook and tie the 3 ft. leader about 12 in. above the sinker. The sinker should be heavy enough to bounce along the bottom, as the boat moves as slowly as possible. If you feel a bite, let out some slack line to give the fluke time to swallow the bait.

To catch fluke from shore or a pier or jetty, use a surf spinning rod. Cast your bait out and then start reeling it back slowly. Lift your rod and lower it at regular intervals, so that your bait rises and sinks in an attractive manner. If you feel a bite, stop reeling, and give the fluke a few seconds to swallow the bait before you set the hook.

One "offbeat" method of fluke fishing is often effective when used in shallow water. This requires the use of a float on the line high enough to allow the bait to just clear the bottom. The hook is baited with a killie or spearing. The rig is fished from an anchored boat and is allowed to drift down with the tide.

When you catch a skate, dogfish, or sea robin, don't throw it back into the water. Instead, cut some strips from their white bellies and use them for fluke. They are extremely tough and will stay on a hook for a long time.

A fluke will often grab a bait and the first indication of a bite is a series of sharp tugs. Lower your rod immediately and let out some slack line, or do both. This gives the fish some time to mouth the bait. Then if you feel a weight as you reel in slowly, lift the rod sharply to set the hook.

Although most fluke are caught on natural baits, they will sometimes hit an artificial lure. Best lures are underwater or sinking plugs, metal squids, spoons, and jigs. These should be worked deep and close to the bottom and retrieved slowly.

Pacific Halibut

A good bait for Pacific, or California, halibut is a small shiner perch about 3 or 4 in. long. They can be caught on tiny hooks and pieces of shrimp. Hook them through the back, in front of the dorsal fin. Fish the shiners with a light ½ oz. sinker about 3 ft. from the hook.

Halibut like a moving bait and will take a live baitfish on a drifting boat best. If you are anchored or fishing from a pier, cast out and slowly reel in your bait along the bottom.

Pacific halibut will often take a chrome or light-colored metal lure if it is lowered to the bottom and "jigged" up and down.

BLACKFISH

Blackfish or tautog are usually caught from boats, but jetty or breakwater fishermen can often catch them from the rocks. The smaller blacks are usually found in the shallow water close to the rocks or even between the rocks in holes. The bigger ones are usually out near the end of the longer jetties and breakwaters.

When you go after blackfish, take plenty of bait and rigs and sinkers. These fish are expert at cleaning a hook and you will soon run out of bait if you don't bring enough. And since blackfish are found around wrecks, rocks, barnacles and mussels, or oysters and piles, you lose a lot of rigs and sinkers. If you make up a dozen rigs in advance you will save time and temper on the fishing grounds.

Blackfish move inshore in the spring and again in the fall. Offshore in deeper water they gather around wrecks, mussel beds, and over rocky bottoms. Inshore you'll find them around breakwaters and jetties, piers, bridges, and over shellfish beds. In no other fishing is it so important to pin-point the best spots and fish right in them.

When using green crabs as bait for blackfish, use the small ones whole. The bigger ones should be cut in half or quarters after you remove the claws and legs; this way they stay on the hook better and are less likely to be stolen by the fish or bothered by bergalls.

There are 3 blackfish baits which can often be obtained along sandy beaches with rock jetties. One is the green crab which is found among the rocks of the jetties. They can be obtained by searching among the rocks or in little pools of water. Another blackfish bait which is not too well known is the sand bug which buries itself in the sand at the surf line. They can be caught by probing in the sand with your fingers as the waves recede. The remaining blackfish bait is the big sea clam or surf clam called the "skimmer." These are sometimes washed up on the beach during a storm and can be gathered at low tide.

When blackfishing, some anglers use 2 hooks. This is okay when fishing in open areas and on clean bottoms. But when fishing around rocks, jetties, wrecks, or rocky bottoms, a single hook is better. You'll lose a lot of rigs in such waters and a hooked blackfish may foul your second hook on a rock or pile.

As the water gets colder in the late fall and early winter, blackfish will head for deeper water around wrecks and offshore banks. Blackfish which are caught in shallow water by a quick freeze may be killed by the low temperatures. But during mild winters, they are often caught even in December and January in deep, offshore water.

Blackfish usually do not take a bait and swallow it quickly; instead, they peck at it with their front teeth a few times before they actually inhale the bait. Most of the time you should wait while the fish is pecking or nibbling. When you feel a solid tug or pull indicating the blackfish has actually mouthed the bait, you can strike to set the hook.

Chumming often works when seeking blackfish. Scatter crushed clams or mussels around the boat, or lower a burlap bag or chum pot filled with the crushed shellfish. Mussels and clams can also be used as bait for the blacks, but bergalls, small sea bass, and crabs steal it too readily, so most anglers prefer crabs.

PORGIES

You'll catch more porgies if you move your bait at regular intervals. This can be done by raising and lowering your rod tip. If the tide is running, use a sinker just heavy enough to hold bottom but light enough to move with the tide when you lift it off the bottom. This way you can bounce your sinker away from the boat so that it covers more area. Another trick is to cast your rig to one side into the current and let the tide move your rig along the bottom.

There are still many anglers who think that porgies can only be caught with natural baits such as worms or clams. More knowing anglers now use diamond jigs. Porgies, especially the big ones, will often go for these shiny lures. They work best when the water isn't too deep or the tide isn't too strong. For real sport use a light, one-handed spinning outfit with 6- or 8-lb.-test line and a diamond jig weighing about 1 or 2 oz.

Porgy fishing usually isn't too good when the tide is slack and there is little or no current; it is also poor when the tide is too strong and you can't hold bottom with your sinker. Fish between these two extremes, if you want to catch porgies.

Sheepshead

Sheepshead are real masters in the art of stealing baits off the hook. The best bait for these fish is a fiddler crab which has had its large claw removed. When you get a bite from a sheepshead, don't set the hook immediately. Instead, at the first bite give a few inches of slack line for a second, then come back with the rod tip.

Look for sheepshead under piers, bridges, around jetties, breakwaters, submerged rockpiles, and sunken wrecks.

An effective and handy chum for sheepshead are barnacles which are scraped off pilings or rocks. Keep them in a container filled with salt water until ready to use.

A fish-finder rig is best for sheepshead because you can give the fish slack line when you feel the bite so that he can get the bait in his mouth.

Sheepshead can be caught in the surf in southern waters if you fish the front of jetty where there are holes scooped out by the tide. Cast your rig so that your bait sinks into one of these depressions.

Cod and Pollock

When using skimmer clams for cod, you can use the whole insides of one clam. However, there are times and places when a smaller bait is better; then you can cut the hard part of the clam into 2 or 3 slices. But always add some of the softer portions of the clam to the hook. Cod prefer the bellies or softer portion over the hard tongue or leg.

Cod in shallow water over a clean bottom often act jittery and can be frightened by too much activity and commotion. Too many boats, noisy anchoring, and too many rigs and baits don't help the fishing much. The angler is better off if he fishes his own private area quietly at anchor or while drifting. In other words, find your own fish and stay away from the fleet.

One hook or 2 or 3 hooks—that is the question codfishermen have to ask. For cod, 2 or 3 hooks can be used when fishing at anchor. However, over a rocky bottom or around wrecks one hook is better—you won't get hung up as often and lose too many hooks. One hook is also best when drifting for cod since there is less chance of the leaders twisting and tangling together.

Chumming for codfish works best in shallow water where the chum can reach the bottom in a small area. In deeper water or in strong tides, the chum is carried too far from the boat to be effective.

You can use crushed mussels, crabs, conch, or clams for chum. These can be scattered around the boat. Or you can fill a potato sack with the chum and lower it to the bottom. It takes a while before the cod locate the chum and move in.

If you are bothered by ling, whiting, blackfish, dogfish, or bergalls while codfishing, it usually means that the cod are either not around or you are fishing in a poor spot. Usually when big cod are present in large numbers these other fish stop biting or are chased away by the bigger fish.

Most codfishing is done during the daytime, but these fish can also be caught at night. Anglers who fish at night for silver hake or whiting in deep water often hook cod. Party boats have also made special night trips for cod.

The oldtimers say that codfishing remains good until the first heavy snowfall. After that it tapers off as the fish move out into deeper water where they remain until spring, when they return inshore for a short period. As a general rule, the cod are fairly plentiful during the whole month of December off New York and New Jersey waters.

Cod usually swallow a baited hook pretty deep and it is often difficult to remove the hook. It's a good idea to carry a hook disgorger with you on every codfish trip. You can easily make such a hook disgorger by taking a wooden stick about 12 in. long and cutting a notch on one end.

When jigging in deep water with diamond jigs for cod or pollock, it is important to find the level at which the fish are hitting. Once you hook a fish it's a good idea to quickly mark your line so that you can lower it again to the same depth. A short piece of plastic tape is good for this.

Big pollock like offshore wrecks in deep water from 100 to 200 ft. deep. Here, they lie and feed over and around the wreck. A big diamond jig anywhere from 8 to 14 oz. jigged down deep will attract and hook them.

Pollock will come into the surf in certain New England areas to chase baitfish during high tide, especially if it occurs during daybreak and dusk.

Silver Hake or Whiting

Although whiting are usually caught with casting rods, spinning rods, boat rods, and even surf rods, you can also use a cane or glass pole. Such a pole around 18 or 20 ft. long is best used from a low dock, jetty, or bulkhead where you are close to the water. Fish there at night when the water is calm. You can also use a cork or plastic float about 5 or 6 ft. above the hook. The long-shank hook is baited with spearing or sand eels and is lowered into the water. When a whiting grabs it, you merely yank it out with the pole.

Whiting often come close to shore at night to chase baitfish such as spearing, sand eels, shiners, and other small fish. While doing this, they sometimes become stranded high and dry on the beach or get trapped in shallow water. On certain nights you can pick such fish up without any trouble. Many "frostfish" fans bring along a strong headlight and a long-handled net or spear to catch whiting in the shallow water.

Baits used for whiting include small baitfish such as silversides, sand eels, and shiners; they'll also take pieces of clam or squid. The toughest baits are thin strips cut from a fresh herring or the whiting itself.

When going fishing for whiting from a pier, dock, bridge, or bulkhead, bring along a bright light or two and suspend it over the water. This will attract spearing or silversides, which in turn will attract whiting. You can also fish close to a light on a pier or bridge.

VARIOUS BOTTOM FISHES

When seeking reef fish such as grouper, snapper, and grunt in the Florida Keys, look for light-colored, sandy patches surrounded by darker bottom. There should be some rocks in order to attract these fish. Even a single rock in such a sandy patch will often attract a surprising number of fish.

Grouper will often take a trolled bait or lure. In the Bahamas, they often use barracuda or king mackerel as bait. These will weigh from 5 to 15 lbs. For best results, the backbone should be removed from the bait and 2 or 3 hooks inserted and sewn so that the points and barbs protrude from the belly of the bait. Troll the baits at depths from 150 to 400 ft. down with weights or wire line.

Croakers bite best when the day is cloudy or overcast; on bright days, fish for them in the evening and during the night. The best baits are shrimp, pieces of clam, squid, or shedder crab on a small No. 1 or 2 hook.

Sea bass are most plentiful over rocky bottoms, shellfish beds, around piles and sunken wrecks. The smaller sea bass are found in shallow water near shore in bays and inlets. The larger "humpback" sea bass prefer the deeper waters offshore around wrecks. Best baits for sea bass are sandworms and shedder crab in bays and squid, clams, or small fish offshore. They like a moving bait, so best results are obtained from a drifting boat. If anchored, lift and drop your sinker at regular intervals.

The best bait for kingfish (northern whiting) in the surf is usually a piece of bloodworm; but you can also try a small piece of shedder crab or a chunk of shrimp. A pound of shrimp bought in any fish store will last you a long time, and you'll have less trouble with crabs than when you use worms.

CHAPTER 19

Other Saltwater Fishes

Pacific Salmon

When trolling or mooching for salmon, vary the depths at which your lure or bait travels. This will, of course, depend on the area and waters being fished and the species of salmon present. Silver salmon are closer to the surface, and here you can work your lure or bait anywhere from 10 to 30 ft. down. Chinook salmon lie deeper and closer to the bottom, and here you may have to go down to 80 or even 100 ft. in some places to get action.

If you are using a "spinner"—a fillet cut from the side of a herring, you can troll it in swift rips and channels so that it will spin and look alive. One trick to try is to reel it fast then let it out again. Keep doing this several times. Someimes a silver salmon will strike when you do this.

In saltwater passages, king salmon feed on herring schools and move around in search of these fish. A good time to fish for them is just before and just after high water, when there is enough tide to activate your herring bait or lure.

A good time to fish for salmon at river mouths and estuaries is in the fall of the year when the first heavy rains raise the water level. Then the salmon move in from the sea and head upstream.

King salmon are caught at varying depths in salt water. They are closer to the surface—about 20 or 30 ft. down, early in the morning, in the evening, and on cloudy days. On bright, sunny days or during the middle of the day they may be down at 100 ft. or more.

FLY TROLLED BEHIND BOAT

Coho or silver salmon are great sport on a fly rod. They hit streamers, usually while trolling. One trick is to use two fly rods, one with a fly being trolled behind the boat, while the other rod is used for casting from the side of the boat. A salmon will often follow the fly being cast and then hit the trolled fly in back of the boat.

An effective way to catch both king and coho salmon is to drift with the tide or current. A herring bait is used about 6 ft. behind a trolling weight. The cut herring should spin slowly like an injured baitfish for best results.

Coho and king salmon will often chase small herring toward shore and feed on them in certain places; this often happens around Vancouver Island. At such times, lures such as spoons and spinners cast into the surfacing fish will catch the salmon.

SHARKS

During the summer and early fall sharks appear in good numbers along the Atlantic coast and can provide good sport on rod and reel. The best way to catch them is to chum with ground bunker, and bait large hooks on 15 ft. wire leaders with a whole fish. You can use a whole bunker, mackerel, butterfish, bluefish, whiting, or ling on the hook. Chunks cut from tuna or albacore are also very good. The boat can drift and you can let out 2 or 3 lines. It is a good idea to add a cork or plastic float to 1 or 2 of the lines. The float can be set about 20 or 25 ft. above the hook. The other line or lines can be used without a float, to allow the bait to drift deep.

A good bait to use for sharks is a live eel, used offshore from a drifting boat without any weight. A live eel can also be used for sharks from piers, bridges, shore, and surf. In the surf you may have to use them with a bottom rig and sinker to get the best results.

Try adding some strips of newspaper to the chum slick when fishing for sharks. The white strips drift and flutter and attract the sharks.

One of the quickest ways to draw sharks to a spot is to cut open the bellies of any school tuna, bonito, or albacore you have caught and hang them over the side of the boat. The blood dripping into the water will bring the sharks, and then you can drift out a small whole fish or chunk of fish with a hook in them.

To make a chum can for shark fishing, get a large metal can or pail, and solder a small spigot near the bottom. Then fill the can with fish oils or blood and open the spigot so that there is a steady drip into the water.

If you are bothered by sharks when fishing and want to get rid of them, you can try the following methods. If you have plenty of time, you can bait a heavy outfit with long wire leader and a fish bait, hook the shark, and bring him up to the boat where he can be killed. If there are no other boats in the line of fire, you can try shooting the sharks with a rifle if they are on the surface. Or you can try trying a length of wire leader to an empty can, cork, wood buoy, or empty Clorox bottle, bait it with a fish, and drift it toward the shark. If he swallows the bait and gets hooked, he'll usually take off dragging the float or buoy with him.

BARRACUDA

Barracuda are usually easy to locate. Or rather, they will locate you if you are in a moving boat. They are attracted by the wake and propellers of a boat and the shadow underneath the hull; thus, trolling is a good way to take them. They are most numerous around offshore reefs, wrecks, lighthouses, or beacon markers, oil rigs, piers, and bridges.

For trolling for barracuda, use such lures as feathers, jigs, spoons, plugs, and a whole fish or strip of fish behind the boat. Usually a fairly fast speed is best for these fish.

Although barracuda are bold and curious fish, they can easily be spooked on flats or in shallow water. Never cast too close to the barracuda; instead, cast from 10 to 15 ft. ahead or beyond him and retrieve the lure in front of him.

Barracuda often follow a lure but fail to strike. When this happens, speed up your retrieve and give the lure a crazy, erratic action.

Surface plugs such as poppers can be used to tease a barracuda until he strikes. If you see a barracuda, keep casting until the fish finally gets angry and charges the lure.

The best tide for barracuda in inshore waters is usually around high tide. That's when they move in on the flats and under the mangroves to wait for fish to swim by.

California Yellowtail

The preferred bait for yellowtail is a live sardine or anchovy. Choose the liveliest baitfish in a tank and hook it through the nose. If yellowtail are showing on top after chum, cast the live bait as far as you can. Usually no sinker is required, but there are times when the yellows are down deep. Then a half-ounce of lead clamped on the leader a few feet above the bait will take it down.

When yellowtail move away from the boat or go down into deep water, jigging will often take them. Here you use a shiny chrome or silver finish metal spoon or squid or jig, cast it out, and then reel it back as fast as you can turn the handle. A reel with a fast gear ratio is best for this fishing.

Yellowtail will take a live mackerel hooked through the lips. Since such baits often run from 1 to 2 pounds in weight, you have to let the yellowtail run with it long enough to swallow it before you set the hook.

Most of the time, let the live sardine or anchovy swim around freely and naturally to tempt yellowtail. But there are some days when working the rod in short jerks will get more strikes. This works best with dead or dying bait and when the fish are sulking down below the surface and not boiling on top.

When yellowtail refuse to strike the regular chrome or silver jigs or spoons, try an all-white or all-yellow or blue and white, or even a brown or black lure. Such colors often do the trick so the wise jig fisherman carries them in various colors.

When a yellowtail takes your line into the kelp beds, give him slack line and wait. Many times the fish will leave the kelp and swim out into open water where you can continue the fight with a better chance of success.

Pacific Albacore

A good way to locate and attract albacore in Pacific waters is by trolling a feather or plastic jig. At the same time, you can toss a live anchovy into the wake at regular intervals. If you get a strike on the lure or see an albacore boil on the surface for an anchovy, you can stop the boat and start chumming with anchovies and cast out hooks baited with the small fish. The angler who gets the bait out the fastest has the best chance for a hook-up.

Albacore can sometimes be located by watching for diving gulls, boils, or leaping fish. You can troll along the edges of such a school or cut the motor up-wind of the fish and drift toward them.

You have to work fast when fishing on a live-bait party boat for albacore. With all those anglers lining the rails, competition is terrific. You should be ready to cast out your bait the minute the boat stops. That means you should keep an anchovy on your hook and be ready to go.

When you hook an albacore, don't try to stop his first run or try to hold him near the boat. Let him make a long run or two. This takes some of the steam out of him, and you will have better control of the fish as you work him toward the boat. A fish that is too fresh and lively near the boat will tangle with other lines and make a mess of things.

Cobia

Look for cobia under buoys, seaweed, logs, crates, piers, offshore oil rigs, or any other shady spot. They like to lurk in such spots and will often dart out to grab a lure that is trolled or cast there.

The best way to catch cobia along Florida's Gulf Coast is to first spot them swimming in clear water, and cast a lure such as a large jig or underwater plug several feet ahead of them. Then work the lure in short jerks; if the cobia grabs it, set the hook hard 2 or 3 times.

Cobia will often hit artificial lures such as spoons, jigs, and plugs. However, they like their lures down deep and if you see a cobia follow your lure but refuse to strike, let it sink and the fish will usually go down after it and take it.

If you are fishing in waters where cobia are found and you spot a manta ray on the surface, cast a lure next to him and let it sink. You'll often hook small cobia which are found following the manta.

Cobia can be attracted to an area with ground bunker chum. You can ladle the stuff out loose and also lower a chum pot or bag full of the bunker under the boat. Best baits in the Chesapeake Bay for these fish are live eels, live spot, and live bluefish. Strips and chunks cut from a bunker can also be used for bait.

When surf fishing for cobia from a beach, choose the calm days when there is little or no wave action. Then the cobia move closer to shore.

COMMON MACKEREL

Mackerel go for almost any small, shiny metal lure such as a diamond jig, metal squid, or spoon. These can be jigged up and down at the level where the fish are feeding; or you can cast out and reel the lure back with regular jerks of the rod tip.

Besides hitting small artificials, mackerel also go for natural baits drifted on a small hook. Use a fine leader and bury the hook in a small piece of bunker, clam, shrimp, or a strip of squid or a piece of mackerel. Small spearing or silversides or sand eels or pieces of these fish are also good. Let the bait drift naturally in the chum slick.

Chumming is the best way to bring mackerel under the boat where they can be hooked on lures or bait. Bunker, finely ground, works best, and this should not be ladled overboard too liberally. A small dipper full every so often will spread and hold the fish near the boat.

If you can't get menhaden or bunker for chum for mackerel, don't give up. Catch a few mackerel by casting or jigging, and grind or mash them up to use for chum. If you can't catch mackerel, do some bottom fishing and catch bergalls, whiting, or ling or any other fish and grind them up for chum.

KING MACKEREL

Most king mackerel or kingfish are caught by trolling or drift fishing with bait, but you can also use light tackle and cast from a drifting boat. Using such lures as jigs or feathers, you can cast in front of a drifting boat, let the lure sink deep, then jig, and reel it back to the surface.

King mackerel in the Gulf of Mexico are most plentiful over reefs and around offshore oil rigs. Trolling in these areas or casting around the base of the oil rigs with jigs, spoons, or plugs will take these sporty fish.

Kingfish will often hit a surface plug if you chum and bring the fish up to the surface near the boat.

King mackerel can be caught at night in many places. Best spots are coral reefs and offshore oil rigs. Chumming with ground fish can be done first to bring the kings up to the boat. Then they'll take baits such as ballyhoo and lures such as jigs.

An East wind often produces good fishing for king mackerel on the outer coral reefs. Some of the biggest fish are caught when the water is rough.

SNAPPERS

Most red snappers are caught on chunks of fish bait, but there are times when more red snappers, especially big ones can be taken on live baitfish. Grunts, pinfish, and blue runners from 4 to 7 in. long are good to use for them.

Big mangrove snappers are cautious and wary fish and no cinch to catch. One way to make them less suspicious is to chum with chunks of cut mullet or pilchards or shrimp or crabs. When they congregate and grab the chum, you can drift a baited hook into their midst. Use a small hook and fine leader or line for best results. Live shrimp also fool good-sized mangrove snappers at times; and if you can't get them to bite during the daytime, come back at night when they are easier to fool.

After you catch one or two mangrove snappers, the rest usually become suspicious and refuse to bite. Then it's a good idea to move the boat or if on shore, walk to some other spot where you can try a new school of fish. By making a move to a new location every time the fish become wise, you can sometimes wind up with a fair string of snappers.

POMPANO

Pompano in canals, inlets, and other narrow waterways tend to travel in schools. Then you have to wait until the school passes by and sees your bait before you get action. If other anglers around you are getting strikes from pompano, it means the school has arrived and you can get set for a bite. At such times it often helps if you let your bait drift with the tide; or raise it slowly off the bottom if fishing with a sinker. A movement of the bait catches the attention of the pompano quicker than if it were lying still on the bottom.

Look for pompano in the surf along the edges of breaking waves, along outer sand bars, in sloughs, and along the beach itself. These fish don't mind a rough surf as long as the water isn't too dirty or too cold.

When surf fishing for pompano with sand bugs, use a round egg-shaped sinker, and when your rig hits bottom don't just let it stay there. Instead, reel in slowly so that it drags bottom and makes the bug look alive. This catches the attention of the pompano and they pounce on the bug.

The best lure for pompano is a small yellow jig. This should be cast out and allowed to sink to the bottom. Then it should be retrieved in short hops along the bottom. This raises puffs of mud or sand and imitates a sand bug.

Permit

Permit will often be found on the same flats as bonefish, but they usually prefer the deeper water along the edges of the flats. They will also feed on rocky bottoms.

Permit travel mostly in small schools and move up and down the flats to feed when the water is high. You can sometimes spot them by looking for their tails and dorsal fins sticking out above the water.

Artificial lures sometimes take permit, but more fish are caught on natural baits such as spider crabs, finney crabs, shrimp, and spiny lobster tail. Try to drop the bait in front of the permit so that he either sees it or is in a direct line below it to come up on it.

Various Fishes

Jewfish or giant sea bass hang around rocks, reefs, sunken wrecks, deep holes, breakwaters, and bridge pilings. Using heavy tackle and a whole live or dead fish for bait, you can often hook one—but if he gets into an obstruction he usually cuts a line or breaks off. The trick is to lure the jewfish away from his hiding place into the open to take the bait, then prevent him from running into it.

If you want to catch the larger Spanish mackerel, fish during the spring of the year and watch for surface feeding fish. At such times the larger fish will strike surface plugs, bass bugs, and other lures.

Look for beaches where clam diggers have worked along the Pacific coast, if you are surf fishing. On the incoming tide, sea perch and other surf fish move in to feed on broken clams or small clams left behind by the diggers.

The best time to catch hickory shad in salt water is usually early in the morning from daybreak to about 9 A.M., then again in the late afternoon and evening.

Artificial lures used for albacore, jack crevalle, Spanish mackerel, or any of the members of the tuna family should be trolled or reeled as fast as possible for best results.

CHAPTER 20

Other Saltwater Tips

STRONG tides, currents, and rips often create favorable fishing periods for saltwater gamefish. At such times striped bass, bluefish, weakfish, tarpon, snook, and other fish chase smaller baitfish or forage for shrimp, crabs, and other marine life being tossed and swept by the strong currents.

Surf anglers casting from a beach should keep their rod tip high at the end of the cast so that the line clears the breaking waves and the lure travels high. But as the lure approaches the beach, lower your rod tip so that the lure stays under and works right up to the sand.

If you want to cast from either side of your boat while drifting, use a drag anchor. This can be a sash weight or similar weight tied to the bow of the boat. Just enough line should be let out so that the weight drags bottom, slowing the drift, and keeping the bow of the boat into the current or tide rather than broadside. Then you can cast from either side of the slow drifting boat.

When fishing Southern waters, look for big flying fish being chased and taking off from the water. This often indicates that gamefish such as dolphin, sailfish, or marlin are feeding on them.

When a wire leader becomes badly kinked or twisted, it is best to remove it and replace it with a new one.

Does a light frighten saltwater fish? Yes and no, depending on where you are fishing, the fish being sought, and the type of light. Lights from bridges, piers, and docks often attract baitfish, squid, and smaller fish. These in turn attract the larger fish and this makes for good fishing. Most of the party boats fishing at night are brightly lit and it doesn't hurt the fishing, but rather improves it. Most surf anglers, however, believe that moving lights such as flashlights and auto headlights may frighten or alert striped bass if they suddenly appear in places where it was formerly pitch black. So surf anglers use light only rarely and do not shine into the water unless it is necessary to land or gaff a fish.

When bottom fishing with bait, it's usually a good idea to drop your rod tip a couple of feet or so as soon as you feel a bite. This gives the fish a chance to swallow the bait.

If you happen to put down a school of surfacing fish by running through them either on purpose or by accident, while trolling, slow down the boat and drop back your lines. The fish may scatter or sound at first but will usually group together and rise again often in time to see your lures go by.

If you see even a single tern or gull hovering over a spot and dipping, make a cast there or troll past the area. This means there is bait below, and some of it is being driven toward the surface by gamefish.

During the summer and early fall months, there is usually a lot of phosphorescence in the sea, and a lure that is reeled or trolled lights up and looks much larger and unnatural at night. The line also lights up and can be seen clearly. Then it is usually a good idea to fish on a moonlit night or early in the morning at daybreak or at dusk when the phosphorescence isn't as noticeable.

Fish in narrow, shallow tidal rivers or creeks are more easily frightened than those found in the larger rivers, bays, or open ocean. So when boat fishing for them, anchor, drift or use the oars instead of the motor. Or you can fish from shore by casting into the likely spots.

Does the moon affect saltwater fishing? There is much evidence from oldtime and expert anglers that it does. To a lesser degree when seeking bottom fishes, but a more important role when going after predatory gamefish. The moon affects tides, as everyone knows, and the strongest tides and currents occur during the new moon and full moon periods. Surf fishing is often good then. So is trolling or casting lures from a boat. Gamefish such as striped bass, bluefish, weakfish, channel bass, tarpon, snook, and even tuna seem to be more active and hit better during the full moon period.

If a hooked fish reaches a rock, weeds, or piles and fouls the line, slacken the line immediately and wait. The fish will often swim out and free the line.

When fishing tidal rivers, a knowledge of the location of the channels and holes is valuable. You can locate these at low water by studying the currents and the color and depth of the water. Each spot in such a river produces best at a certain stage of tide. Once learned, you can move up and down trying different spots which produce best during those stages of the tide.

When jigging with diamond jigs, hammered squids or bucktails, it is necessary to find the depth where the fish are feeding. First let the jig down to the bottom and work that depth; then reel in a few turns of line and jig there. Keep on doing this almost to the surface.

The angler who is afraid to lose an occasional lure or rig never catches many fish. Most fish hang around weeds, rocks, piles, wrecks, and other obstructions. If you reel or troll your lure so that it passes too far away from such fish hide-outs, you'll get few strikes. The idea is to work your lure as close as possible to the obstruction without actually hanging up. In doing so, you'll occasionally lose a lure or rig—but you'll also get more strikes and fish. The shrewd angler carries plenty of spare lures and rigs so that he can afford to lose a few.

Take along some cans of cheap sardines. Then when you want to chum all you have to do is punch some holes in the can and drop them into the water. They will sink to the bottom and the oils and bits of sardine meat will ooze out and attract saltwater fish.

A good time to locate the best surf fishing spots is at low tide, especially when the moon is new or full. At such times, the extra low tide will reveal sand bars, cuts, sloughs, and holes which can be fished later. If you plan to come back the same day or night, you can even mark the spots with a stake pushed into the sand above high-water mark. Or you can line up the spots with sand dunes, buildings, or other landmarks.

Saltwater fish feed at different levels; but depending on the species and prevailing conditions at the time, this takes place most of the time either on or near the surface or near the bottom. Fish spend most of their time feeding or resting on or near the bottom. Or they rise to the top to chase baitfish. They find less food and therefore spend less time in the intermediate depths between the surface and the bottom.

A form of slow trolling done from bridges, piers, and bulkheads is often a deadly method of taking saltwater fish. Here you simply lower your lure into the water and walk along the bridge or pier dragging the lure. Usually you get better results if you also quickly raise and lower your rod tip at regular intervals. The best lures for this fishing are spoons, jigs, and plugs. This method can be used up North for striped bass and down South for sea trout, snook, tarpon, and ladyfish. Night tides usually produce better than daytime fishing.

If there are a lot of baitfish such as mullet, menhaden, herring, shiners or other baitfish in compact schools, you can quickly get some live bait to use for larger gamefish. Just cast a weighted treble hook or two into the baitfish or even a lure and snag one. Then let it sink and swim around under the school of baitfish. Chances are that there are some larger fish lurking below which will grab the snagged baitfish.

The secret of catching fish on lures in the surf is to "work" them so that they look alive or simulate a small, crippled fish. This isn't always easy because of wave action. An incoming wave tends to kill the action of the lure as it sweeps it in toward the angler. An outgoing current or backwash also tends to ruin the action of a lure by making it spin or twist. The correct procedure is to reel faster when the lure is swept toward you and then reel slower as the lure is caught by the backwash and is pulled from you.

Severe storms will often change the formations along a sandy beach. Sand bars may shift, disappear, or new ones may be formed. Sloughs, holes, and cuts may be filled in or new ones may appear. This is especially true if there are 2 or 3 storms, one after another. Then the surf angler may have to scout around for new spots to fish.

When you can't obtain bunker for chum, get some canned cat food made from fish and mix it with oatmeal. It's a fair substitute chum to use for many saltwater fishes.

When surf fishing along the beaches, two tide periods are usually most dependable. One is the low-water "change" when the tide just starts to come in. The other is the high-water "change" when the water starts to move out. Of course, fish are also taken during the incoming tide and outgoing tide on many days in many areas. Slack water is a poor time to fish in most places. When fishing inlets, usually the last of the outgoing and the start of the incoming is best.

The best time to fish inshore is when the water is slightly murky, or at daybreak or dusk. And, of course, during the hours of darkness. At such times, the fish cannot see the line, leader, snaps, swivels, or the details of the lure.

If the fish aren't biting directly under the pier, try casting away from the structure into deeper water at the end; or do the same thing from the sides of the pier. If you know of a deep hole, rocky bottom, or a mussel bed near the pier try to reach that spot with your bait or lure. Naturally, overhead casting should be done only when no other anglers or bystanders are behind or near you.

When casting lures in the surf, don't cast in front of an incoming wave. Wait until it breaks and then cast *behind* it. If you cast in front of the wave, the onrushing water will kill the action of the lure and create slack line; casting behind the wave, however, will give the lure better action and keep the line taut.

If you are fishing an area where there are already several boats on the scene, find out how they are fishing and use the same method. If they are anchored, then you should do the same. If they are drifting or trolling, you can follow suit. Most of the time, the method being used by most of the boats is paying off. Besides, if you use a different method you may interfere with the other boats. If you want to fish in a different way, it is best to go away from the rest of the fleet in an area which isn't crowded.

When you are bottom fishing and you get a bite, but fail to hook the fish, wait a minute or two; and if you have no more bites, reel in your rig. Chances are that your hook will be cleaned, or only a small piece of bait will remain. Many anglers waste valuable time waiting for bites that will never come because there is no bait on the hook.

Party-boat anglers lose many big bluefish and false albacore because of weak lines and tight drags. When big blues and false albacore are running, use at least 40-lb.-test monofilament line. Beginners may be better off with 50-lb.-test line. And fish with the drag set, so that some line will come off the reel when the fish runs.

When surf fishing and casting against a strong wind, keep your casts low. A side cast is often best then to carry your lure on a low trajectory over the water. Another tip is to cast directly into the wind and not at an angle. This way you avoid a belly in your line, and your casts will be farther and more accurate.

When straight trolling doesn't produce, try a zig-zag or "S" course. This will vary the action and depth of the lure and often bring strikes when straight trolling doesn't work.

If you run out of bait when saltwater fishing, take one of the fish you have caught and cut it up into small chunks or strips and use it for bait. Most fish are cannibals and will eat their own kind. A piece of fish bait is usually light in color, gives off a fresh scent, and often flutters attractively in the water if cut into a long, slim strip—and it is tough and stays on a hook a long time. Best of all, it catches other fish.

During the summer months, the winds are usually stronger in the middle of the day and afternoon. So if you are fishing from a small boat, go out early in the morning around daybreak when it is more likely to be calm. And come in before noon to avoid the increase in wind and waves.

When hurricanes or storms create ground swells or a heavy surf, fishing may be difficult or impossible along the open beaches. Then it's a good idea to try the protected waters of inlets. Here the bait-fish often take shelter or congregate to wait until the surf calms down. Striped bass and bluefish may also move into the inlets and can often be caught.

Most saltwater fish hit better in shallow waters when there is a slight breeze which ripples the surface of the water. When there is little wind and the water is flat and calm, the fish see you and are spooky.

During the hot weather, night fishing is usually more pleasant than in the broiling sun during the day. And you will often catch more fish since striped bass, bluefish, weakfish, and sea trout, tarpon, and snook are often more active at night than during the day. Even such day feeders as fluke and porgies can often be caught at night.

The direction and velocity of the wind can make or break a fishing trip. Surf anglers know that a moderate onshore wind creates white water and often good fishing for striped bass and bluefish. A strong onshore wind will make casting and working of lures difficult. An offshore wind tends to flatten the surf and clean the water. Fishing is usually poor during the day, but a few fish may be caught at night. A strong wind can also hamper boat anglers by making it difficult or impossible to troll, chum, or drift. A light wind or no wind is poor for drifting, but is good for fishing at anchor. If the wind is strong during the day, wait until evening or nighttime when it usually moderates or dies.

One way to get plenty of exercise and increase your chances of catching fish in the surf is to "work" a mile or two of beach. You cast 2 or 3 times in one spot, then move about 50 ft. down the line and do the same thing. And instead of just casting straight out, make a cast or two at an angle. In this way you cover more spots and increase the chances of a fish seeing your lure.

Chumming is usually done from boats, but it can also be done from shore. One problem when trying to chum from a beach or jetty while surf fishing is to get the chum way out and keep it from washing back inshore. To avoid this, look for a current or rip which carries such chum out to sea. Another trick is to freeze your chum into small blocks and throw these out as far as you can. As they melt, small chunks of bunker, fish, clams, or what have you, will break off and spread all around to attract fish to the area.

Best results are obtained when fishing from a drifting boat when there is a light or moderate wind or tide. The boat should move steadily—not too slow or too fast. If there is no wind or the tide is weak, the boat stays in one place. If the tide or wind is too strong, the boat moves so fast that your sinker doesn't stay on the bottom. Then you should add more weight and let out more slack line.

When fish are breaking or feeding on top, trolling or running a boat through them or near them will put them down. The correct procedure is to slowly run your boat up to about 100 ft. from the edge of the surfacing fish, then cut the motor and drift. This doesn't frighten the fish, and they'll often break right near your boat. They'll also stay up on top longer than if you frighten them with a moving boat or loud motor.

Day in and day out, bottoms with sea weed, kelp, or rocks produce more fish than barren sand or mud bottoms. Bottoms with rockweed, kelp, eelgrass, and rocks harbor shrimp, crabs, worms, and small baitfish which attract the larger fish.

There's an old saying that for every fish seen breaking on top there are 10 or 15 down below. In other words, there are always more fish below the surface than those actually breaking and feeding on top. So trolling deep or casting and working your lures below the surface will usually produce more fish than lures worked on top.

When trolling, it is important to check your terminal rig and lure at regular intervals. The lure may be fouled and not working properly. Or there may be some seaweed, sea lettuce, or other debris on the lure or leader. Remove this stuff completely before you let the line out again.

It always pays to keep on the lookout for any terns or gulls diving and wheeling. Offshore, this could mean a school of tuna, albacore, bonito, or bluefish. Inshore close to the beach along the Atlantic coast, it usually means a school of stripers or blues.

A surf angler working a stretch of beach can try one lure on his way down. Then on the way back it's a good idea to switch to a different lure. Unless, of course, you obtained strikes or caught fish, in which case you can stay with the successful lure.

If you see any baitfish concentrated in a cove and milling around, try fishing at the entrance to the cove. Usually the baitfish have been driven into the cove by gamefish which may be waiting at the entrance for the baitfish to come out.

When fishing from a jetty or breakwater, choose a rock that isn't too high above the water yet is high enough to be safe when the big waves come in. And, if alone, place your gaff near enough so that it can be reached without any trouble. Also work out a plan of bringing your fish into a pocket or between rocks before you hook it.

Who says fish aren't smart? In many clear tropical waters there are snook, sea trout, snappers under a bridge or pier which are almost impossible to catch. You can throw shrimp, small fish, or pieces of fish into the water and these fish will grab the free handout without hesitation. But when you use the same bait on a hook, these "educated" fish won't even look at it. These wary fish are sometimes hooked when the water turns murky or by some skilled angler fishing at night.

Tarpon and bonefish are easily spooked by a boat racing near or over them, especially in shallow, clean water. If you see a school of tarpon rolling or swimming, cut the motor and pole the boat quietly. In deeper water, anchor the boat, or drift with the tide or wind near the fish.

The stubborn saltwater angler who refuses to change his ways or listen to good advice seldom catches many fish. On almost every party-boat you'll see a few anglers who are using the wrong tackle or rig or refusing to fish like everyone else. Then they wonder why everyone else is catching more fish than they are. On charter boats you'll see "know-it-all" anglers who refuse to follow the captain's or mate's advice. The really "smart" angler always follows the advice of the party boat or charter boat skippers. They fish almost every day and know what's going on. They aren't always right but they have a higher batting average than the "casual" or "Sunday" fisherman who fishes only occasionally.

Fish hit more often and with greater fury when competing with other fish for food. That is probably why a surface lure which makes a big commotion or splash attracts fish to the top. They see the big splash of the lure and think another fish is feeding. This makes them rise to the top where they see the lure kicking up a fuss, then they rush and grab the lure before the other fish can do so.

Ponds near the ocean which have no opening to the sea usually contain baitfish or young fish. If these ponds are opened by a storm or by man, they can create some fast surf fishing. It doesn't take long for striped bass or bluefish to gather at the inlet or outlet to such a pond.

When trolling, it is always a good idea to watch your rod tip not only to tell when a fish hits, but also to see if the lure is working right. If the rod tip stops vibrating or has a "different" look, reel in and check the lure. It could be fouled and not working properly, or the lure could be heavy with weeds.

Keep a record of your fishing trips if you have the time. Such a record should note the place, time, weather, moon phase, water temperature, wind direction and velocity, waves, tide, bait, and any other helpful information. If this is done for several years, you acquire a valuable guide which can be used for future fishing trips. Then it can be used as a quick reference to recall the fishing conditions and size of the fish caught on a given day. If you depend on memory alone, you're likely to forget or guess at what really happened.

In shallow, clear water it is usually a poor policy to anchor directly over the spot to be fished. The movement and shadow of the boat will frighten the fish away. Instead, anchor about 30 or 40 ft. away from the area to be fished, and cast your bait toward it.

One way to attract fish to a pier, dock, bridge, or jetty is to scrape the barnacles off or smash up some mussels attached to the piles, supports, or rocks. This acts as chum which attracts crabs and baitfish and small fish, which then draw the larger fish.

Find the baitfish first and then you'll usually locate the bigger fish too. Look for concentrations of baitfish in coves, between jetties, in inlets, along the beaches or shore, or even out in the open ocean. If you stay with the baitfish or return later, you'll have a good chance to be there when the gamefish arrive and tear into the smaller fish.

When you hang up on the bottom with a sinker, weight or lure, you can often break free when in a boat by running it directly over the rig or lure and then in the opposite direction. However, when fishing from a party boat, shore, pier, or bridge, it is usually best to break off as soon as possible so that you don't waste valuable fishing time.

One reason why the larger breakwaters provide good fishing is because many of them are built adjacent to an inlet. Smaller fish, baitfish, crabs, and other creatures move in and out with the tides, and this attracts the larger fish.

When trolling, it often pays to vary your speed at times, by slowing down or speeding up your boat. Fish will often hit a lure that is sinking when the boat turns or slows down. Other times they'll grab a lure that is rising when the boat speeds up.

One of the best ways to guarantee a good day's fishing on a party boat is to check the catches of anglers returning from a trip. If their bags are full or the fishing has been good, try to go out the very next day. If the weather doesn't change and the wind doesn't shift or increase, chances are good that excellent fishing will continue.

A big fish hooked from a pier or bridge should be allowed to run away from these structures so that he can be played at a distance. Once the fish stops or tires, you can try to gain back some line. But try to avoid bringing an active or "green" fish near the pier where he can run among the pilings and cut you off. Wait until the fish quits and turns over on its side before you attempt to land him.

Most surf anglers tend to crowd a fishing spot and line up next to each other when fish are hitting. This may be necessary if that spot is the only one that is producing fish; but most of the time you are better off if you go to another spot down the beach where you can fish alone or with just 1 or 2 other anglers. Then if a school of fish comes in, you will make a better catch than if you have to compete with too many other anglers.

When you are wade fishing in the bays found along the Gulf of Mexico, look for oyster and weed beds, holes, sloughs, and sharp drop-offs. This is where the best fishing for redfish, sea trout, and snook will be found.

Saltwater fishermen often find their quarry too far away to reach with a fly rod, especially on windy days. One good way to bring the fish closer within reach of a short cast is to chum. The chum will often attract the fish up to the boat or where you are standing, if wading. Then you can present your fly to the fish of your choice at close range.

To locate fish in southern waters, look for a shrimp fleet. They keep the shrimp, but throw trash fish and other sea creatures overboard. This acts as a chum and attracts king mackerel, cobia, dolphin, bonito, and other fish. By fishing near the shrimp boats, you can often have fast action.

ANOTHER 1001 FISHING TIPS AND TRICKS

Contents

Preface

When *1001 Fishing Tips and Tricks* was published in 1966, it met with wide acceptance by freshwater and saltwater anglers all over the country. This new book, with 1001 *more* fishing tips and tricks, is almost identical in format and organization to the first book, except that its tips and tricks are all new and different.

Wherever possible the book reflects recent developments in fishing. When the first book was published, for example, coho salmon were just being introduced to the Great Lakes and there was nothing among the original 1001 tips about fishing for coho in fresh water. This new book contains tips and tricks about this type of fishing.

And, of course, there have been many developments and refinements in fishing tackle, lures, baits, rigs, and techniques and methods in freshwater and saltwater fishing. A great number of these are included here.

As in the previous book, I would like to thank the following editors and publishers for permission to use material that appeared in their publications: Henry Lyman and Frank Woolner for items and illustrations that appeared in the "Tip of the Month" section of *Salt Water Sportsman* magazine; Fred Walczyk and Mike Zicarelli for tips used in the "Fishing Know-How" column of their weekly publication *Anglers News*; Dick Wolff and Robert Stankus of the Garcia Corporation for the use of tips and drawings published in *Garcia Fishing Annual*; and Richard Reina for permission to use tips and drawings from the "Rigs-Baits-Lures" column published in the weekly *Long Island Fisherman*.

And, as always, thanks are due to the many anglers and readers who have sent in tips and ideas which were used in the publications above and in this book.

Pompano Beach, Florida   VLAD EVANOFF

Another *1001*

FISHING TIPS AND TRICKS

CHAPTER 1

Freshwater Fishing Tackle

RODS

Three fly rods will handle most of your freshwater fishing if you want to be fully equipped. One should be a 7 or 7½ ft. fly rod for dry flies, and small fish in small streams. The second is an 8 ft. fly rod, which is a good all-round rod for dry flies, wet flies, streamers, and bait fishing. Finally, an 8½ or 9 ft. fly rod can be used for big trout on large rivers, for bass, salmon, and other large freshwater fish.

Short, light fly rods are best for dry fly fishing because they work best with the tiny flies and light leaders used in this technique. They also enable an angler to cast all day without tiring his wrist or arm.

When fishing for big bass in heavily weeded waters or lakes filled with cypress trees or stumps, use a short 5 ft. bait-casting rod, a bait-casting reel, and a line testing 15 or 20 lbs. With such an outfit you'll make more accurate casts and be able to turn a big bass away from obstructions.

When using bottom-bouncing lures for black bass, you need a bait-casting or spinning rod with plenty of backbone to set the hook and fight the big ones, but at the same time the rod should be limber enough to feel every movement of the lure as it bounces and creeps along over the crevices, ledges, underwater banks, and sunken logs. And a limber tip also helps you to feel the pickup of the lure by a fish.

The best outfit for catching trout on the tiny midge flies is a light fly rod 6½ or 7 ft. long with a fly line to match it. Leaders should be long and have a fine tippet.

If you plan to do a lot of casting for muskies with big, heavy plugs, choose a spinning rod or bait-casting rod stiff enough to handle such lures. Pick one with a longish handle, so that you can use two hands when casting lures too heavy to cast with one hand. The longer handle or butt will also help you to fight a big fish better.

You can use a spinning outfit for trolling, and it is especially effective near the surface or at moderate depths. The light lines usually used are less visible to the fish, but, remember, this same weak line is a handicap when trolling deep near the bottom. If you hang up you'll often break the line and lose the lure or rig. So for deep trolling use a heavier rod and line, or change to a bait-casting or regular trolling outfit which has a heavier line.

A "one rod" man often misses a lot of good fishing and usually doesn't catch as many fish as an angler who uses all three of the basic freshwater outfits: the fly rod, the spinning rod, and the bait-casting rod. With these you are prepared for almost any freshwater fish or any type of water in any part of the country.

For casting lures choose a spinning rod with a fairly stiff action and no vibration in the tip. A quick test can be made by holding the rod directly in front of you and then moving it briskly back and forth. Then stop the movement abruptly. The rod tip should stop vibrating quickly.

Panfish can be caught on almost any kind of freshwater tackle, but if you want to catch them on tiny lures and have good sport, use an ultralight spinning rod about 4 or 5 ft. long, with a soft action. Get an ultralight spinning reel for this rod and fill it with 3 or 4 lb. test line.

When you buy a rod and reel, make sure in the store that the reel fits into the reel seat of the rod you choose. The reel foot on many reels may be too wide, too narrow, or too thick to fit into the reel seat.

For certain kinds of freshwater fish and fishing, a saltwater outfit can be used. Some anglers fishing for lake trout, big catfish, sturgeon, and coho, for example, use saltwater rods and reels for casting and trolling.

REELS

If you do a lot of casting at night, choose a good spin-casting reel and rod and you'll have no trouble with line loops, snarls, or tangles with loose line, as so often happens with a regular, open-faced spinning reel.

Although a cheap, ordinary fly reel is good enough for most trout, bass, and panfishing, you will need a better model when you go after Atlantic salmon, steelhead, pike, or even big trout in fast, heavy rivers. Then a fly reel with a good drag and size enough to hold 100 yd. of extra backing line should be used.

When fishing for big black bass in weed-filled waters around obstructions, use a bait-casting reel and tighten the drag if it has one so that the line barely slips off the reel under tension. This is necessary to pull a bass away from stumps, pads, or weeds when you first hook him.

A bait-casting reel requires oiling more often than does a spinning reel. In fact, when you are fishing for hours, you may need to oil the level wind on the reel two or three times during the day. The end bearings should be oiled before you start fishing each day.

LINES

When using nymphs or wet flies, carry a floating fly line on your reel for fishing in shallow water or for going after trout that are taking flies near the surface. But you should also carry an extra reel spool with a sinking fly line, or another fly reel with such a line, for fishing nymphs and wet flies down deep.

Monofilament lines for spinning vary in diameter, and it pays to buy a brand that is thin rather than thick. With this you can use a slightly heavier test and still get the same amount of line on your reel and cast the same distance.

To keep a fly line from slipping out when running it through the guides, double the line about 4 or 5 ft. from the end. The loop makes the line easier to hold and to see. Also, if it slips from your fingers, it won't fall out of the guides.

When using a braided line on a bait-casting reel, always tie a monofilament leader on the end. It takes wear and tear better than the braided line and is less visible to the fish.

Use separate lines for trolling and casting. Trolling stretches a line, which makes it unsuitable for casting, since it tends to get stiff and lose some of its strength.

To obtain the maximum distance and depth when fishing for steelhead or big trout on a wide river, use a 30 ft. shooting-head sinking fly line tied to 100 ft. of 20 lb.-test monofilament.

For fishing surface bass bugs, get a floating fly line, but for fishing wet flies and streamers (either when casting or when trolling with a fly rod), a sinking fly line is usually better.

When using bottom-bouncing lures, check your leader and the first few feet of your line as often as possible. In this kind of fishing, the line tends to get tiny nicks or scrapes when it is dragged over rocks, trees, or logs, or when a fighting fish runs you around obstructions.

Buy your spinning line on bulk spools so that you can fill your reel several times during a fishing season. You are wise to replace old, worn, or damaged line every few fishing trips with brand-new line.

LEADERS

Long, light leaders from 10 to 12 ft. in length are best when you are using nymphs. Besides being less visible to the trout, they also give the fly a more lifelike action during the drift.

When tying leaders for fly fishing and using the pound test as a guide, be sure all the leader material is from one manufacturer so that you will not encounter variations in size.

Fly leaders should be tied according to the size of the waters fished, the size of the fish to be caught, the size of the fly you will use, and the water conditions encountered. So even when fishing the same stream you may need different lengths and strengths.

For smooth fly casting, make certain that the butt section of your leader (the thickest part) is close in diameter to the end of your fly line.

If you are trolling deep for lake trout, landlocked salmon, or coho with wire or lead-core line, use a monofilament leader on the end of the line and then attach the lure. This leader is less visible and more flexible than the wire line. Such mono leaders will vary from a few feet up to 20 or more feet, depending on the lure or rig used.

OTHER TACKLE

A change purse is a handy container to carry in your pocket on a fishing trip. It can hold snaps, swivels, split-rings, small sinkers, and other items.

One of the easiest ways to carry a few hooks is to place them on a length of transparent tape, then cover them with a second length of tape. The hooks can then be carried in your pocket without catching on your clothes or body.

One of the most important items an angler can carry on a fishing trip is a hook sharpener. And he should use it often to sharpen the hooks on flies and lures. More fish are missed on a strike because of a dull hook or bent point than for any other reasons.

To keep clincher sinkers from sliding down on your line or leader, fold one ear down on the line, wrap the line completely around the sinker, then fold the second ear down on the line; it will stay in place perfectly.

CHAPTER 2

Freshwater Lures

DRY FLIES

When choosing a dry fly, look for one that has stiff hackles with a sheen. Hackles that are soft become soggy and do not float high. The wings on a dry fly should be evenly matched and balanced, so that the fly doesn't spin when cast and will float in an upright position rather than off to one side.

It pays to carry some oversize dry flies especially when fishing the big, rough western rivers. They attract big fish, float better and higher than the smaller, light-hackled flies.

When trout are feeding on midges they usually ignore other flies and baits. In this case you need the tiny midge flies tied on a No. 20 or 22 hook.

If you want to dispense with buying and carrying a lot of dry fly patterns to match the various hatches of natural flies, use mostly variants. These flies do not imitate any particular fly but look like many different kinds of flies. An assortment of variants in different sizes will take care of many fishing situations.

WET FLIES AND NYMPHS

Many commercially tied wet flies are too bulky. A wet fly that is
sparsely dressed is much better. You can often take a small pair of
scissors and trim a heavily dressed wet fly.

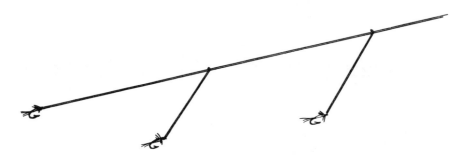

Try fishing three nymphs at the same time instead of just one. This
combination usually attracts and interests trout more than just a single
nymph.

You can quickly make a fly that imitates a big nymph or a woolly
worm, caterpillar, or grub by trimming the hackles on a bi-visible dry
fly and then fishing it wet for trout or bass.

If you are getting short strikes from trout or bass and can't hook
any fish, try adding a smaller trailing hook to the bigger one on a wet
fly or streamer.

Don't throw away your wet flies or nymphs because they are old or chewed up. Such underwater flies usually produce better than new ones.

A highly effective way to use a wet fly for trout is to strip the line in with short, fast jerks. Hold your rod tip low over the water when you do this.

When choosing nymphs, try to pick those that are tied for a specific area. Different kinds of nymphs are found in different waters and local patterns are usually most effective.

STREAMERS AND BUCKTAILS

When adding weight to a streamer, put the split-shot right next to the hook at the eye. This makes it easier to cast and gives the fly a better action in the water than when the weight is placed up on the leader.

Since streamers and bucktails are usually tied to imitate minnows or small fish, the addition of a bit of silver or gold to the body helps. The addition of Mylar strips makes a flashing fly which draws strikes from many freshwater gamefish.

Try fishing two streamers or bucktails, with a smaller one tied just behind the larger one up front.

Weighted streamers and bucktails are great for trout or bass when you want to fish the deeper spots and holes, especially in a current where ordinary streamers don't sink deep enough.

Small streamers work best in small streams where trout aren't too big. Fish them on light leaders for best results.

Bass Bugs

Bass bugs are usually most productive toward evening. They should be fished very slowly, allowing plenty of rest periods. When retrieving the bug, give it a few short jerks or twitches, then stop and let it rest again.

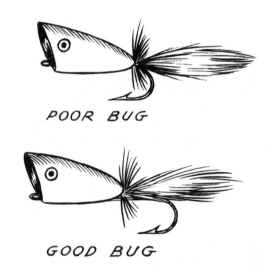

POOR BUG

GOOD BUG

When buying a bass bug or making one, be sure that the bend and point of the hook is well behind the body of the bug, where it will hook a fish more readily.

Some of the smaller bass bugs used for bass will also take big brown trout at night. Those that imitate big flies or bugs, minnows, frogs, or mice can all be tried.

Instead of using bucktail or ordinary feathers when tying a minnow-type bass bug, try adding some marabou herl around the hook. Such a bug will often take bass, pickerel, and panfish better than the regular bass bugs.

PLASTIC LURES

When rigging a plastic worm, place the hook at the head, and if two hooks are used add the second one right behind the first. This allows the tail of the worm to wriggle freely and results in more hits.

Plastic worms are often effective for trout, especially after a rain or shower, which raises the water level and washes food into the stream. In shallow water, drift the worm naturally down with the current. In deeper water and pools, retrieve it slowly along the bottom.

CORK
STOPPER

A quick way to turn your plastic worm into a surface-popping lure is to add a cork stopper in front. This will help keep your worm on top and it can be popped occasionally to create a disturbance.

Spoons and Spinners

Spoons are usually fished below the surface, but there are times when a spoon skittered fast on top of the water will get more action from bass or pike.

One highly effective way to fish a weighted spinner deep near the bottom without hanging up too often is to add one of the casting plastic bubbles about a foot or so ahead of the spinner. The float enables you to reel in the spinner slowly along the bottom to catch trout, bass, and walleyes.

A spoon can be used down deep near the bottom if you choose a heavy-gauge type that sinks fast. Let it go down and lie on the bottom, raise it, let it go down again, raise it again, and so on until it is near the shore or boat.

A good lure for channel catfish is a weighted spinner with a strip of pork rind. It should be worked slowly along the bottom with a stop-and-go motion.

When using a spinner on a fly rod, choose one with tiny, thin blades. This kind casts better and spins more readily than one with thick blades.

A small spinner added in front of a streamer fly often makes it more attractive to the fish. The blade flashes and gives it a more lifelike appearance, especially in quiet pools or lakes where there is no current.

Use light, thin-gauge spoons in still, quiet water, since they sink more slowly and have a fluttering action. But when fishing fast water with a strong current, use a heavier, thicker spoon to get down more quickly.

RUBBER BAND

A quick, easy way to make your spoon weedless is to pull a short rubber band through the eye of the spoon, then run one end of the rubber band through the other end and pull to form a single loop. Now stretch the band and catch it at the barb. It also helps to bend the hook point a bit inward with a pair of pliers.

Don't polish all your spoons and spinners or use brand-new ones every time you go fishing. Let a few of these lures get dull and tarnished. Under certain conditions they catch more fish than the bright, shiny ones.

You can use two spoons by removing the hooks from the first spoon and adding a trailer with another spoon on the end. The first spoon can be larger than the second one and you can use different colors or finishes.

JIGS

The small jig known as a "shad" dart is not only good for shad but can also be used for black bass, herring, white perch, crappies, and other panfish.

A good lure for jigging for bass around stumps near shore in muddy water can be made by using a jig head and adding some plastic worms with split tails. Or you can add a couple of live nightcrawlers to the lure.

Jigs are not too expensive and many can be made cheaply at home, so it pays to carry a wide assortment in different sizes and colors and to use them often to catch a wide variety of species. Don't hesitate to use them around obstructions, or in weeds, or on the bottom, even if you lose a lure every so often. You'll catch more fish if you sacrifice some jigs.

PLUGS

The light balsa wood and plastic plugs that have a natural, lifelike appearance and action are killers for bass and other fish when fished on top. Here you get the "floating" model, and instead of reeling steadily or fast to make it dive below the surface, you use a different technique. Cast out and let the plug rest on top for a while. Then twitch it and reel only a turn or two of the handle. Rest it and repeat. The plug will create a ripple and wake, and look like a crippled minnow struggling on the surface.

Some light surface plugs are so delicately balanced that the addition of a wire leader, trace, swivel, or snap will change or even ruin the action. Such plugs work best tied directly to the leader or line. If you must add a snap swivel to the end of your leader, choose the smallest one you can find.

Deep-diving or deep-running plugs usually require fast reeling or fast trolling to get down to their maximum depths.

Small, light plugs are best to use in waters which are clear and calm and in which fish get frightened easily. They land with less splash and noise and do not scare the fish as much as would a big plug.

A surface popper or splasher is most effective in fairly shallow water where it can be seen by the fish and bring them up. It is also good near shore, where it draws fish out of hiding places such as overhanging brush, lily pads, hyacinths, or logs.

Bass will often hit a plug that is lying stationary on the surface and that dips or "nods" every so often. The best plug to use for this is a slim type that has a propeller in the rear and is weighted so that it rests on top, partly submerged, with the head out of the water. A skilled angler can make this plug seem alive by twitching it so that it dips and nods in one spot without moving ahead more than a few inches.

A floating-diving plug is a good one to use near shore, where the water varies in depth and there are scattered boulders or sunken weed beds. Reel slowly over the shallow spots to make the plug travel near the surface, but speed up over the deeper spots and holes to make the plug dive.

Various Lures

Even on the same stream trout fishermen may run into various kinds of waters—smooth or rough, clear or roily, fast or slow, shallow or deep. A complete fly box with a wide assortment of patterns and types of flies enables an angler to meet changing conditions more readily.

All-black flies and jigs are effective for many freshwater species and are especially good when used for smallmouth bass in rivers where they feed on hellgrammites and small catfish that are black in color.

A combination lure can be made by tying a fly around a spinner shaft ahead of a lure such as a small spoon or plug. The combination looks like a minnow or small fish chasing a fly or bug and catches walleyes, bass, and pike.

Cut some toy balloons into strips and put them on the tail hooks of a spoon or plug. They are lighter and have more action than pork rind and do not change the lure to any extent.

Most of the so-called sound lures, which give off vibrations in the water, must be reeled or trolled at fairly fast speeds to be effective. Each lure varies in this respect and some lures will require faster reeling or trolling than others.

When using jigs or weighted plastic worms or eels for freshwater bass down deep, try letting the lure settle on the bottom and lie there a second or two. Bass will often follow the lure down and hit it while it is on the bottom or the second it leaves the bottom.

To give your pork-rind strips and frogs a better flavor, try soaking them in brine with some Italian anisette added.

CHAPTER 3

Freshwater Rigs

This rig can be used to drift a bait for channel catfish close to the bottom, but the float will keep it from hanging up on a rock or log. Add a small clincher sinker on the leader to keep the bait down.

A good rig to use for bluegills or bream when they are down deep makes use of a light ⅛ or ¼ oz. sliding sinker on your line, a small barrel swivel to act as a stop, and a small hook on a 12 in. leader baited with a worm. This is cast out and slowly reeled along the bottom.

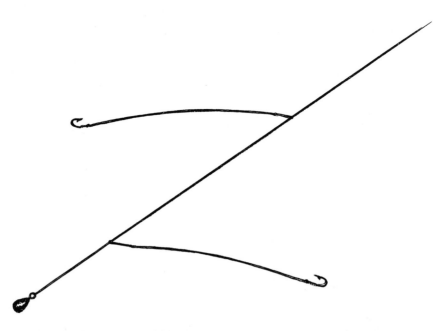

A bottom rig for bullheads and catfish can be made by tying a dipsey sinker on the end of the line, then one hook on a short leader a few inches above the sinker, and, finally, another hook about a foot above the first one.

A highly effective rig used when trolling for walleyes is made by tying a long "pencil" type sinker up to 15 in. long to one of the eyes of a 3-way swivel. These sinkers are usually made by casting lead around a heavy wire such as a coat hanger. The other eye of the 3-way swivel holds a 3 ft. leader and the lure on the end. This rig works best when trolled slowly in water from 8 to 30 ft. deep.

Another walleye rig makes use of a dipsey sinker attached to a 3-way swivel. A longer leader has two spinners with a tandem hook on the end. These can be baited with nightcrawlers or a minnow. The rig is trolled slowly along the bottom.

Still another kind of walleye rig is a combination-lure type where a 2 ft. leader is tied to one eye of a 3-way swivel and a light plug of the floating type is attached to the end of the leader. Then a jig on a short 12 in. dropper is tied to the other eye of the swivel. The jig provides weight to get the lure down and give the fish a choice of two lures. The jig also gets hung up less often with its single hook riding up. But in case it should, you can tie it on a lighter line, which will break and save the plug and the rest of the rig.

Take a deep-diving plug and remove the hooks, then tie a 3-ft. leader behind it and attach a floating plug. The deep-running plug will go down and bump bottom or move through the weeds without fouling while the trailing plug will clear the weeds or bottom and bring strikes from fish.

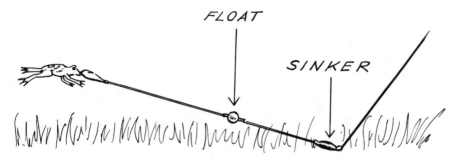

Hook a small frog on a weedless hook about 12 in. ahead of a small float; then add a clincher sinker a few inches ahead of the float. This rig can be used for very slow trolling or drifting over weed beds, since the float will tend to keep the frog above the weeds, and even if it goes through some weeds the weedless hook will help it to keep from fouling.

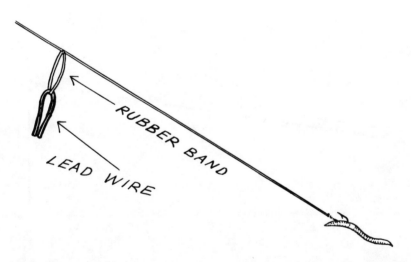

A rig for drifting baits or lures along the bottom can be made up by tying a rubber band 18 to 20 ins. from the hook and then cutting a length of heavy lead solder wire and bending it onto the rubber band. By cutting the lead wire into different lengths you get varied weights according to stream or river conditions.

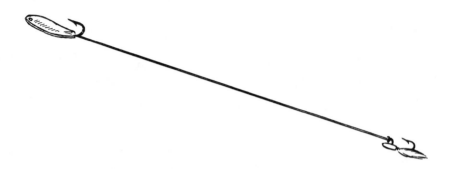

A combination lure that can be used when trolling for shad is made by tying a small spoon on the end of your line. Then add a 2 ft. leader to the spoon and a tiny white or yellow jig or shad dart. Although primarily used for trolling, this rig can also be cast from boat or shore into a river where shad are migrating.

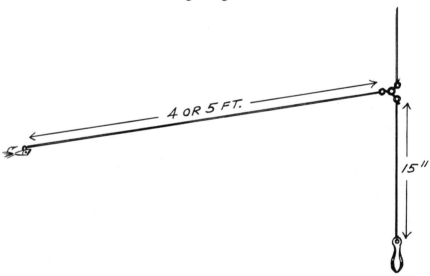

Another shad rig that can be used for trolling in a river is tied with a 4 or 5 ft. leader and a shad dart on the end. The sinker is attached to a 15 in. dropper and ranges from 1 to 4 oz., depending on the depth of the water and strength of the current.

4 TO 6 OZ.
KEEL SINKER

4 FT. WIRE LEADER

A muskie rig can be made by tying a 4 to 6 oz. keel sinker to the end of the line, then attaching a 4 ft. wire leader with the lure on the end. This rig is used for fast trolling on large lakes and rivers with a short length of line out.

When trolling for landlocked salmon use this rig, which presents three different streamers at varying levels. It gives the fish a choice and also simulates a small school of baitfish.

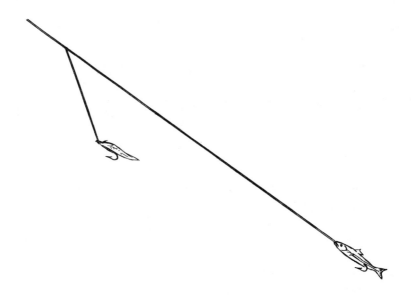

Another effective rig used in trolling for landlocked salmon is made by tying a streamer fly on a short dropper and then sewing a smelt about 3 ft. behind the fly.

This steelhead rig can be used when drift fishing for these fish. Tie a barrel swivel on the end of the line. Then tie an 18 to 20 in. leader with the hook. Next attach a short dropper with a short length of surgical tubing. Push a pencil sinker into this tubing and the rig is ready to go. If the sinker gets hung up on the bottom, a yank on the line will pull it out of the rubber tubing and save the rest of the rig.

A good deep-trolling rig for lake trout is illustrated above. This makes use of a triangular wire spreader. Attach a 6 ft. leader with a spinner and minnow to one eye of the triangle. Then attach a dropper of 4 ft. to hold the sinker. The remaining eye holds a barrel swivel to which the fishing line is tied.

Another lake trout rig, which is often called the "cowbells" or "Christmas tree" rig, makes use of several spinners on a leader ahead of the lure. This is attached to a rudder to prevent line twist. A sinker ranging from 3 to 8 oz. on a dropper is also tied to the rudder. For best results troll this rig with a lead-core line in depths from 50 to 150 ft.

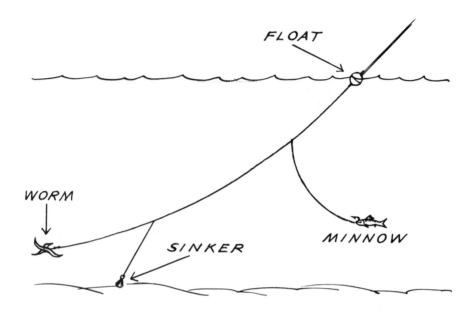

If you want to fish two different baits at different levels with a cane pole and still use a float or bobber to indicate bites, tie up the rig shown. A light sinker is used to keep the baits down. The float should be adjusted to the depth of the water being fished so that the sinker lies on the bottom and the float is on top.

CHAPTER 4

Freshwater Natural Baits

WORMS

The time to stock up on earthworms and nightcrawlers is during the spring months. The ground will be damp and the worms will be closer to the surface, where they can be dug. At night the big nightcrawlers will be out and a good supply can be gathered for future use. Later on, when the ground dries, it will be difficult to obtain worms.

To hook a nightcrawler for trolling or casting, run the hook into the mouth of the worm and bring it out near the head.

MINNOWS

The best places to keep minnows for long periods of time are cold springs and brooks, or streams with running water. A wood-topped box with fine-mesh wire around a frame makes an ideal container. It allows a free flow of water through the box, and the wooden cover provides shade.

When trolling a minnow, rig it by running the hook through the mouth and out the gill opening twice, then push the hook through the body near the tail.

Golden shiners used to catch big Florida bass can be 7 or 8 in. long.

FROGS

When fishing a frog among lily pads, hyacinths, saw grass, or other dense weeds, use a weedless hook and run it through the frog's lips. When a fish grabs it, give it plenty of time to swallow the frog before trying to set the hook.

To catch frogs for bait along a lake or pond shore, chase the frogs into the water and watch where they hide in the weeds or mud. Then reach under the water and grab them quickly.

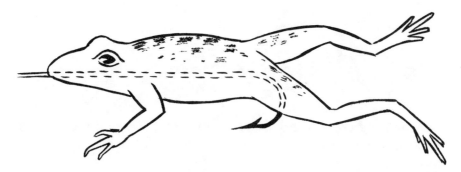

A dead frog makes a good bait for catfish, especially during the summer months. Run a long-shanked hook into the mouth of the frog and push it out at the crotch. Naturally, it has to be fished with a sinker or weight to keep it near the bottom, where catfish normally feed.

One good trick when fishing with dead frogs that have to be worked for bass or pike is to pull the boat up to shore and cast out into deeper water. Then reel in your frog toward shore in a stop-and-go action. That's the way frogs usually swim when trying to escape fish in deeper water.

Tadpoles, which are young frogs with a tail, often make good bait for trout, bass, and catfish. Hook them through the lips or the base of the tail for best results.

CRAYFISH

An excellent bait for channel catfish in streams and rivers is a crayfish. Hook it through the tail and drift it into spots where the catfish lie.

Although crayfish are easiest to obtain at night, when they come out of hiding, you can also obtain this bait in the daytime by turning over rocks in brooks and streams and by digging them out of burrows in mud or clay.

When using a hard-shelled crayfish for smallmouth bass, break off the big pincer claws and also crack the shell on the back of the crayfish. Bass pick up the scent and can taste the bait better when you do this.

If you get a crayfish that is too big for trout, break off the tail and run a hook under the skin on the underside of the tail as shown. Then drift this along the bottom.

INSECTS

During the Japanese-beetle season, trout and bass often feed on them. Then you can chum by dropping some of the beetles into the water. When you see a fish take them, you can float one of the beetles on a tiny hook toward the fish.

One of the best baits to use when fishing the small meadow brooks is a live grasshopper or cricket, since these insects are plentiful in such areas and are always falling into the water, where trout feed on them.

Take a glass jar and nail a stick to the inside of the lid. Punch some holes in the lid and catch some grasshoppers and put them in the jar. Then when you want bait, unscrew the lid; the hoppers will cling to the stick and can be grabbed easily.

OTHER BAITS

Even live baits such as worms, minnows, and crayfish fished deep for bass catch more fish if you give them some rod action instead of just letting them swim or hide on their own. Of course, with live baits the rod action will be slow and mostly in one spot.

The small freshwater shrimp found in some lakes makes a good bait for bluegills and crappies.

A good winter bait for bluegills is the larvae found in the nests of wasps and hornets.

Use a toothpick or a thin stick to push the eye of a tiny short-shank hook into a salmon egg so that it is buried completely.

Beef liver makes a fine bait for many freshwater fish. Cut it into long, narrow strips to look like a worm and use it for trout and bass. Use tiny pieces for panfish, and bigger strips or chunks for catfish.

Freshwater clams and mussels found in the mud and sand of streams and rivers can be used for catfish, carp, buffalo, and panfish. The meat must be removed from the shells before using.

If you want to try fishing for panfish or bullheads and have no bait, try a tiny piece of hot dog, ham, salami, or similar meat.

One of the easiest baits to obtain in a trout stream is a caddis worm. The worm, or larva, builds a case from tiny sticks, stones, sand, or leaves. They can be found on the bottom or clinging to stones. Break open the case and use either a single worm on a tiny hook or two or three on the same hook.

Water dogs, which are large salamanders, make good bait for bass. Those about 4 or 5 in. long are best, and they should be hooked through both lips.

A can of corn—the whole-kernel type—should be carried on a freshwater fishing trip. It comes in handy if you run out of bait or can't obtain any. One whole kernel on a hook can be used to catch bluegills and other panfish. Several kernels of corn can be threaded on the hook to catch carp, bullheads, and even trout if you drift the corn in a current.

Sturgeon feed a lot on vegetable matter in certain freshwater rivers, so here a good bait is the green moss or algae found growing on rocks. This moss can be gathered along the shores of a river and then rolled into a ball and put on a hook.

When using doughball bait for carp, form a pear-shaped ball that covers the entire hook right up to the eye. You can also use a small treble hook, which is also covered completely up to the eye.

Spring worms, which are brown-black grubs found in the mud of spring creeks, can be used for smallmouth bass in many rivers. Drift them near the bottom for best results.

If you are fishing near wooded areas and want to obtain a good bait, just break up some rotted logs and look for the grubs found inside.

Chicken blood that has been allowed to coagulate can be cut into strips, threaded on a small treble hook, and used to catch catfish.

A good bait can be made quickly and easily by mixing equal parts of peanut butter and flour and moistening the mixture with a bit of hot water. You can form this into doughballs of various sizes and use it to catch carp, catfish, bullheads, and panfish.

Marshmallows can be used to catch trout, panfish, bullheads, and carp if cut up into various-size chunks depending on which fish you are going after. When using the bait for trout, drift it in a current. For panfish let it sink and give it a bit of rod action with short jerks. And for bullheads and carp, just let the bait lie on the bottom.

Even when using such baits as salmon eggs or nightcrawlers for steelhead, it's still a good idea to tie some red yarn around the hook as an added attraction.

CHAPTER 5

Trout

BROWN TROUT

If you know that a heavily fished stream or river contains big brown trout, which are rarely caught during the day, try fishing for them at night. Big brown trout come out at night to feed, are less wary and easier to fool at this time.

If you do fish any waters at night for big brown trout, don't flash any lights on the water. This will frighten the trout or make them wary for the next hour or longer.

Brown trout in big lakes and reservoirs will often hit a streamer trolled fairly fast using a fly rod, a sinking fly line, and a long 50 ft. monofilament leader on the end.

A prime period to catch big brown trout on streamers or bucktails is right after a rain or shower, which discolors the water slightly.

You can also catch big brown trout in lakes and reservoirs by trolling deep with small plugs, spoons, spinners, or bait.

The best way to catch big brown trout in a stream or river is first to locate some fish by scouting the water to discover their hideouts. Then try drifting a worm or minnow to the fish, especially in the late afternoon or evening.

A good way to locate the hiding spots of big brown trout is to work a spoon or spinner alongside logs, roots, crevices, undercut banks, and other spots where the trout like to lie. Often you will see big trout come out of these hiding places to look or make a pass at the lures. Then you simply have to come back and fish that spot every chance you get.

Rainbow Trout

Rainbow trout in lakes are usually easier to catch in the spring and fall, when they come into shallow water; during the hot summer months they go deep and are more difficult to locate. Look for them at depths where the temperature ranges from 50 to 60 degrees. An electronic fish-finder is a big help in locating them in deep water.

Fish the slower pockets in a rapid, where rainbow trout are holding between boulders and rocks, which break the current in a stream or river.

Rainbow trout usually prefer larger rivers and streams with fast currents, but in some waters that warm up during the summer months, they may enter the feeder streams and tributaries, where the water is cooler.

When looking for rainbow trout in a pool, fish the head of the pool, where the fast water enters, and the water below the pool, where it picks up speed.

BROOK TROUT

Brook trout usually leave the larger streams and rivers during the summer months if they become too warm, and head for the deeper lakes, springs, and brooks. But they return to such waters in the fall, when the waters cool. They also are found there in the spring, when the water is still cold.

Although brook trout will rise to a dry fly on many occasions, you'll usually catch more fish with wet flies, streamers, underwater lures, or bait fished below the surface.

Look for brook trout in the inlets and outlets of a lake or pond. Some of the biggest brookies are caught in streams or rivers emptying into large lakes.

Streamers can be trolled for brook trout, or you can anchor in a river or wide stream and cast downstream and retrieve the fly against the current.

Choose a streamer or wet fly with red and white or a combination of these for brook trout.

Since brook trout like cold water, you'll find them around springs, especially during the summer months, if the water is low and warm.

When fishing for big brook trout, you can't go wrong by using streamers or bucktails. They usually feed on smelt and minnows and these lures imitate these baitfish. Fish them deep in pools and holes for best results.

Small brook trout often bite all day, but if you want to catch the bigger ones, wait until the late afternoon and evening, when they move into the shallows near shore to feed on flies, insects, and minnows.

MORE TROUT TIPS

If trout strike short or swirl near your dry fly without taking it, you probably have too large a fly on your line. Change to a smaller size in the same pattern.

Willow trees hanging over a trout stream or river often have good trout lying in the water below the branches. The willow tree provides shade and food for the waiting fish.

Big trout are usually more plentiful in the lower portions of a stream or river, especially early in the spring, when they stay in the larger, deeper pools, where the water is warmer and the food more plentiful.

Early in the season, when trout are sluggish and lying on the bottom, a nymph should be fished deep, almost on the bottom, for best results.

To catch big trout consistently you have to concentrate on them and use somewhat heavier tackle and bigger lures to attract and hold them. Most important, you have to locate big trout or know where they lie in a stream or river.

When fishing for trout lying under grass-covered overhung banks, it is important to cast your dry fly as close to the bank as possible. It should float no more than a few inches from the shoreline.

On the larger western rivers, float fishing with a guide often pays off in good trout fishing. Here you usually get only one chance at each spot and you have to make a good, accurate cast.

When dry fly fishing, you have to avoid drag to get rises from trout. Try making short casts and floating the fly for a short distance. It also helps to keep the line that is out off the water.

During the hot summer months, fish the limestone trout streams. These waters are usually higher and cooler than other trout streams at this time.

When the water is high and fast, look for trout in pockets behind rocks or boulders, along undercut banks or among washed-out tree roots, and in deep, quiet holes. There they can avoid the full strength of the current.

If the regular retrieves fail to work, try skittering your wet fly on top. This often wakes trout up and excites them.

Once a trout is disturbed or frightened, it will take a long time before he gets over his fright. Even when he does, he may be wary and hard to fool. A trout that hasn't been disturbed is more likely to hit a lure.

Since you cannot see where you are casting at night for trout in a stream or river, one good system is to cast across the current slightly downstream, starting with short casts and gradually lengthening them. Then move down a few feet and repeat the process. In this way you cover most of the water and stand the best chance of a fish seeing your lure.

Trout in a lake or quiet pool are harder to catch because they have plenty of time to look over a fly or lure before taking it. When using underwater flies or lures in such waters, try a faster retrieve to give the fish less time to examine a lure.

It is rarely necessary to cast more than 30 or 40 ft. when fishing with a dry fly. Shorter casts will enable you to cast more accurately and more delicately, and to control the float of your fly better.

When trout are lying deep they aren't too interested in a dry fly. They are most likely to take the floating fly during a hatch of insects. But if there are no hatches, you can try casting the dry fly toward likely spots in the shallower portions of a stream.

Fishing upstream is usually best when using dry flies, but even when casting dry flies or nymphs you can approach a trout from behind with less chance of frightening him by working upstream.

A good place to fish for trout is a narrow portion or constricted area connecting two bodies of water, especially if you can cast across it from land or anchor in the middle and reach both shores. Trout cruise through this narrow spot sometime during the day or evening and you can be there waiting for them.

When trout are striking short or just following a streamer or buck-tail without taking it, try slowing down the retrieve to give the fish a chance to catch the lure.

If you are casting spoons or heavy spinners for trout in quiet water, make long casts well beyond the area you want to fish. This way there is less chance that the splash of the lure will frighten the fish.

Fly fishing for trout is usually best when water temperatures are between 55 and 65 degrees. That is when most fly hatches occur and trout do a lot of feeding.

To work a bait or lure deep when trout fishing, cast it upstream and slightly across. This cast should be well above the spot you actually want to fish, so that it can sink and drift into it. As the lure or bait drifts, take up slack line. When it passes opposite you, let out line until the bait or lure is down deep. Then you can retrieve it slowly against the current. You can also try releasing line every so often, letting the lure or bait drop back toward the bottom.

Trout will sometimes feed and swim in the fastest, most powerful currents in a stream or river. But most of the time they will be lying near the bottom or along the edges of the main current, where the flow is weaker and they do not have to fight the current continuously. That's where to work your lure or bait in a trout stream.

Pools usually hold the biggest trout and they will often be found at the head of the pool. Look for them along the edges of the main current where there are eddies or obstructions that break the force of the current.

When the trout season is still open, you can have good fishing during the fall months. There are fewer fly hatches in the cooler weather, so most of the action will be on small spoons, spinners, streamers, and lures that imitate minnows. Live baits are also good at this time. Best fishing will usually take place on the warmer days and during the middle of the day.

During the hot summer months try fishing the pockets found between rocks and boulders in a stream or river. These small pools are often fairly deep, cool, and well aerated. Good-size trout often lie in them and wait for food to drift in.

If trout in a lake are feeding on large insects or bugs, try a small panfish or bass bug when you see the fish breaking and feeding on top.

When the trout season first opens in the northern states, conditions in rivers, streams, and brooks are usually unfavorable for good fishing. The water may be too high, too muddy, or too cold. Instead try fishing the lakes and ponds, near shore, where the water is usually clearer and warmer.

The best time to fish the quiet, glassy meadow streams is when it is cloudy and there is a breeze to ruffle the surface. If insects are also hatching you have an excellent chance to catch some nice trout.

Early in the trout season use a white marabou streamer. A weighted model works best—one that has lead wire wrapped around the hook. To fish it, cast across and upstream and let it drift with the current. When it has completed most of its swing, start retrieving it very slowly with short twitches of the rod tip.

You can often locate big trout at night by listening for the splashes when they are feeding.

Most trout seek the shady spots of a stream, especially during the middle of the day when the sun is high and bright. Toward evening or early in the morning, when the light is low, however, they are more likely to leave this cover and be found in more open waters.

The headwaters or upper portions of a stream or river are usually best for low-water hot-weather fishing. Here the water is cooler than in the lower sections.

One way to locate big trout during midsummer or early fall is to walk along a meadow bank and kick the grass and shake the bushes along the stream. If grasshoppers or beetles or other bugs fall in the water, watch them drift downstream. Should a fish rise and take the insect, mark the spot and fish it with a live grasshopper or an imitation.

While big streamers and bucktails are often effective in the spring and early summer months, when the water is high, it's a good idea to change to smaller streamers and bucktails during the hot summer months, when the water level drops.

Fishing with a dry fly for trout in a lake is usually a waste of time if you just cast at random. It pays to wait until you see insects hatching or hovering and fish actually feeding before using the floating flies. Or if you see a trout cruising you can cast a few feet ahead of him and then make the fly move in short spurts to imitate a helpless insect.

Trout are warier and more quickly frightened during the low-, clear-water periods in July and August. At such times stalk the fish and keep hidden or make long casts. Use longer leaders, up to 12 or 15 ft., and fine tippets.

When fly fishing at night for big trout, it is important to avoid slack line, especially when fishing with a free-floating dry fly or bug. Night-feeding trout often take such flies lightly and since you can't see the strike you have to feel the fish take the lure in order to set the hook.

When trout streams are high or slightly discolored early in the season, worms, spinners, and spoons are better than flies. You can also try using the tiny balsa and plastic plugs that have silver or gold bodies and a brisk lifelike minnow action. Use them on a light or ultralight spinning outfit to get casting distance.

When fishing mountain lakes at high altitudes, you'll usually have the best fishing during the middle of the day, when the sun warms up the air and insects hatch and fly over the water.

Nymphs aren't too productive when the trout season opens, especially if the stream or river is high or roily. Larger, more flashy lures are better then. But as soon as the water drops, clears, and warms up a bit, nymphs start to take some good-size trout.

When fishing a wet fly for trout, it's a good idea to strip in a couple of coils of line and then, as the fly drifts directly below you, release the coils so that the fly drops back downstream. Often a fish will follow the wet fly, then decide to take it when it suddenly drops back.

Weighted streamers or bucktails can be cast out a good distance with a spinning outfit. They sink fast to reach the bottom in holes, pockets, or deep runs where big trout lie.

A good way to work a spoon, spinner, or underwater plug for trout is to get above your fishing spot, then cast beyond it and reel in your lure slowly near the bottom.

If you hook a big trout in a stream and the fish tries to sulk or rest on the bottom, throw a rock behind the fish to start it moving again.

CHAPTER 6

Black Bass

LARGEMOUTH BASS

A largemouth black bass isn't very active if the water temperature is below 60 degrees, so in the early spring it's a good idea to carry a thermometer and take a reading. If the water temperature is above 60 degrees, use lures. But if it is colder, use live baits such as minnows and fish them deep.

When fishing heavily weeded bottom that covers a wide area, look for clear spots or patches where there are no weeds. Largemouth bass often like to gather in such places.

Some of those plastic "worms" or "eels" are no doubt mistaken by largemouth bass for small snakes, especially when they are fished on top or just below, where snakes usually swim. Another deadly way to use these worms or eels is to rig them with a weedless hook and then reel them across the top of the lily pads. When you come to an opening or clear spot, let the lure sink before you resume reeling.

Bullhead minnows make a good bait for big largemouth bass in

Florida, especially when found in the same waters as the bass and the bass are on the spawning beds.

Weedless lures are often needed for big bass under the lily pads in weeds or grass. But you miss a lot of fish, which fail to get hooked. When buying a weedless lure or hook, test the wire guard to make sure it is not too stiff. Choose weedless lures or hooks with softer, more flexible wire guards.

Daytime fishing during a full-moon phase is likely to be poor or slow. Bass feed at night more then and are not too hungry during the daylight hours. However, you can often have good fishing at night under the moon. Or you can wait until the dark of the moon to fish in the daytime.

A highly effective way of using bass bugs is to cast into a likely spot and let the bug lie motionless as long as 4 or 5 minutes. Then twitch it a bit and let it lie again.

The largemouth black bass is one of the smartest fish in fresh water and soon learns to avoid certain lures that are fished often in a lake. Your best bet in such a heavily fished lake is to use "strange" or new lures. Or you can wait until the season opens, when bass tend to forget past experiences and hit well during the first day or two.

One of the best ways to use a weedless spoon with a skirt or pork rind or plastic worm is to cast it right into the weeds and reel it back fast so that it skims along on top of the pads and water.

When fishing for big bass on spawning beds in Florida, don't cast your bait or lure directly at the fish. This can frighten the bass. Instead cast several feet beyond the bed and work it toward the fish.

SMALLMOUTH BASS

Unlike largemouth bass, which often hit a stationary or slow-moving bug, the smallmouth bass prefers a somewhat faster-moving bug, especially when fishing rivers. Here, because of the moving current, the fish have to make up their minds fast and move quickly. So you can work your bass bug by popping it steadily with only short pauses every so often.

When fishing for smallmouth bass in a river, it is vital to discover where they are lying. When working a good-size pool, you can start at the head where the pool begins and work downstream toward the tail, casting at various angles and working various depths until all the water is probed. Once you get a hit or catch a fish, keep working that spot, because you can often catch more than one fish there.

During the hot summer months smallmouth bass go deep, and one of the best baits to use at this time is a live frog fished near the bottom.

One of the most effective surface lures for smallmouth bass is a tiny plug with a propeller at the rear. This can be worked with plenty of erratic rod action to simulate a crippled minnow.

There are times when smallmouth bass will take a dry fly and provide great sport on a fly rod. This usually happens when they are feeding on a hatch of flies or such insects as grasshoppers.

When fishing the smaller, shallower rivers for smallmouth bass, more caution is needed than when fishing larger rivers or deeper lakes. In the smaller streams, wade upstream and cast into likely spots. Move and fish slowly and quietly so that you don't frighten the bass.

A good lure for smallmouth bass when they are in rocky or weedy areas feeding on crayfish is a twin spinner in a black finish with a green pork frog added to the hook. This is cast as far as possible and is allowed to sink to the bottom and reeled very slowly, bouncing bottom all the way in. Evening, sunrise, and night are best for this fishing, since that is when crayfish are most active and bass come looking for them.

If you like fly fishing for smallmouth bass, try a streamer or bucktail in your favorite stream, river, or lake, especially in the late afternoon and evening. Try to imitate the local baitfish with your fly pattern.

You can also try a wet fly and just let it sink in a lake without any rod action. Smallmouth bass will often hit such a wet fly as it is slowly sinking.

A jig can be worked slowly along the bottom to imitate a crayfish. Jigs dressed with brown, green, or black hair are best.

A good way to use a spoon for smallmouth bass over a sandy bottom is to cast it out and let it sink until it lies on the sand. Then raise and bounce it along the bottom so that it stirs up the sand.

When smallmouth bass are feeding on hatching mayflies in a river, they can be located by looking for rings formed on the water by rising fish. Then you should cast your fly just above the ring so that it floats into it.

When using surface plugs or bass bugs in a lake for smallmouth bass, work them more gently than for largemouth bass. The smallmouths respond better to ripples, wakes, and tiny splashes than to loud pops or big splashes.

A key time to fish a river for smallmouth bass is right after a thunderstorm, which dirties the water along the shore but leaves the midstream section clear. At such times cast your lure or bait into the clear stretches.

MORE BASS TIPS

If you see a bass following your surface plug when it is being retrieved at a moderate or fast speed but refusing to hit it, try stopping the lure so that it floats without moving. The fish may hit then or when the plug starts moving again.

One effective technique when working a jig is to let it sink and rest on the bottom as long as 30 seconds. Then raise it off the bottom and let it drop back again.

When fishing for bass in the late fall—October or November—concentrate on the deeper holes and drop-offs, where the water is from 15 to 30 ft. deep.

During a cold front in Florida, black bass will head for the deeper canals and holes. But they will return to the shallows after the cold front passes and the weather warms up again.

When bass are schooling and chasing shad minnows, try plugs that look like these silvery fish and work them just below the surface. However, bigger bass may be lying down deep at such times, so a lure allowed to sink will often draw hits.

Bass can be caught during the summer months in many shallow-water areas if you fish the stumps, logs, overhanging trees, bushes, docks, and any other hangout where there is shade.

Usually when bass are down deep you must use underwater lures or bait to get them. But one trick that sometimes works is to cast a noisy surface plug or big bass bug repeatedly to the same spot. Bass have been known to come up from pretty deep water to grab such a lure.

When fishing for bass in canals, you'll often find them lying along the drop-off. Here you can cast a sinking lure into the shallow water near shore, then work it and let it sink so that it works into the deeper water.

One effective way to fish a gravel bar or rocky point in a lake for smallmouth bass is to run the boat up to shore and then cast out into deeper water with a deep running lure.

A bass bug can be worked and popped steadily for 15 or 20 ft. Then stop it and let it rest before you pick it up for the next cast. Often a bass will follow a moving bug without taking it, but if it stops he'll often hit it.

Anglers fishing the Saint Johns River in Florida chum with small menhaden to attract big black bass. Then they hook one of the menhaden and drift it toward the waiting bass.

If black bass are inside reeds or other heavy growth where they can't be reached with lures, try casting to the edge of such weeds. Cast to the very same spot several times. This will often draw a fish out of the heavy cover to investigate the disturbance and will bring a strike. Surface lures or bass bugs are best for this.

In lakes or reservoirs the good places to fish for black bass are slide areas—places where trees, rocks, or debris have fallen into the water.

Black bass feed heavily during fall months, and good fishing can be had at this time. Some of the top spots include the small streams and creeks entering into the larger rivers, lakes, or reservoirs. Bass move into these waters to look for crayfish, minnows, and frogs.

Although bass usually like a lure worked slowly or at a moderate speed, there are times when a lure that is trolled or reeled fast is best.

When bottom bumping for big bass, most of your strikes will come when the lure moves over an underwater object such as a rock, a sunken tree trunk, or stumps. The strike usually comes just as the lure clears the obstruction and starts to sink.

River bass often lie in the crevices under rock ledges or in holes or eddies beneath an undercut grassy bank. These places are fished best from the opposite side of the river, casting toward the ledges or under-cut bank.

A good fishing spot should be fished at different times of the day to find out when the bass are feeding. It pays to return to the same spot at intervals and give it a good workout.

Big bass like to lie in the shade of the hyacinth beds or islands found floating or growing in many rivers, canals, and lakes in Florida. The best way to catch these bass is to lower a live shiner at the edge of the hyacinths, which are usually too thick to cast lures into. Try positioning your boat so that it is close to the growth at the sides of the patch of hyacinths, then cast a plastic worm or plug near the vegetation and retrieve the lures along the edges.

To work a shoreline for bass, move slowly and cast your lure ahead of the boat. An electric motor is best for such fishing.

Usually a bass bug popper should be worked slowly, but on days when it is windy and the water is riffled, a fast retrieve with loud pops is better. Then the added commotion and noise are more likely to be seen and attract the bass.

When a bass in lily pads or other weeds hits your plug or spoon but fails to get hooked, try changing to a plastic worm and cast it into the same spot. Often the same bass that refuses the rigid lures will grab the soft worm.

A good spot to fish for bass is by a tree that has fallen into the water and is lying mostly submerged. Cast your lures over and around the sunken trunk and the branches. Several bass can often be caught in such a spot.

The best time to catch a big bass in Florida is in the late winter or early spring, when huge largemouth bass are "bedding"—preparing their nests prior to spawning. Try to find a few such nests and keep casting your lures or baits to the fish. Sooner or later the big bass guarding the nest will get angry and grab the lure.

In many of the southern states, where winters are mild, bass fishing is good even during the winter months. But even there the bass tend to be sluggish and stay in deep water. To make them hit, you have to work your lures right on the bottom as slowly as possible.

The quiet approach is always best when fishing for black bass in shallow water. Loud outboard motors, waves, splashes, banging objects against the boat, and similar disturbances forewarn or alert a bass or frighten it so that it won't strike your lure or bait and may even leave the area.

Bass fishing may vary from lake to lake and river to river. If one lake is poor, try another one nearby and keep trying until you find one that is producing. Try different stretches of a river or even different rivers. Bass feed at different times and on different foods and in different places and depths, depending on water temperatures and prevailing conditions. This can vary from one body of water to another. Fishing may be poor or slow in one lake, but another one, not far away, may be hot.

You can sometimes stir up lethargic bass in a lake by whacking the water with an oar or a board. Then leave the area for a few minutes, after which you can go back and start fishing.

If you are using a plastic worm over a submerged weed bed, let the lure sink until it reaches the tops of the weeds, then retrieve it slowly with jerks just over the weed bed.

Streamer flies are effective for both largemouth and smallmouth bass. Fish them deep near the bottom in deep holes and pools during the daytime and just below the surface in shallow water at daybreak, dusk, and night.

The best way to catch a trophy black bass in Florida is to fish a live shiner up to 8 or 10 in. long under a float or bobber. Hook the shiner through the back or lips and fish it along the edges of pads or hyacinths and in open water among this vegetation.

When fishing surface lures for bass at night, don't be afraid to pop them loud and often. This gives the fish a better chance to locate the lure. Also it's a good idea to cast your lure into the same spot several times.

When fishing in lily pads with a plastic worm, try casting into an opening between the pads and let the worm sink toward the bottom. Often a bass will grab it before it reaches the bottom.

The best points to fish for bass in lakes and reservoirs are those that slope gradually for 40 or 50 ft., then drop sharply. If there are sunken trees, bushes, or weeds at the drop-off, you have a real hot spot.

Some of the best fishing for bass is found in the saw grass shallows and patches in Florida. But saw grass can be rough on your line and leaders. You should cut off a few feet of line every so often to eliminate the weak line or leader nicked by the saw grass.

CHAPTER 7

Muskellunge, Pike, Pickerel, and Walleyes

MUSKELLUNGE

Not all muskie waters are suitable to the same methods and techniques. Casting may produce best on some lakes and rivers, trolling is best on other waters, and bait fishing with suckers or other fish is most productive in other spots. So rather than waste your time on strange waters, it pays to hire a guide or find out which methods and techniques work best in the waters you plan to fish.

Muskies often start hitting just before and during a storm or in bad weather. Many veteran muskie fishermen and guides go out at such times, but caution is in order if the water gets too rough.

A good way to catch muskies is by drifting with the current in a river or a breeze in a lake with a live sucker. This can be done in the daytime or at night.

To catch muskies, you have to put in a lot of time and concentrate on them with the right tackle, lures, and baits, not wasting time fishing for other species.

Muskie lures should be trolled deep during the spring and late fall, but during the summer and early fall they can often be taken near the surface or in the shallows, especially in the evening and at night.

Trolling is usually the most effective way to catch muskies on the larger lakes and rivers where there is mostly open water with no islands, lily pads, rocky points, or logs to cast around.

In muskie fishing don't quit after making one or two casts in a spot. Keep casting in a productive spot for long periods. A muskie may be present but may not strike on the first few casts. Before trying a new spot, keep casting until you are convinced the fish isn't interested.

Muskies will often hit surface plugs that make a lot of commotion, such as poppers, wounded minnow types, flaptails, swimmers, and wobblers. These are best when fished in fairly calm water along shorelines, over weed beds, and in shallow coves.

Not too many muskies are caught early in the morning. You'll get your best results after 9 or 10 o'clock and up until dusk. They are also caught at night, but not too many anglers want to fish for them in the dark.

When fishing for muskies in rivers, use a float above a hook baited with a big minnow or small sucker and drift the rig toward a log, sunken tree, or brush pile.

When hooked, muskies have a favorite trick of swimming toward the angler faster than he can reel, and the resulting slack line enables them to throw the hook. A reel with a high gear ratio will help to prevent a slack line.

The easiest muskies to hook are those that haven't been exposed to lures or baits. Once they have been hooked or cast over by many fishermen, they tend to become wary and less inclined to strike. So it pays to look for new waters or new fish if you want real action.

In a lake a prime spot for muskies is by a tree overhanging the water. A muskie will often be found lying under such a tree waiting for something to fall off the branches into the water. Try to cast under the branches extending over the water.

In rivers look for muskies around fallen trees, logs, boulders, rock ledges, springs, and mouths of tributaries or feeder streams.

PIKE

Unlike muskies, pike usually prefer smaller lures. Plugs in the ½ to ⅝ oz. range and spoons weighing from ½ to ¾ oz. are usually more effective than the larger sizes.

If a pike takes your line into the weeds and fouls it, give him some slack line. He'll often come out into the open water again.

During the summer months, when pike are down deep, try still-fishing or drifting with live baits such as big minnows, chubs, or suckers.

Pike can be caught during the winter months in many rivers and streams, especially those that flow into a lake containing pike. Many of these moving rivers are free of ice and can be floated in a small boat.

In the winter, river pike often lie under the ice formed along shore and in quiet coves and backwaters. Cast your lure along the edge of an ice shelf and retrieve your lure as close to the edge of the ice as you can.

Live baits used for pike include big minnows, suckers, yellow perch, and bullheads with the spines cut off.

The best seasons to fish pike, especially the big ones, are spring and fall.

Good pike spots in rivers are along shorelines and in slow waters and backwaters, where the pike doesn't have to fight the current and where minnows, suckers, and small fish are plentiful.

Fishing for pike tends to slow down during the summer months, but in colder waters in the far north—for instance, Canada—they can often be caught during July and August.

Fishing a streamer or bucktail for pike requires a fast retrieve. This is best done by stripping in line in rapid spurts.

If you hook a pike in weedy waters or around obstructions, try to get your fish out into the open water, where you can fight him better. Of course, to do this you need stout tackle such as a bait-casting rod and a reel filled with 20 or 25 lb.-test line.

During the hot summer months troll at depths of 10 to 30 ft. for pike, especially along sharp drop-offs.

Pike can be caught on a fly rod if you use big streamer flies, up to 5 or 6 in. long. All white, all yellow, or red and white and red and yellow are good colors to use in these large flies.

When pike refuse to hit a spoon retrieved in the regular manner, try casting it and letting it sink to the bottom. Then wait a few seconds and raise the spoon quickly off the bottom, letting it settle again. Keep doing this during most of the retrieve.

Pike can be caught through the ice. Use a big minnow or a small sucker for bait and fish it close to the bottom.

PICKEREL

Pickerel are usually found near such cover as rushes, lily pads, weed beds, logs, and sunken trees. In rivers and streams look for them in the quieter waters—coves, pools, and eddies.

Pickerel often follow a lure for long distances without hitting it. If you see a fish following your lure, speed up the retrieve, and chances are good that he will grab it.

Streamers and bucktails fished with a fly rod make good lures for pickerel. The red and white streamer and flies with silver bodies produce especially good results.

Pickerel are more active and hit better on cloudy or rainy days than on bright, sunny days.

WALLEYES

When choosing plugs for walleyes, pick those that sink or dive deep on the retrieve or when trolled. They should also have a lot of action even on a slow retrieve, which is best for these fish.

The strike or bite of a walleye is slower and less noticeable than that of many other gamefish, so there is less chance that he will hook himself. The best procedure is to set the hook with a sharp sweep of the rod at the slightest indication of a hit.

In rivers walleyes lie in the deeper holes during the daytime. In the evening and at night, however, they move into the shallow riffles to feed on minnows.

Since walleyes are school fish, it pays to carry a buoy attached to a weight which can be tossed overboard when you get a strike while trolling. Then you can cast or troll in the spot marked by the buoy.

Walleyes tend to feed better on the side of the reef where the wind is blowing rather than on the opposite or lee side.

Walleyes in a river like to lurk along the edges of a current or in eddies, where they don't have to fight the strong current but are still in a position to dart into the fast water for food.

Although most walleyes are caught by trolling or casting, try drifting next time. Use a spinner and minnow combination and let it down near the bottom while the boat drifts with the wind.

Walleyes are rarely caught on fly rods, mainly because they are usually deep and do not rise to dry flies or even wet flies fished on or just below the surface. But you can catch them on a fly rod in the shallows toward evening if you use a streamer on a sinking fly line and work it slowly near the bottom.

Usually all walleyes in a single school are of the same size. Thus if you are catching small ones of 2 or 3 lbs. and you want to catch bigger ones, it pays to leave the spot where the small fish are and look for another where big ones may be congregated.

Some lakes and rivers contain good populations of walleyes, but not too many are caught because most anglers insist on fishing during the daytime, even though the walleyes feed mostly at night.

In a lake fish for walleyes in the deep waters along rock ledges. In a river fish the deeper eddies and deep holes below rapids.

You can often locate walleyes by trolling deep with a plug, spoon, or a spinner and minnow combination. Then when you find them or hook a fish, stop the boat and try jigging just off the bottom with a jig.

Walleyes will often take a sinking or deep-running plug cast or trolled near the bottom. They are especially partial to red plugs.

If you must fish for walleyes during the daytime, fish the deeper waters and try to choose a cloudy, overcast, or stormy day.

Walleyes are lazy feeders—in the sense that they do not like to cruise around and chase baitfish as other fish often do. Instead they prefer to stay in one place and wait for the food to come by. Then they grab it with a quick rush. That is why, when fishing them with lures, you have to get the lures down deep near the bottom and work them slow.

CHAPTER 8

Panfish

BLUEGILLS AND OTHER SUNFISH

When fly fishing for bluegills, use surface bugs in the morning and evening. During the middle of the day and when the water is rough, use wet flies or sinking bugs below the surface.

During the hot summer months you'll catch plenty of small bluegills near shore in shallow water. But if you want the big ones, fish the deeper-water drop-offs, especially those next to weed beds.

One of the best times to fish for bluegills is toward evening, right up until dark.

A top natural bait for bluegills and other sunfish is a "bonnet worm," which is found in the upper stalks of "bonnets" or lily pads.

Even with bluegills the quiet approach is best, especially if you want to catch the big ones. Too much noise or splashing will frighten them or make them wary.

A deadly fly for bluegills is one resembling a bee. It should be tied on a No. 8 or 10 hook. Half of the body is dressed with yellow chenille or wool and the other half with black chenille or wool. Add some black shoulder hackle and tie off with a fat black head.

When using wet flies for bluegills or sunfish, try putting a small maggot or grub on the hook.

In the spring, when bluegills are spawning, they are easy to locate. Just look for the light-colored nests near shore along sandy or gravel bottoms.

A good way to fish a wet fly for bluegills is to let it sink without any rod action in the beginning. When you reach the depth where the fish are, twitch the fly gently and let it sink again, then repeat the rod action.

During the summer months bluegills can be found among the deep weed beds and along drop-offs, steep banks, and wooded shores with shade.

Good baits to use when fishing through the ice for bluegills are waxworms and mealworms.

You can chum for bluegills and other sunfish and bring them up to the boat. Mealworms, chopped-up worms, tiny pieces of fish or meat, and various cereals and grains, such as oatmeal, boiled rice, or corn flakes, can all be used to draw in the bluegills.

YELLOW PERCH

Some of the best fishing for yellow perch takes place early in the spring soon after the ice is out. Then they come close to shore and into streams and creeks to spawn.

Yellow perch can be caught by trolling. Best lures for this are tiny spoons, weighted spinners, and spinners with a worm behind them. Troll at the slowest possible speed close to the bottom.

Yellow perch rarely bite at night, and the best fishing is usually from sunrise to sunset. Occasionally there will be some action around dusk if you locate a school on the bottom near shore or in a hole and drop the bait among them.

You can often catch yellow perch two at a time by using a two-hook rig such as the one illustrated above.

When fishing for yellow perch in rivers, look for them in the deeper, quieter sections where the current isn't too strong.

Small live minnows are one of the top baits for yellow perch. But they will also take worms, tiny frogs, grasshoppers, crickets, crayfish tails, and nymphs.

White Perch

On some of the larger lakes you can often locate schools of white perch if you look for gulls swooping and feeding. The white perch feed on small smelt or other baitfish, driving them to the surface, where they are picked up by the gulls.

Catch your first white perch on a worm, minnow, or tiny lure, then fillet it and cut it up into small strips. Use these on a hook to catch more white perch.

A good time to fish for white perch with such lures as wet flies or small streamers is early in the morning, from daybreak to a couple of hours later. That is when they are schooled and chase minnows.

A good bait for white perch in many lakes in Maine is a small whole smelt or pieces of a big smelt.

An effective rig for white perch is a gold spinner about 20 to 24 in. ahead of a hook baited with worms. Troll this very slowly at various depths until a school of fish is located. Then troll in the same spot at the same depth.

You'll often see schools of white perch moving slowly along the surface in a lake. You can try trolling or casting at such times.

White perch move into shallow water near shore at dusk and usually remain there until daybreak. They bite well at night and can be caught at such times.

You can catch white perch with a fly rod using tiny panfish bugs or large dry flies. This is usually best in the late afternoon and evening, when the fish are feeding on insects.

White Bass

When white bass move up rivers to spawn, look for them in the quieter eddies and pools, below boulders, and in other spots where the current weakens and the fish can rest or mill around before moving upstream again.

Choose dark, cloudy, or rainy days when fishing for white bass. Then they often rise to the surface to feed.

White bass move widely over a lake or reservoir and range from shallow water to deep water. When they are down deep, look for them over sand and gravel bottoms. Closer to shore they prefer sand and gravel bars or points and drop-offs to deep water.

Find schools of gizzard shad, and you'll usually find the white bass chasing and feeding on them.

Trolling is a good way to catch white bass. When they are on top, a tiny plug, spoon, or spinner can be trolled 10 to 15 ft. in the wake of

the boat at a fairly fast speed. If they are down deep, you have to use
a weight or a wire line to get from 30 to 50 ft.

CRAPPIES

Tiny underwater plugs often work well for crappies. Those with
silvery sides, which match the small minnows on which these panfish
feed, are usually best.

Crappies often bite better early in the morning or in the late afternoon. They can also be caught at night.

If you see some twigs, brush, or branches sticking out of the water,
try a few casts for crappies. They like to spawn and feed among submerged trees and brush.

When fishing for crappies, it's a good idea to move around and try
different spots until you get a bite. Then anchor there and keep fishing
as long as the action lasts.

Crappies can often be caught through the ice during the winter
months. Small, live minnows make the best bait, but crappies will also
hit ice flies or jigging spoons at times.

When crappie fishing, try beating the water with your cane pole or
rod. This often brings crappies to the scene, and you can then fish for
them.

When the sun is bright, fish for crappies under your own boat. They
often congregate in dark, shady spots.

In the fall crappies will return to shallow water to feed on minnows.
Then they will hit live minnows, spoons, spinners, or jigs.

Try cutting a thin, tapered strip from the sides or belly of the first crappie you catch. Then run the hook through the widest part of the strip and cast it out. Let it sink without any weight and give it a little action with the rod tip to make the strip flutter and move.

It doesn't pay to stay too long in one spot if you get no bites or catch no crappies. Move around, trying different spots until you locate a school of fish.

Crappies will often take insects such as grasshoppers, crickets, and cockroaches when used as bait. And one of the best baits of all is the larva of a drone honeybee.

OTHER PANFISH TIPS

You can often locate or follow a school of panfish by catching one and hooking it gently to a bobber or float on about 4 or 5 ft. of line. Then put the fish back into the water and watch where the float goes. When it stops or slows down, fish near it.

One of the best times to fish for shellcrackers in the south is three days before the full moon and three days after it.

In lakes look for rock bass over rocky shoals and bars, along rocky drop-offs, and among big boulders and rocks near shore.

Warmouth bass are usually found in quiet, shallow waters with muddy bottoms and weeds. So look for them in the weed beds and around lily pads and other vegetation.

CHAPTER 9

Other Freshwater Fishes

Atlantic Salmon

In salmon fishing the color or pattern of the fly is less important than in trout fishing. For Atlantic salmon you don't try to match any special fly or insect since these fish rarely feed when in fresh water. Instead you concentrate on presenting the fly properly.

Atlantic salmon may rise to a dry fly, but that doesn't mean they'll take it. They often just play with the fly, bumping it but not mouthing it. In order not to frighten the fish at such times, you have to avoid trying to set the hook, hoping he'll take the fly later on.

Although Atlantic salmon prefer a steady current, they usually lie in the slack or weaker flow behind such obstructions as boulders, rocks, shelves, and logs.

Atlantic salmon are rarely hooked when they are actually migrating or moving upstream. You have to wait until the fish is resting or holding in a spot before you can drift your fly over him.

321

Some Atlantic salmon rivers with gravel or sand bottoms may be gouged out and changed in the spring by moving ice and high water or floods. The former salmon resting places or lies may be barren, and new holding spots will be created. So when fishing such waters don't expect to find the salmon in the same spots as last year.

If an Atlantic salmon shows interest in your dry fly but refuses to take it, try changing to a small wet fly and cast it to him.

Some Atlantic salmon rivers are known as "early" rivers, meaning that the fish move up them to spawn in the greatest numbers in the spring or early summer. Other rivers are known as "late" rivers, and here the salmon move up in the fall. So when planning your trip, find out the time of year when salmon will be most plentiful in the river you intend to fish.

While Atlantic salmon are usually hooked on a drifting wet fly with no rod action, there are times when a few short twitches as the fly ends its drift will bring a strike.

Atlantic salmon fishing is usually best in the spring and fall months, when the rivers are high and the water is cool. Not only do the rivers have more salmon at that time, but the fish are also more inclined to hit a fly. When the water gets warm and low during the summer months, they do not take flies too readily.

In hot, sunny summer weather Atlantic salmon fishing is usually poor during the middle of the day. Try to do most of your fishing early in the morning or in the evening.

Unless you know an Atlantic salmon river well and have taken many fish from it, it's a good idea to hire a guide. He will know where the salmon lie, which flies have been taking fish, and how to present them in each spot. This can save you time, especially if you have only a short time to fish.

LANDLOCKED SALMON

If spring is late and the water remains cold, you can often take landlocked salmon in shallow water near shore as late as July on some lakes in Maine and Canada.

Landlocked salmon will often chase smelt to the surface in the spring. By watching for smelt skipping or skittering on top, you can locate salmon and then cast or troll in the area.

If landlocked salmon refuse to hit a plain streamer fly trolled behind the boat, try adding a small 3 in. minnow or smelt to the hook. Hook the baitfish through the lips.

Even when landlocks are chasing bait near the surface, deep trolling is still a good way to catch them, especially the bigger ones. Use sewed smelt or shiners or plugs or spoons.

When trolling for landlocked salmon, try using three streamer flies on the end of your leader. These can be attached on 12 or 14 in. droppers to the main leader. You can use three different patterns of streamers. The whole rig looks like a small school of baitfish swimming by and can attract more salmon than a single fly.

When landlocked salmon are in rivers and rising to dry flies, it is important to drop the fly in the water lightly. Look for a feeding salmon and try to figure out which way it is moving, then cast in front of it.

When using a sewed smelt for landlocked salmon, troll it slowly close to shore or around streams or rivers entering a lake.

A dry fly fished for landlocked salmon in a lake must be given some movement or action to draw strikes. Make it quiver, skip, and skate across the top of the water.

When trolling for landlocked salmon with streamer flies, keep one of these lures in the prop wash near the boat. Many times the land-locks will grab this fly rather than one trolled on a longer line.

Also, when trolling for landlocked salmon with a fly rod and stream-ers, extra action often produces more strikes. You can pull on the line or raise and lower the rod tip.

You'll usually get best results by following a zigzag course when trolling for landlocked salmon. You cover more water and swing the lure closer to shore as well as cause the lure to sink and rise to different depths.

COHO SALMON

To locate coho salmon, find the concentrations of bait. They feed mostly on alewives and smelt and follow these baitfish in the lakes.

Look for coho salmon early in the season, soon after ice-out, in the shallow waters in the southern part of Lake Michigan. They also feed closer to the surface then than later in the year when the water warms up.

Coho usually move quickly through a school of small fish, hitting them on the run. Then they turn and pick off the cripples. So when you get a hit while trolling, it's a good idea to drop back your bait or lure to make it act disabled.

In the late summer and fall coho salmon will be most numerous off the mouths of the rivers where they will spawn. This is when some of the biggest fish are caught.

When coho run up rivers to spawn, they hit smaller and more colorful lures than they do in lakes. Fluorescent orange and red work well. Spoons, spinners, and plugs in these colors can also be used.

If coho are deep, a saltwater-type trolling rod with a 3/0 or 4/0 reel filled with solid Monel wire line is needed. To this you add a trolling weight up to 12 oz. to reach down to depths of anywhere from 50 to 150 ft.

In rivers look for coho salmon in the deeper parts—in holes and channels or under banks, logs, brush, and other obstructions. Work your lure near the bottom for best results.

Many coho are lost when they dive or run at the sight of the boat. So be prepared for this: let the fish run and take line. Better yet, play your fish until it quits; then it can be netted or gaffed more easily.

STEELHEAD

Bring along plenty of rigs, bait, and sinkers or weights when drift fishing along the bottom for steelhead. You'll hang up and lose rigs, but if you don't lose some rigs, you're probably not getting down deep enough or are fishing along smooth bottoms, where steelhead are scarce.

The big winter steelhead rivers are often plagued by muddy water and high water. At such times fish the smaller feeder streams and creeks, which clear faster than the main rivers.

Smaller flies and lures and baits are usually more effective for steelhead when the rivers are low and clear, during the summer and early fall months.

When fishing for steelhead with a rig, using a sinker to keep the bait or lure near the bottom, the weight of the sinker should be changed depending on the depth of water, the strength and speed of the current, the type of lure or bait used, and the diameter of your line. So it's a good idea to carry sinkers weighing from ⅛ to 1 oz. to meet the different conditions encountered.

When the water is low and clear in the rivers during the summer months, wait for a rain or shower that raises the water level or makes it a bit murky. Then you can often catch steelhead throughout the day.

Fish the longer runs, that have fairly deep or moderate currents, when seeking steelhead. If there are eddies or the water slows down in any spot, fish this thoroughly because it is where the steelhead often lie.

When fly fishing for steelhead, match the size of the fly to the weather and water conditions. If the day is cloudy and the water high or murky use a big fly. If the day is sunny and bright and the water clear and low, use smaller flies.

The tail of a pool is a prime spot to fish for steelhead. Here the water gets shallow and speeds up just before it runs into the next riffle or rapids. This slick should be fished along its entire length and width.

It's a good idea to study a steelhead river you plan to fish during the summer months, when the water is low and clear. Then you can pinpoint the ledges, depressions, pockets, boulders, sunken trees or logs, and holes where steelhead like to lie or rest. Later, during the late fall and winter months, when the water is high and discolored, this early reconnaissance will pay off.

During the summer months, when the streams and rivers are low and clear, the best steelhead fishing often occurs at daybreak and dusk.

When a steelhead river gets too high and roily, the fishing usually falls off. Then it pays to wait until the river starts to drop and clear. This is when the best fishing takes place.

Since most steelhead fishing is done in rivers or streams with a fast or moderate current, there's a tendency for a lure or bait to drift just below the surface or not too deep. A good trick here is to give slack line immediately when the lure or bait hits the water after a cast. Then the bait or lure will sink fast and reach a greater depth.

LAKE TROUT

When casting for lake trout, reel your lure in fairly fast for best results. Some rod action also helps to draw more strikes.

Some of the best lake trout fishing takes place in the worst weather. Rough water, snow, rain, cloudy days all seem to produce better than bright, sunny, calm days.

Most lake trout are caught by trolling, casting, or jigging, but lakes with deep canyons between rocky underwater cliffs are good spots to fish with a live 4 or 5 in. minnow. This can be fished with a sinker on the end of the line and a leader with a hook tied above it.

Lake trout are often caught in the early spring in Maine and Canada when fishermen are trolling for landlocked salmon. However, lake trout prefer a somewhat slower-moving lure and one that travels deeper.

When casting for lake trout from shore, use a spoon and let it sink almost to the bottom, then reel it in slowly but with plenty of action.

Anglers fishing for lake trout in Maine have caught most of these fish at depths between 40 and 60 ft. in both summer and winter.

Along their southern range lake trout come into the shallows and can be caught near the surface mostly in the early spring and late fall. But in the far north, in Canada and Alaska, you can often catch them near the surface even during the summer months.

A good lure for lake trout when they are deep is a bucktail jig with a 5 or 6 in. strip of fish belly on the hook. Cast this out and let out line until it reaches bottom. Then work the lure up and down.

Trolling with Monel wire line is a good way to catch lake trout. Attach an 80 to 100 ft. leader of 15 or 20 lb.-test monofilament line to the end of the wire. Then the lure. As you troll, the belly of the wire line will occasionally hit a rock or ridge, so you will know you are down deep enough. But the lure will ride higher than this belly and will clear the obstacles.

SHAD

Shad will often hit a bare gold or silver hook or a similar hook attached to a brass, nickel-plated, or chromed barrel swivel when used with a fly rod.

Shad can be caught on darts or jigs by fishing them from an anchored boat and letting the lure sink to the bottom. Then reel in a few feet so that the lure is suspended just above the bottom. If the water is rough, the rise and fall of the boat and rod will provide action to the jig. But if it is calm, you can raise and lower the rod at regular intervals.

Shad seem to be partial to lures with white, yellow, or red colors. So use shad darts or jigs in these colors. In metal lures such as spoons and spinners, silver and gold are best.

If you fish from shore in rocky rivers, you'll lose a lot of lures, so bring along plenty of shad darts or other lures you plan to use. Also bring along some extra spools of line in case you lose too much line when breaking off.

CATFISH

A sliding bobber or float that can be adjusted to let the bait drift at different depths is a good rig to use for channel catfish. Most of the time they will be on the bottom, but other times the catfish will take a bait drifted higher up.

Some of the best spots for channel catfish in a stream or river are holes where trees, logs, and brush are sunk in the deeper water. These catfish also lurk under banks or shores that have been washed out by the current.

Catfish will sometimes hit a jig with a plastic worm or pork rind on the hook. This has to be worked deep and slow along the bottom to be effective. A good spot for such fishing is below a dam in a river.

The best time to fish for bullheads is from dusk until around midnight. They usually bite best in the late spring months, until the fall.

Fishing is often better for catfish when the river is down or low. This makes the catfish congregate in the deeper holes and channels, where they are easier to locate and catch.

Channel catfish will more readily hit a moving bait than one that is lying still. They like faster currents than other catfish and are attracted by a moving bait.

When fishing for big catfish in deep, strong currents and big rivers, where heavy sinkers are needed to hold bottom, try using a pyramid sinker, which is popular in saltwater surf fishing. They hold better than other types, such as the round or dipsey weights used in fresh water.

In rivers and canals look for bullheads behind points of land, on sandbars, or where creeks enter the main body of water. Here there are usually mud deposits where bullheads congregate.

Channel catfish often show a preference for or feed on a single kind of food to the exclusion of others. Thus when they are feeding on insects, that is about the only food you'll find in their stomachs. Naturally at such times it's a good idea to give them what they want.

Catfish are often slow about taking a bait, so don't try to set the hook at the first signs of a bite. Wait until the line moves out a few feet before coming back with the rod. If you fail to hook the fish, let the bait lie on the bottom to see whether the fish will return. If he doesn't, reel in and put on a fresh bait and cast back to the same spot. The catfish will often return, and then you have a good chance of hooking him if you let him swallow the bait.

In a shallow stream or river a good way to fish for channel catfish is to wade out and let your bait drift downstream in the current. Then you are more able to work the bait toward the hiding places of the catfish and can slow down the drift by snubbing the reel with your thumb.

Channel catfish will often strike lures such as plugs, spoons, spinners, and jigs. These usually work best if reeled slowly near the bottom in the evening or at night.

A top bait for catfish is a soft-shell crayfish. If you can't get soft ones, you can use a hard-shell crayfish, but a good trick then is to crack the shell a bit to make it more attractive to the catfish.

Although catfish bite best at night, you can often have good fishing in the daytime if you choose dark, cloudy, rainy days instead of bright, sunny ones.

A good time of the year to fish for bullheads is in the spring soon after the ice disappears on a river or lake and the water warms up a bit. They are hungry then and come into shallow, quiet waters to look for food.

When fishing for catfish in the daytime or when the water is low and clear, look for them beneath rocks and ledges, in crevices and caves, around stumps, logs, brush piles, and sunken or fallen trees, under tree roots, and in the deeper holes, channels, eddies, and pools.

CARP

A spinning rod is ideal for carp fishing because you can often cast doughball baits without adding any sinkers or weights when fishing in lakes or quiet sections of a river.

If you want to use a float for carp, choose one of the long, narrow types such as the porcupine quill. This float is so light that a carp feels no resistance or weight when it takes a bait.

In a river carp can often be located by looking for mud patches or streaks made by these fish while rooting along the bottom. Then you can cast your bait just upstream of the muddy water.

A handy and simple bait for carp is a loaf of fresh white bread. Simply add a little water or milk to the bread and knead it into doughballs.

Carp will sometimes rise to the surface and take a fly or bass bug. The best lures are those that are tied with deer hair and are on the bulky side to imitate big beetles, grubs, or cicadas, on which the carp feed. And wait until you see a carp near the surface before casting the lure well in front of him, letting it lie still without any rod action.

VARIOUS FISHES

You can often attract whitefish to a spot in a lake by baiting the area with boiled rice, canned corn, cooked spaghetti, or other cereals for a day or two before you fish there.

Whitefish will take a dry fly when they are feeding on top on drowned flies floating on the surface.

You can sometimes catch sturgeon in freshwater rivers by using nightcrawlers or cut fish for bait. It is important to use a sinker that holds the bait on the bottom at all times.

When fishing for suckers, let the bait lie still on the bottom but don't try to set the hook on the first light nibbles. Wait until the rod dips or the line moves out before setting the hook.

Mullet bite best on a hook or tiny fly when they are in fresh or brackish water. Then they will often take worms, small doughballs, grubs, mealworms, or whole kernels of corn.

CHAPTER 10

Other Freshwater Tips

Submerged weed beds attract fish of all kinds, and if you can locate several of these and are able to find them again, you have the best insurance against getting skunked. All you have to do is fish each one until you find one that produces.

Pools below dams and high waterfalls in rivers and streams usually harbor big fish of many kinds because species that migrate upstream to spawn can't pass above the obstructions and congregate in the pools below them.

When fishing with jigs, you can often tell when your lure hits bottom by watching your line. It will be taut and straight while the lure is sinking; when the jig hits bottom, it will sag and go slack.

One of the most effective ways to fish live baits such as worms, crayfish, frogs, or minnows is from a boat drifting slowly in a lake. The bait should move close to the bottom. If the boat drifts a little too fast, try adding a weight to the leader. You can also use a small sea anchor to slow up the drift of the boat.

When trolling with streamers in a stream or river, the best procedure is to troll slowly against the current. This gives the streamers the best action.

If you want to work your lure right up to shore or a boat, lower your rod tip into the water and keep on reeling until most of the line has been retrieved.

When fishing strange waters, it pays to hire a guide or to fish with a local angler who knows the best spots. That way you save a lot of time running around trying to locate the fish. If you are down only for a day or two, you haven't got much time to do this.

Carry a spool of red or orange fluorescent yarn with you when you go fishing. If action is slow, try wrapping some of the yarn around the leader next to the lure or bait. This increases visibility in dark or murky waters and also adds a new color to a bait or lure.

In a large lake look for the shallower reefs when seeking smallmouth bass or walleyes. You can troll around such reefs with deep-running lures, or after you catch a fish or two by trolling, you can anchor or drift over the spot and cast.

When fishing freshwater canals, for best results cast your lures or baits along shorelines with weeds and around the gates or locks, diversions, inlets, and outlets.

An effective way to fish for salmon or steelhead in a river is to wade out into the water directly above the spot you want to fish. Then drift your lure or bait into the spots where fish are lying. You can even let the lure hang in one spot for long periods, letting the current give it action.

Some of the tiny plugs made of balsa wood or plastic can be cast or let out in the current with a fly rod and used to catch big trout, bass, and panfish.

When fishing with lures from a drifting boat, cast them in the direction in which the boat is moving. This way you don't frighten or disturb fish so readily.

Anglers tend to get into a rut when it comes to working their lures and use the same retrieves day in and day out. Every so often it pays to change your style and reel underwater lures as fast as you can turn the reel handle. Or work a popper fast and loud. Or if you normally tend to work your lures fast, see how slow and how long you can retrieve them for a change of pace.

If there have been heavy rains or floods during the winter months or early spring, your favorite trout stream may have changed radically. Then you have to study the stream and bottom to discover the new resting and feeding locations of the trout.

Probably the most important single factor that makes one angler more successful than most of the others is his perseverance and determination. When the average angler quits and goes home, the successful angler is still at it. He puts in more hours and days, casting, trolling, or still-fishing, so he naturally learns more about the waters and the fish and is present when the fish start feeding.

Droughts in south Florida often create good fishing for bass, bream, or bluegills, crappies, and catfish. As the water level drops in the shallows and saw grass area, the fish are forced into the deeper holes and canals, where there is less food and more competition for the available food. This makes the fish hungry and easier to catch.

When fishing in clear lakes and rivers with calm water, it is best to remain seated while casting or even still-fishing. You'll frighten fewer fish and get more strikes or bites if you don't stand up in a boat. It is also safer.

If you want to troll faster, move the boat with the wind, but if you want to troll slowly, run the boat into the wind.

A good bait for catfish is a toad hooked through the lips. You can find sand toads along sandy beaches and among rocks on the shores of a river or lake. Toads also come out at night, especially after a shower, and can be spotted with a flashlight or the headlights of a car. Use the small toads for small catfish and the big ones for larger catfish.

When streams or rivers that empty into the saltwater bays or ocean get low during the summer months or dry up during droughts, do your fishing downstream in brackish waters. Here tides replenish the water, and fish from upstream often move down to these cooler and deeper waters.

While fishing a jig in fresh water along the bottom, it is often difficult to detect a bite. On the slightest twitch, tug, stop, or movement of
the line, you should set the hook. This way, even though there will be
false alarms, you won't miss the real strikes.

When trolling for landlocked salmon or trout, work the rocky points,
submerged bars, and mouths of streams and rivers entering the lake.

If the weather has been warm and calm with little or no wind, wait
for a day when the wind picks up and blows for several hours. This
usually stirs up some of the colder water, and the wave action adds
more oxygen to the surface waters. Then fish that have been sulking
below in deep water will often rise and start feeding.

Once Pacific salmon move into freshwater rivers, they don't feed
much but can still be caught on such lures as spoons, spinners, and
plugs. Fly rod anglers can use big, flashy, silver-bodied streamers tied
with yellow, orange, or red feathers.

On big rivers a boat is handy even when fishing with flies for trout—
not so much for fishing from the boat itself but to reach islands, sandbars, and shores that cannot be reached on foot or by wading.

Usually a streamer or bucktail is retrieved deep or just below the
surface. But there are times when retrieving the fly on top of the water
is best. Here you strip in the fly with the rod held high so that the
streamer leaves a ripple or wake on top like a minnow trying to escape
a larger fish.

When fishing small, narrow streams with dry flies, use shorter fly
leaders. Short casts of no more than 15 or 20 ft. are needed on such
waters, and a long leader is harder to handle and cast than a shorter one.

Fly fishing on lakes will be most productive in shallow water near shore, over and along the edges of weeds, off points, islands, coves, rock and sandbars, and in brooks and streams entering the lake. This is where the insects are most plentiful and where the fish feed on them.

For fishing streamers and wet flies deep in a fast current, try weighting the flies by wrapping lead wire around the hook shank. This can be done to a finished fly, but is best if you wrap the lead around the hook before tying the fly.

Long casts seldom catch as many fish as shorter ones in freshwater fishing. Working lures is more difficult on a longer line, and so is setting the hook. Nowadays, with limber spinning rods and monofilament lines, you'll hook more fish on a short cast than on a long one.

When using surface lures or bass bugs on top, you should always keep your eye on the plug or bug. If a fish hits, you can then set the hook in time. If you are distracted or depend on "feel" to set the hook, it will usually be too late.

When waters become muddy from rain or showers, fish in shallow water close to shore around stumps and rocks. The water is usually less muddy in such areas. Also look for spots where the muddy water is just starting to clear.

Most gamefish are quickly attracted to any unusual movement or vibration that indicates a weak or crippled creature. Thus it is up to the angler to work his lure so that it acts weak or crippled and looks like easy pickings. Usually a slow, erratic, hesitant retrieve achieves this result best.

On days when the wind is strong, choose a lake with plenty of islands scattered throughout its length. Then fish the lee sides of these islands, where you are protected from the wind and the water is calm.

You can't cast a dry fly on a tiny, narrow meadow brook, but if you use a long fly rod, you can dap a fly on the surface. Crouch low or hide behind a bush when you do this.

One good way to cover a long riffle for big trout is by using a streamer or bucktail with a sinking fly line. Start at the head or upper part of the run, cast across stream and let the fly sink and swing downstream. Then retrieve it in an erratic manner with frequent pauses. After each cast move downstream a few feet and repeat.

Most fish go on a feeding spree at least once during a given day. That is why the most successful anglers are usually those who spend the entire day from dawn to dusk on the water, waiting to catch this feeding period.

When fishing in thick cover such as lily pads and hyacinths, one good trick is to run your outboard boat through the weeds for a good distance, then wait and fish your way back along the same route. Bass that were attracted to the scene by the commotion and dislodging of water insects, frogs, and minnows that were hiding in the vegetation will be waiting there or looking for more food.

If you are casting toward shore and get hung up and have to go in with a boat to free your lure, forget about fishing that spot for a while. Move on to another spot and wait about a half hour before you return to fish the spot that was disturbed.

Many big fish, especially bass, pike, and muskies, are lost when you fail to set the hook past the barb. This is usually true when using a limber spinning rod with a surface lure. If you are going after these big fish, get a stiffer spinning rod and stronger line. Or change to a bait-casting outfit with a heavier line so you can drive the hook in.

When drifting in a big trout river in a boat, one good way to use a dry fly is to cast it out to one side and let it move downstream at the same speed as the boat.

When the water is discolored, a good general rule is to use larger, noisier lures to enable the fish to locate the lure. But when the water is low and clear, use smaller, quieter lures and light leaders in order not to frighten the fish.

The position of your rod tip will depend on where you are fishing and the lure you are using. When retrieving surface lures or fishing in weeds or lily pads, hold your rod tip high. When using underwater plugs or a diving plug, hold your rod tip low, almost touching the water. And if you are really going deep with bottom bouncing or deep-running lures, you can even submerge your rod in the water to keep it working at the right depth.

Long casts are sometimes needed on a big, wide trout stream and waters you can't wade. Here it's best to use a powerful fly rod, a spinning outfit with a plastic bubble and fly, or lures.

When the sun is bright, fish the shady side of a lake; then as the sun sets, fish the other side.

One reason why many anglers fail to catch big trout is that they waste a lot of time fishing for the smaller ones. If you want big trout, ignore the smaller fish and cast only where big fish hang out.

When fishing a good spot on a trout stream at night for big trout, don't flash a light on the water or along shore. Instead walk up on shore and turn away from the water, pointing the light toward land. After you are through, put out the light and return to the water's edge.

A highly effective plug for casting upstream into the current of a stream or river is one of the light, floating balsa or plastic models. They can be twitched or activated during the entire retrieve without reeling too fast, as must be done to bring out the action with heavier plugs or other lures.

CHAPTER 11

Saltwater Fishing Tackle

RODS

There is no such thing as a single "all-round" saltwater fishing rod suitable for all kinds of fishing. You need at least two or three rods to be fully equipped for surf fishing. Offshore anglers usually have three or four outfits. Even bottom fishermen are better off with three different outfits. Of course, if you fish for just one kind of fish in one location all the time you may get away with one outfit. But if you plan to fish for several species of various sizes in different locations, you'll need more than one rod to meet the changing conditions.

A bait-casting or "popping" type of rod and a level-wind bait-casting reel with a free spool and drag make a versatile light tackle outfit for many kinds of saltwater fishing. It is especially well suited for accurate casting toward shore under mangroves for snook and tarpon.

To cast a live sardine or anchovy any distance, you have to use the special "live bait" rod, which is longer and has a thin, flexible tip section. Light lines also help to get the baitfish out farther, where the yellowtail, albacore, and tuna may be feeding.

When fishing under bridges for big striped bass, snook, or tarpon, use a fairly heavy rod such as a conventional-type surf rod 8 or 9 ft. long, but with a shorter butt, and a conventional surf reel filled with 30 or 40 lb.-test line.

When choosing a surf rod, you have to decide whether you will be casting mostly lures or heavy sinker and bait. For casting and working lures, a somewhat lighter, shorter, and more limber rod from 9 to 10 ft. long is best. It is less tiring to use, casts lighter lures more successfully, and gives your lures better action. The heavier, longer surf rods up to 12 or 14 ft. long are better if you cast heavy baits and sinkers. They can be used for lures such as metal squids, which don't have to be worked with the rod tip.

Spinning rods can be used with conventional revolving spool reels by just turning them around so that the guides are on top. Conventional reels are better for bottom fishing and drifting baits out in a current and can be used with heavier lines; the more limber tip on a spinning rod is better for casting light, live baits and for fighting certain kinds of fish.

If you do a lot of night fishing with lures and cast a lot, it's a good idea to paint a couple of inches of your rod tip with luminous paint or wrap it with luminous tape. Then you can see the end of your rod at all times.

Surf rods to be used for top-water plugs such as poppers should be somewhat stiffer and have more backbone than those used for underwater lures or with bait. A stiffer rod will enable you to "work" the popping plugs more effectively. The rod itself can still be light, but its action should be on the stiff side.

If you want to catch grouper or red snappers in deep water using heavy sinkers, choose a strong rod with a 4/0 or 6/0 reel filled with 80 or 100 lb.-test monofilament line.

REELS

If you do a lot of surf fishing at night and use a conventional revolving spool reel, choose one that has a somewhat narrower spool than most squidding reels. You'll find that it will be easier to spool your line more evenly on the reel, and you will cast better and get fewer backlashes.

The best reel for deep-water jigging with diamond jigs or other metal lures is a conventional reel with 4 to 1 gear ratio, which enables you to reel in the lure fast to give it action.

The spinning reels with a Teflon drag are best when fishing for fast saltwater fish that make long runs. It is smoother and more dependable than the drag disks used on earlier models.

LINES

Nylon monofilament line will lose some of its strength if exposed to the ultraviolet rays of the sun for any length of time. Thus it's a good idea to reverse your line or put on a new one often when you fish a lot in bright, sunny weather or in the tropics, where the sun is strong.

If you are interested in entering fishing tournaments or trying for a a record catch that will be recognized by the International Game Fish Association, make certain that the fishing line you will be using doesn't exceed the limit set for the various classes. Most American-made lines are OK in this respect, but some imported lines may test from 2 to 4 lb. more than the number on the label.

Most monofilament lines take a "set" or "curl" when left on a spool or reel for long periods. It's always a good idea to let out a couple of hundred feet of line, tie the end to a solid support, and stretch it before fishing or casting.

LEADERS

Although wire leaders are often needed to hold sharp-toothed fish and "shock" leaders are great lure and fish savers, they should be used only as a last resort when fishing with light tackle for wary species. You'll get more strikes, especially in clear water, if you tie your lure directly to your monofilament line. And if you are using a heavy line, you can attach a lighter mono leader to fool fish that shy away from the heavy line or leaders.

When choosing leaders for saltwater fishing, pick the lightest leader that is practical for the fishing to be done. A heavy leader is not only more visible but can kill the action of a lure or bait.

Shiny wire leaders can be a problem for many kinds of fishing. You can paint or spray them with a quick-drying paint in a dull, dark color. Or you can buy the "coffee"-colored wire leaders, which are less visible than the silver ones.

If a single-strand stainless steel leader kinks badly, get rid of it and use a new one. Such a leader is undependable and can break at the kink under a strain or yank.

If you are bothered by sharks taking a bait meant for other fish and don't want to waste time fighting them, use monofilament leaders instead of wire. Then when a shark swallows the bait he will usually bite through the mono leader, and you can resume fishing for more desirable species.

How long a leader do you need for saltwater fishing? It depends on your tackle, the method of fishing, and the fish sought. Surf anglers often use short wire leaders permanently attached to their lures, and these are only from 8 to 12 in. long. But this short leader may be attached to a longer shock leader, up to 15 or 20 ft. long, made up of monofilament. Wire leaders used when trolling for small fish can be only 3 or 4 ft. long. Offshore you can use leaders from 5 to 10 ft. for small and medium-size fish and from 10 to 15 ft. for bigger fish. In some kinds of fishing, such as trolling with wire lines, you may need a monofilament leader up to 30 ft. long on the end of the wire line.

Monofilament leaders are becoming more popular for offshore or big-game fishing. You can use leaders testing 100 or 150 lb. for the smaller billfish such as sailfish, white marlin, striped marlin, and school tuna. Heavier 200 to 300 lb.-test mono leaders can be used for small blue marlin and swordfish. For still bigger fish cable wire leaders are safer.

Hooks

Always discard old, rusty, or doubtful hooks. Or remove them from lures and add new ones. You can lose a big fish on a weak, rusty hook.

Even brand-new hooks from a box or on new lures often require some sharpening. The point may be dull or covered with plating. A minute or two spent with a sharpening stone or file can really improve the point of such a hook.

Other Tackle

STRIPES

It's a good idea to paint your gaff white and add fluorescent tape around the handle. This is especially valuable if you do a lot of night fishing since it enables you to locate your gaff in the dark. If you have stripes on the handle, you know which end to grab.

When fishing for school fish which do not hang around too long, it pays to have two or three outfits rigged up and all ready to go. Then when the fish appear and you hook one and happen to break off, you can grab another outfit and immediately get into action again rather than waste time tying on a new hook or lure.

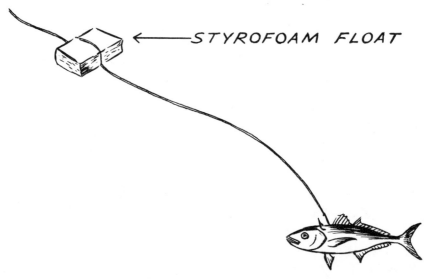

←————— *STYROFOAM FLOAT*

Chunks of styrofoam make good floats for bait fishing. Cut them into squares—small ones for inshore and light tackle fishing, larger ones for heavier tackle and offshore fishing. If you score or cut two sides of the foam slightly, you can tie it better to the leader.

If you have a choice, always use dull, black snaps, swivels, and other hardware on your terminal rigs. Bright, shiny snaps and swivels are more visible and are also hit by bluefish, Spanish mackerel, and king mackerel, which can cut the line or leader with their sharp teeth.

When bottom fishing, paint your sinkers white, yellow, silver, or red. Then as you lift and drop the rig, the bright colors will attract fish to the scene.

CHAPTER 12

Saltwater Lures

PLUGS

When working a surface plug such as a popper or swimmer for striped bass or bluefish in calm, clear water, reel it fast and pop it often. This causes a lot of commotion, which attracts the fish and also confuses them. They don't have much time to examine the lure too long or too closely.

But when using a swimming plug on top for striped bass at night, slow down your reeling. Make it swim slowly, leaving a wake or ripple, and even stop reeling a second or two every so often. You can pop or jerk the plug at night also, but do it more gently and less often than in the daytime. Here you want to attract the fish to your lure, but you also want to give him a chance to see it and grab it.

The mirror-type plugs, which are silvery and shaped like a deep minnow or baitfish, have no built-in action and must be activated by the angler. To make them effective, you have to work your rod so that they rise and sink and dart from side to side. Worked right, they will catch striped bass, bluefish snook, tarpon, sea trout, and many other saltwater species.

Other deadly plugs for saltwater fishing are the balsa wood and plastic models, which are long and slim and have a snappy wriggle underwater. They look like live baitfish. They now come in many sizes and can be cast or trolled for most saltwater gamefish.

Metal Lures

Metal lures such as metal squid, heavy spoons, and diamond jigs can be used in the Pacific Ocean to take such species as yellowtail, albacore, bonito, white sea bass, barracuda, rockfish, and lingcod. When gamefish are on top, cast these lures out and reel them back fast. When they are down deep, cast the lure out and let it go down to the bottom, then jig it up and down.

When after cod or pollock, bring along some 6 to 14 oz. diamond jigs. Use the lighter ones in shallow water and weak tides and the heavier ones in deeper water and strong currents.

If you are using spoons in clear, shallow water, use the gold finish. Silver finishes are usually too bright. However, on overcast days, in murky waters, and when fishing at daybreak and dusk, use the more visible silver spoons.

When using a diamond jig in a riptide or strong current, cast it about 20 or 25 ft. upcurrent or ahead of the boat and when it hits bottom, start jigging it.

Jigs

The size and weight of the jig you use will depend on the fishing tackle used, the depth of the water, the tide, and the method of fishing. When using light tackle and fishing shallow water and flats, the ¼ or ½ oz. bucktail or feather jigs are best. On rivers, canals, bays, and inlets and for surface-feeding fish inshore and offshore, a ¾ or 1 oz. jig is good. When trolling offshore for larger fish or jigging in deep water and strong currents, jigs from 1 to 3 oz. may be needed.

A jig should be used with either a snap swivel or a loop knot, both of which give the lure more action than a leader tied with a tight jam or clinch knot against the eye. A snap swivel will serve if you are fishing in rough surf, in murky or roiled water, or at night. But when fishing in clear water or for wary fish, tie the jig directly to the mono with a loop.

When it comes to choosing jigs for saltwater, you can't go wrong by picking those that are mostly white or yellow. These two colors will catch most saltwater species in most waters.

Although jigs are usually fished with some rod action, you can also drift a jig completely "dead" in a current. Here you cast across or upcurrent and let the tide swing the jig in an arc. It works best in inlets, rivers, and canals where there is a strong tide.

Heavy jigs up to 2 or 3 oz. can be used for deep jigging in water up to 150 ft. deep. Lines testing 15 or 20 lb. work best on spinning, heavy bait casting, or conventional saltwater rods. You can catch barracuda, amberjack, king mackerel, bonito, false albacore, grouper, snapper, and many other species in southern waters with the deep jigging.

PLASTIC LURES

One of the top lures for striped bass, snook, tarpon, bluefish, cobia, and other saltwater fish is a plastic eel with an action head up front such as a small metal squid or a heavy spoon. A slow or moderate retrieve is best—try to "feel" your lure working at all times. The plastic eel can be cast or trolled in the daytime, but is particularly effective at night.

Another good way to use a plastic eel is to raise and lower your rod at regular intervals as you reel in to make the eel rise and then dive. You can also slow it down or speed it up every so often.

The plastic tube lures often called "Norwegian" or "Norway" eels, up to 5 or 6 in. long, are killers for striped bass, bluefish, pollock, and even cod when trolled deep on wire lines near the bottom. They come in various colors with white, yellow, pink, orange, and red the most popular.

Such billfish as sailfish and marlin will often hit and mouth soft plastic lures again and again because they feel natural to them, unlike the harder lures made of wood, metal, or rigid plastic.

A short tail of plastic on a jig head makes a deadly lure for many saltwater species. It can be used in many of the same ways as a bucktail or feather jig and is especially productive when used around bridges or bounced along the bottom. The tails are now sold in various sizes and colors.

COMBINATION LURES

Remove the hook from a diamond jig and attach a nylon leader about 2 ft. long. On the end of the leader you can tie either a feather teaser or a light jig. The diamond jig provides casting weight and an added attraction with its bright flash.

You can make up a trolling rig using two or three Japanese feathers by attaching a hook on a wire leader and sliding one feather lure down to it. Then, a few inches above this end lure, attach a barrel swivel to the wire and another wire leader above it. Now slip on another feather lure to rest against this swivel. Then repeat the process by adding another lure, and you're all set.

Saltwater Flies

When snook or small tarpon are feeding on tiny fry in canals, a small fly is usually more effective than a big one.

Carry an assortment of streamer and bucktail flies in different colors and sizes when fishing with a fly rod for striped bass or other saltwater fish. You can never tell what kind of bait will show up, and you can match the food the fish are feeding on best if you have a varied selection of flies.

Saltwater flies with marabou wings are good for bonefish and permit on the flats. These should be tied in white, yellow, and brown colors.

Other Lures

When choosing lures for saltwater fishing you can't go wrong by sticking with those that are predominantly silver, white, or yellow. Most saltwater baitfish and small fish have silvery sides and white or light yellow bellies. A touch of blue, green, or brown on the back or top of such lures will add a more realistic touch.

Tie some white or yellow feathers around a 5/0 or 6/0 hook and keep them in your tackle box. You can tie one or two of these on short droppers above a sinker or diamond jig and use them for jigging. Add an egg sinker on the leader ahead of the feather hook, and you have an excellent trolling or casting lure. Add two or three sea worms to the hook, and you have an excellent striped bass trolling lure for shallow waters and rocky areas in bays, inlets, and rivers.

Leaping fish get rid of heavy lures much more easily than light ones. Hook a tarpon or billfish on a plug, spoon, or other heavy lure, and the fish usually throws it. Hook the same fish on a plain hook or a light lure such as a fly, and your chances of boating the fish is much better.

One way to get your lure down to the bottom in a fast-running canal or river is to cast out into midstream and then walk slowly along the bank, reeling in slack but keeping the lure deep as it drifts downstream. The best lures for this are jigs, heavy spoons, weighted eelskins, and sinking plugs.

A novel snook lure can be made by cutting a thin cardboard as shown above. It should be about 3 in. long and taper on both ends. Then attach it to the hook of a jig and fish it so that it skims along the surface around piers, docks, and bulkheads at night.

Two easily made pork-rind lures are shown here. The top one is made with a single large hook to which a tail-hook pork rind is added. The lower one has two large hooks, one slipped on the other. Then you add a long pork-rind strip over both hooks. Use the top lure for striped bass, weakfish, and fluke or summer flounder. The bottom one is good for bluefish, school tuna, albacore, bonito, and stripers.

Always test your lure alongside the boat just below the surface to see whether it is working properly and has good action at the speed the boat is moving. You may have to slow down the boat or speed it up or adjust the lure before letting it out on a long line.

To make a cheap, quick lure use a clincher or clamp-on sinker and wrap it around a hook shank. Then tie a few feathers or bucktail hairs at the tail of the lure. You can paint or spray the sinker body white, yellow, silver, or any other color. This lure can be used for casting or trolling with different-size hooks and different-weight sinkers.

If you use a lot of lures in saltwater, often it's a good idea to have a pail or bucket filled with fresh water on board a boat or on shore. Then when you remove a lure from the line, you can rinse it in the fresh water before you hang it up to dry. The hooks and other metal parts won't rust or corrode as badly as when you let the salt water dry on the lure.

CHAPTER 13

Saltwater Rigs

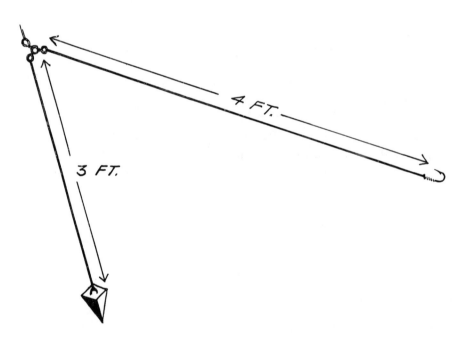

The snook rig shown above can be used from piers, bridges, and boats. A pyramid sinker weighing from 1 to 4 oz. is used, depending on the strength of the tide. A 4 ft. leader holds the hook while a 3 ft. dropper holds the sinker. You can bait the hook with a live pilchard or mullet, a pinfish or shrimp.

This rig is used for trolling for striped bass in the Chesapeake Bay area, where there are rocks, stone piles, or other obstructions. It has a long 10 to 20 ft., 30 lb.-test monofilament leader to which the lure is attached. A shorter 2 ft., 10 lb.-test dropper holds a sinker, which may be from 4 to 20 oz. depending on the current. This light line will break if the sinker snags, saving the rest of the rig. A small spoon is attached to the long leader.

This rig is used when fishing for bonito in California waters. Use a fluorescent orange or red plastic float and 3 ft. below a 20 lb.-test mono leader attach a jig. The rig is reeled in fast so that the float splashes on top.

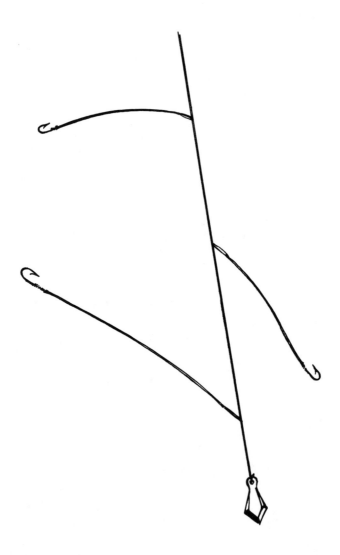

To fish for whiting and cod at the same time, the rig pictured above is the one to use. The two upper hooks can be short 10 or 12 in. leaders with 4/0 or 5/0 hooks tied to the ends. The lower hook is on a longer 18 or 20 in. leader and larger 6/0 or 7/0 hook. The upper hooks can be baited with spearing, squid, or fish strips. The lower one can be baited with a whole skimmer clam for cod.

The rig shown here can be used in California while drifting for striped bass with live shiners or anchovies. The hook on the long 4 to 9 ft. leader is tied to one eye of the 3-way swivel while a dropper of from 8 to 12 in. can be tied to the other eye to hold the weight. This will vary from a few ounces to a couple of pounds depending on where you are fishing.

The rig shown above permits you to cast a bait with a bobber or float to keep the bait drifting with the tide. A sinker is clamped about 2 ft. above the hook, and the float is added on the line above the weight. Then wrap some thread or plastic tape around the line about 6 ft. above the sinker. This acts as a stop just like the sinker. The float drops down to the sinker when you cast, but in the water the sinker will pull the line through the float until it stops at the thread or tape.

BARREL SWIVEL

EGG SINKER

The drift rig presents two baited hooks at different levels—one on the bottom and the other about 18 in. above it. To tie it, attach your fishing line to one eye of a 3-way swivel. A short leader and hook is tied to the second eye and a length of leader material to the remaining eye. Then slip an egg sinker on this leader and tie it to a barrel swivel. Now you tie the second hook to the barrel swivel to complete the rig. Although primarily designed for croakers, this rig can also be used when drifting and fishing for fluke or summer flounders, sea bass, porgies, snappers, and other bottom species.

When trolling a surgical-tube lure for striped bass or bluefish near the bottom, it's a good idea to add a weighted keel even if you are using a wire line. Tube lures turn and can twist a line. Also, the keel enables you to bounce bottom and know you are down deep enough.

A good combination rig when fishing North Atlantic waters in the winter months is illustrated here. The top hook on a long 2 ft. leader holds a 5/0 or 6/0 hook baited with clam for cod, while the lower hook in size 1/0 or 2/0 can be baited with a green crab or fiddler crab for blackfish or tautog.

Another good combination rig offers a fluke or summer flounder three baits to choose from. Use a 3 ft. leader and tie one hook on the end and two hooks on short droppers into the leader. You can put a live killy on the end hook, a strip of squid on another hook, and a strip cut from the belly of a fluke or sea robin on the remaining hook.

The rig illustrated here is popular for fishing king mackerel from a pier. You use a large plastic float about 5 or 6 ft. above the hooks. A big hook about 6/0 or 7/0 in size is attached to the wire leader, and a few inches below it you attach a treble hook. A live bluefish or other baitfish is hooked with the big hook through the back.

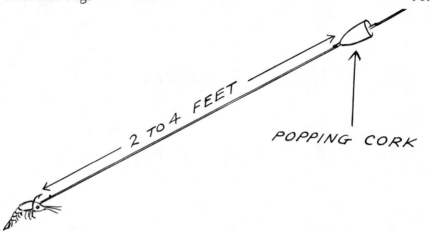

An effective rig to use for sea trout is made by adding a popping cork to your line and then attaching a small hook about 2 or 3 ft. below it. You can bait this hook with a live shrimp. When using this rig, pop or jerk it every so often so that the cork throws a splash. This draws the sea trout to the scene, and they then see the shrimp and grab it.

The sliding sinker rig is popular in southern waters for use from drift boats, party boats, piers, bridges, and small boats when bottom fishing for various species. To make it, slip an egg sinker on the line, tie a barrel swivel, and then tie your hook to this swivel on any length leader you desire. This is a good rig to use for slow biters or fish that shy away from heavy weights. It lets a fish take line through the hole in the sinker without feeling the weight.

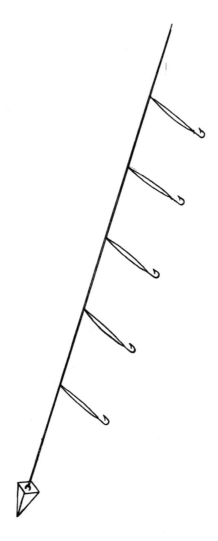

This pompano rig is used when fishing in the surf or from piers for these fish. It consists of a long 30 or 40 lb. leader with anywhere from three to six gold-plated No. 1/0 hooks on short droppers spaced equal distances apart. On the end you attach a pyramid sinker from 3 to 5 oz. in weight depending on the surf and tide. The hooks are baited with sand fleas, bugs, or pieces of shrimp.

Another striper rig is this one, which is popular when trolling for Pacific bass. The wire spreader has a longer leader on top to hold a plug, while the shorter lower leader holds a jig.

This rig is used along the Pacific coast when fishing in the surf for surf perch. It has the lower hook on an 18 in. leader tied about a foot above the sinker and the second one of the same length tied about 18 in. above the first hook. For sandy beaches and rough surf, the sinker can be a pyramid type or a bank or round type in rocky areas or when you want the bait to roll around in the wash. Clams, mussels, or pileworms can be used as bait.

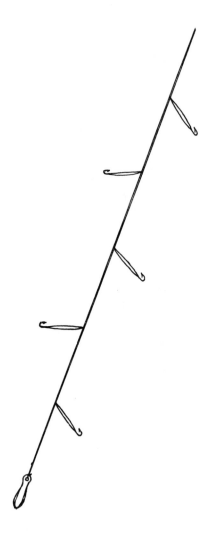

Use this rig to catch small fish for bait. Just tie a series of short loops on the light monofilament leader or line and add tiny No. 8, 10, or 12 gold-plated or silver hooks to each loop. Then attach a ½ oz. sinker to the end. This rig can be jigged up and down from a pier, bridge, or small boat, and baitfish will often bite the bare hooks. You can also add tiny bits of clam, shrimp, worm, or other bait to each hook.

The "umbrella" rig, which was developed at Montauk, N.Y., is a multilure device making use of a spreader that holds several small plastic tube lures and is trolled deep on wire line. The idea is to imitate a small school of baitfish. It works best on bluefish, often hooking more than one fish at a time. It also catches striped bass, pollock, and a few other species.

CHAPTER 14

Saltwater Natural Baits

BAITFISH

The mossbunker or menhaden is often used as chum, but it also makes an excellent bait. It can be used in chunks or strips for striped bass, bluefish, channel bass, and other fish. Whole bunker can be used for big striped bass, tuna, and sharks.

Soft baitfish such as sardines, bunker, shad, and herring often fall off the hook or are easily stolen by the fish or crabs. You can avoid this by wrapping these baits around the hook with maline or fine netting.

EGG SINKER

You can add an egg sinker to a mullet to use in rough seas and to help keep it from flying out of the water too often. Just slit the belly

370

of the mullet and push the eye of your hook into the hole and into the bait's mouth, then slip an egg sinker on a wire leader and run it through the lower jaw and out at the top of the head. Form a loop and close it with the regular wire leader wrap.

The small fish called the spot can be used live to catch king mackerel, tarpon, and cobia or used dead and cut into two or three sections to catch channel bass.

Deep trolling with weights or wire line over reefs will take grouper, using a barracuda or king mackerel weighing a few pounds for bait. Rig such baits with two or three hooks.

Dead baitfish, whether cast or trolled, are most effective when they look natural. To add weight without changing the appearance of the baitfish, use the two methods shown. In the top drawing a clincher sinker is wrapped around the shank of the hook and then inserted into the mouth of the baitfish and out of the belly. To keep the hook in place, sew the eye into the closed jaws of the bait. The lower drawing shows a quick way to add weight to a large baitfish. Here cut a small slit near the anal fin and insert a diamond jig and wire leader into the baitfish's belly. Pull the leader out through the mouth and sew it into the jaws of the baitfish. The size and weight of the diamond jig will depend on the size of the baitfish used. Here, too, you can sew up the slit and the mouth.

Alewives or herring can be used for striped bass, and you'll hook more fish if you use a 3/0 or 4/0 treble hook to hold the herring. Hook it in the mouth and troll it slowly on a lead-core line or drift with the herring.

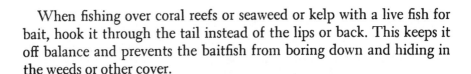

When fishing over coral reefs or seaweed or kelp with a live fish for bait, hook it through the tail instead of the lips or back. This keeps it off balance and prevents the baitfish from boring down and hiding in the weeds or other cover.

If you are using anchovies or herring for Pacific salmon, cut some gashes in the sides of the baitfish to give it a wounded appearance.

When using a live baitfish, especially a good-size one such as a bunker, mullet, herring, pinfish, blue runner, or mackerel, give the fish time to swallow the bait before trying to set the hook. One good procedure is to let the fish run with the baitfish until it stops. When it starts to move again, set the hook.

A good way to rig for fish that are likely to grab a baitfish head on is shown here. Run a short-shanked hook through the tail, then wrap it around the body and into a gill opening and out the side of the mouth.

When using a delicate baitfish such as a small bunker, herring, or sardine, you can prevent the hook from tearing out of the flesh by threading your line through a small button, then tying a treble hook on the end. Use a needle to thread the line or leader through the baitfish's body and out on the opposite side, then into the gill opening and out at the mouth.

If you are using live anchovies for yellowtail, albacore, or tuna in the Pacific, make only one cast with a live bait. And keep it in the water for a few minutes before replacing it with a new bait. Lively baitfish get more strikes or pickups than sluggish or dying baits.

You can give a dead baitfish more action by crimping the tail at an angle with thin, soft wire. This gives the bait a darting movement that is especially deadly when you are mooching for Pacific salmon.

A good rig for amberjack, tarpon, barracuda, king mackerel, and other fish in southern waters is a jig to which you add two more hooks as shown; hook a ballyhoo through the head with the jig hook and into the belly with the two trailing hooks. This should be used from a drifting boat and lowered into the depths, then raised and lowered to give it some action.

EELS

When using live eels for striped bass, let the eel swim naturally from an anchored or drifting boat. An eel will usually head for the bottom and this is what you want. But don't let it hide in the kelp, weeds, or rocks. When you feel the eel bump bottom, lift your rod tip to keep it away from any obstructions.

Live eels used in bays, in inlets, or around bridges should be smaller than those used in the surf. Those ranging from 6 to 10 in. are ideal. When big stripers are expected along the beaches or rocky shores, you can use 12 to 18 in. eels.

The smaller school tuna will often take a live eel live-lined out in a chum slick or let out into the depths from a drifting boat.

CRABS

In the fall small calico crabs are plentiful along the Atlantic coast and can be raked out of the sand in shallow water around jetties and on sandbars. The crabs can be used to catch blackfish and striped bass; use one small crab for blackfish and three or four on the hook for striped bass.

When drifting out live soft-shell crabs for stripers, it's a good idea not to run the hook through the crab. Instead use rubber bands to hold a long-shanked 7/0 hook against the crab's body.

Big black drum can be caught on blue crabs. Use half of a big crab or a whole small one. Crack the top shell of a whole crab before using it.

SHRIMP

One of the best ways to catch grass shrimp for bait is to tow or drag a fine-mesh net around a frame along the edges of marsh banks or through eelgrass and other spots where the shrimp hang out.

A good way to fish a live shrimp in a saltwater canal is to cast it upcurrent and let it drift naturally while you take up slack line.

When using live shrimp over weedy bottoms, pinch the head of the shrimp before you put it on the hook. This will weaken the shrimp so it won't hide in the grass where fish can't find it.

Small grass shrimp make the best bait for sturgeon in the saltwater bays of California. Two of these on a hook should be used, with the first one impaled tail first and the second one head first.

Sand shrimp dug from muddy sand at the mouths of bays and rivers along the West Coast make good bait, especially for surf perch, but they are somewhat soft and should be tied to the hook with light thread.

Two good ways to hook big shrimp are shown above. In the top drawing the hook is run through the hard, bony section of the head. But avoid running it through the dark spot if you want the shrimp to stay alive. The lower drawing shows how you run the hook from the end of the tail, through the tail, and out of the body on the underside.

Shrimp can be kept alive in an insulated ice chest or styrofoam container. Place the shrimp in a small plastic container and then place this inside the chest or larger container. Pack some ice around the shrimp. The shrimp should never come in direct contact with the ice or fresh water if you want them to stay alive.

Squid

Squid makes a good all-round bait for surf fishing and will catch striped bass, channel bass, bluefish, weakfish, and kingfish from the beaches. From jetties, breakwaters, and piers you can use it to catch sea bass, porgies, fluke or summer flounder, and silver hake or whiting.

Squid also make good bait for California yellowtail. Net the squid under a spotlight shining into the water at night. When the squid are attracted to the light, scoop them up.

A quick and easy way to rig a whole squid for swordfish is illustrated above. Use a long-shank No. 10/0 or 12/0 hook and a No. 12 wire leader. Slit a tiny hole at the tail of the squid about a hook length from the end and insert the hook into the squid so the eye rests in the tail end. Then take the wire leader and run it into the squid's tail, through the eye of the hook, and out on top. Form a loop and wrap the wire around itself several times to secure it.

Look for schools of spawning squid in Pacific waters and fish under them with one of the squid on a hook for white sea bass, halibut, and black sea bass.

When using squid for bait, cut it into long, narrow strips either rectangular in shape or tapering like a pennant. You'll get more bites on such long strips than on short chunks, which are lifeless and do not attract gamefish the way that the longer ones do.

STRIP BAITS

A fast way to attach a fish strip bait to a hook is to put a big hook on a snap swivel and then impale the strip on the snap and hook and close it.

When using long strips of fish or squid in bottom fishing, make a double hook rig like the one above, with a small hook up front wrapped to a long-shank larger hook. Then impale your strip with both hooks so it lies straight.

CHUM

When fishing in southern waters for snappers and yellowtail, use ground fish as chum to bring the bottom fish closer to the surface and your boat. Then use a live shrimp or pilchard as bait.

To make bunker chum float closer to the surface, mix it with sawdust. To make it sink faster, mix it with sand.

Crushed mussels or clams make a good chum for flounders. But if you can't get them, you can try such substitutes as canned corn kernels, canned dog or cat food, or boiled rice mixed with sardines. This kind of bait can be scattered around the boat or placed in a mesh bag or chum pot and lowered to the bottom. Shake the bag or pot every so often to release some of the chum.

You can make a good chum by mashing an oily fish such as a menhaden, herring, anchovy, or sardine and mixing the hash with corn meal or oatmeal. Then roll this mix into small balls and throw them overboard.

When cleaning or preparing baits for saltwater fishing, save the remains to use later as chum. When cutting up a mullet, bunker, herring, or any other fish, save the head, tail, and entrails. When opening mussels, clams, or oysters, save the shells and the meat attached to them. When preparing squid for bait, save the tentacles, the insides, and fins. All of these remains can be chopped or ground up and used to attract fish under your boat.

OTHER BAITS

Clams can be preserved for a length of time by removing the meat from the shells and putting it into a container with salt. The same thing can be done with mussels to toughen and preserve them. Use coarse kosher salt rather than fine table salt.

Always keep live saltwater baits such as clams, seaworms, crabs, shrimp, and most baitfish away from fresh water or rain. It won't take long for the fresh water to kill such baits.

To keep a sandworm or clamworm alive on a hook for a long time, do not run the hook into its head or body. Instead use a couple of small rubber bands to hold the worm against the hook.

The big sea scallops make good bait for flounders. Here you use mostly the mantle or stringy lips along the edge of the shell.

Pale or grayish mussels can be dyed yellow. Simply shuck the mussels, put them in a jar with salt brine, and add some yellow food coloring.

A good bait for red snappers is a southern porgy cut up into chunks or squares an inch or two across.

If you can't get bunker chum to use for mackerel, take along any fish, grind or chop it, and throw it into the water as chum. After you catch the first mackerel, you can grind it up and use it as chum to catch more mackerel.

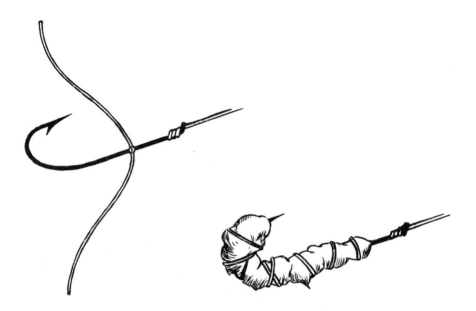

When using soft baits such as crab meat, the insides of a mussel, or the softer portions of clams, and shrimp, tie a short length of nylon thread to the shank of the hook. Then wrap the thread around any of these baits to hold them in place.

One of the top baits for bonefish in Bermuda waters is a green worm that is dug from the mud in bays.

Freshwater crayfish can be used in salt water to catch such fish as pompano, snapper, grunts, and other fish.

CHAPTER 15

Striped Bass, Channel Bass, Bluefish, Weakfish, and Sea Trout

STRIPED BASS

Water temperatures affect the movements and feeding of striped bass. In the early spring, when the water is cold, striped bass seek warmer waters and feed little or at irregular intervals. They start feeding more as soon as the water goes above 41 degrees, and they start migrating when it reaches 50 degrees. During the summer months stripers seek colder and deeper waters.

Many anglers seem to think that bloodworms and sandworms are good for striped bass only in the spring, but stripers will take these worms right up until the late fall months.

Popping plugs are most effective during the daytime but will also take stripers at night, although they should be worked more slowly then. A surface swimmer is even better at night if reeled just fast enough to bring out the action.

Chumming for striped bass with skimmer clams is a deadly method during the summer and early fall months. You can shuck the fresh clams for chum, but frozen clams or the trimmings are also used. The clam meat can be put in chum pots and lowered under the boat. You can also dribble it over the side or stern at regular intervals. Use the softer "belly" portions of the clam for bait and drift this out in the tide with the chum. The best fishing usually occurs during tide changes and when the tide isn't running too strong.

Up in New England around Cape Cod, live herring or alewives make good bait for striped bass in May and June. Usually the best procedure is to drift in a boat in a bay or around a river or brook, for herring usually gather at the mouths of rivers and brooks. You can also cast a live herring from shore and let it swim around. In a canal, river, or inlet with a current, you can walk along the bank while the baitfish drifts. Live herring can also be trolled slowly.

When using a surface plug for striped bass and a fish follows the lure but doesn't hit, try stopping the plug for a second, then start retrieving it fast as if it is trying to get away. This often draws a smashing strike from a striper.

Look for eelgrass in bays. There you have a good chance of locating striped bass. The eelgrass forms a natural hiding place for grass shrimp, crabs, sea worms, killifish, spearing, and small fish. Stripers know this and feed along the edges and in the eelgrass.

When stripers are feeding on sand eels or sand launce, long narrow lures such as the tube lures and plastic eels are very good in the smaller sizes.

Big striped bass often go for big lures and baits. A good plug is the big jointed minnow that is about 12 in. long. Rigged eels and plastic eels up to 18 or 20 in. can also be used. Live mackerel or menhaden a foot or more in length take the big cow stripers.

When fishing for striped bass, many fishermen use live eels from boats drifting with the wind or tide. If there is an inlet or very strong tide, you can anchor and let the eel out in the current. If a striper grabs the eel, let it run with it a few seconds before setting the hook.

Striped bass along the California coast feed in the surf during the summer months, chasing smelt or other baitfish right up to the breakers. At such times lures resembling the baitfish are most effective.

Live eels can also be trolled slowly down deep at night to catch big stripers. Hook the eel through the upper jaw for this kind of fishing.

Coves, inlets, and river mouths are great fishing spots for striped bass, especially during a storm or blow. Baitfish are usually present in such waters or take shelter there during a storm. Stripers will follow or hang around to feed on the baitfish.

Which color is best in a striped-bass fly? You can't go wrong by using an all-white or all-yellow streamer or bucktail. Those dressed with light green, blue, or black backs are also good. Also, flies tied with silver bodies or Mylar strips are effective because they imitate the silvery baitfish that stripers usually chase. You can imitate such baitfish better if you carry the flies in different sizes and lengths.

When using a live bullhead—a sculpin—for striped bass on the Pacific coast, hook it through the lips and fish it with a sinker on the bottom in sloughs, rivers, and deltas. But every few minutes reel in the baitfish a couple of feet so that it doesn't bury itself in the mud.

The sandbars found in most inlets are wonderful striped bass fishing spots. They are especially productive on an outgoing tide when waves break over the shallow bars. Cast a plug or metal lure into the white water and retrieve it into the deeper water. These areas are also danger-ous spots when a heavy surf is running and should be avoided then or fished with extreme caution.

If stripers are present but not feeding on top and if few baitfish are around, the bass are probably seeking food on or near the bottom. At such times natural baits such as sea worms, clams, shedder or peeler crabs, and squid should be tried.

White water and striped bass go together wherever there is any surf breaking. If you see white water spots on sand or rock bars, at rocky points, alongside rocks, or at the ends of jetties, work your lure through them.

When you are surf fishing for striped bass along a sandy beach and the fish are not hitting near the surface, try letting your metal squid or jig sink to the bottom. Then raise it quickly, reel in a few feet, and let it settle into the sand again. This trick will help you simulate a sand eel, sand bug, or crab, for they often bury themselves in the sand to hide from their enemies.

When fishing tidal bays, creeks, sloughs, and flats, it's a good idea to be there at the start of the incoming tide, since stripers will move in from the deeper water to feed in the shallow water as soon as the flats get covered by the tide.

Live eels can be used on the bottom for striped bass when fishing from a boat or shore. Use a fish-finder rig and hook the eel through the tail to avoid tangled lines.

When trolling a lure for striped bass and fish are around, but not hitting too well, try dropping your lure back and letting it sink a few feet by throwing the reel into free spool and thumbing it to let line out. Then engage the drag and reel in fast to make the lure rise as if trying to escape.

On dark nights in the late summer and early fall, the phosphorescence in the water lights up the line and lure, leaving a streak in the water. At such times stripers do not hit readily and are hard to catch. To overcome this situation, do your fishing on moonlit nights, at dusk and daybreak, and during the daytime.

One trick that will bring more strikes from striped bass in the surf is timing your casts to the breaking waves. Wait until a wave crests and breaks and turns the water white. That is the time to cast your lure just behind the wave. You'll get more strikes in the foamy white water than you would in clear water. Your lure also has better action behind a wave than in front of it.

Striped bass like to lie close to the marsh banks in tidal bays and rivers. Your lures or flies should be cast right up to the shore in such spots.

Big stripers feeding on bunkers or menhaden that are swimming or dying on the surface will often go for a surface plug. One of the top plugs for this is a big swimming model that wriggles on top yet can also be popped to throw a splash when jerked. It can be used for trolling or cast from a jetty or a boat, especially at daybreak or dusk.

If you want small stripers, especially during the summer months, do your fishing in tidal rivers, bays, sounds, and inlets. If you want big stripers, stick to the mouths of rivers and inlets and the surf along beaches and rocky shores.

When trolling with jigs for striped bass, you'll get more strikes and hook more fish if you "work" the rod. The best way is to stand up at the stern, lower your rod toward the water on the side of the boat, and then with quick, short jerks move your rod tip back and forth.

As a general guide use white or silver plugs, plastic eels, and surgical tubes when trolling for stripers at dusk, at daybreak, or at night. Use the natural-color or darker lures of the same type during the daytime.

When striped bass are feeding on shrimp, a short fly dressed to look like a grass shrimp is often a killer. A slow retrieve with short jerks is usually best with this fly because shrimp swim this way.

If you are trolling deep with spoons, surgical tubes, underwater plugs, or rigged eels for striped bass and you get a fish on, slow down the boat. Then have the other anglers on board grab the other rods and reel them in slowly, giving the lures some rod action. Many times you'll hook a second or even third striper that has been following the first fish.

When you are fighting a big striper, always keep a tight line, and if it suddenly goes slack, don't stop reeling. Instead speed up your reeling to take up the slack. Chances are good that the bass is still there but running toward you.

CHANNEL BASS

The best months for big channel bass in Virginia are May and June in the spring and September and October in the fall. This is when the big red drum feed in the surf along the barrier islands and in the bays and inlets along the coast. In North Carolina, April, May, October, November, and sometimes early December are best for the big channel bass.

When fishing in the surf for channel bass, try to get down to the beach a couple of hours before high tide and fish for two or three hours after high water.

When searching for channel bass schools from a boat, choose sunny days when there is not too much wind. Wear Polaroid sunglasses and look for the fish just below the surface. A school of channel bass may look pink, brown, reddish, purple, or like a dark patch. Investigate any water that looks "different" or varies in color from the surrounding water. As you get closer, you can usually see the individual fish. But do not approach closer than about 200 ft. in order not to spook them.

Big channel bass will sometimes rise for a surface plug, but most anglers prefer deep-running or sinking plugs as well as metal lures such as metal squids, casting spoons, and similar lures. One of the best techniques is to let the lure sink to the bottom and then retrieve it slowly.

Channel bass and sharks don't mix too well. Usually when there are a lot of sharks in the surf, channel bass are not around. But there are times when you will hook big channel bass and sharks will cut them off your line or mutilate them.

Channel bass in the surf will often bite at night, especially moon-lit nights during the period just before and after the full moon.

In the fall, schools of redfish or channel bass show up in the Gulf of Mexico along Florida's west coast. They are especially plentiful in the waters outside the Ten Thousand Islands, where they will be around the oyster beds and rock bars.

A good tough bait for channel bass in the surf is salted mullet. You can get the mullet when they are fresh and plentiful, clean and cut them into the right sizes and shapes for bait, then salt them away in jars for future use.

Channel bass can also be caught by casting from a boat toward the beach with a bait on a bottom rig. You can use the same baits—mullet, spot, menhaden or bunker, shedder or soft crabs—as you do when casting from shore.

Big channel bass feed along sod banks and in many tidal creeks, marshes, and sounds in Virginia and North Carolina. They can be caught with natural baits and bottom rigs. If you can spot schools of these fish, you can also cast metal lures into them.

When fishing for the smaller channel bass or redfish in Louisiana during the winter months, try the deep bayou holes, especially in spots around bends where the reds often gather in schools. Baits fished on the bottom work best here.

If you are using small mullet for channel bass, slash the baitfish with a knife in several places before putting it on the hook. The blood and liquids oozing out will attract channel bass more quickly.

You can catch channel bass along Florida's east coast from August to October at the mouths of inlets and along the beaches. Fish the high tides from the beaches and the outgoing tides at the inlets for best results.

BLUEFISH

Surfacing bluefish should be approached with care in order not to spook them and cause them to sound. Either troll along the edges of the school or cut your motor 100 or 150 ft. from the fish and cast into them.

If the butterfish or bunker bait being used for bluefish becomes old or ragged, replace it with a fresh one that looks neat and gives off a fresh, oily scent. It is also important to cut the bait cleanly with a sharp knife.

When chumming for bluefish, try throwing some spearing or shiners into the chum slick to excite the fish and make them more eager to take your bait.

Bluefish will move up rivers that are salt, but they don't go into fresh or brackish water as many other saltwater fish do. When a river gets high from recent rains or a dam is opened, releasing fresh water, the blues leave and head back to the saltwater bays or the ocean.

When chumming for bluefish, you usually get the best action if you drift the bait out on a free line with no weight. But if the tide or current is strong and the fish are deep, you can add a clincher sinker above the hook. If the tide is slack or very slow, you can add a small float a few feet above the hook.

Big bluefish can often be taken with a bottom rig and a fish chunk or fillet as bait. A piece of butterfish, bunker, herring, mackerel, or porgy can be tried.

When using a heavy diamond jig for bluefish in a fast tide and deep water from a drifting boat, let your jig down fast and when you hit bottom reel it in fast for a few feet, then let it go down again to the bottom and then reel in fast again. Keep repeating this until you have drifted away from the payoff spot.

If you have a choice, always take along freshly caught menhaden or bunker when chumming for bluefish. This is much better than iced or frozen bunker. Of course, once you get the fresh bunker, keep them on ice or grind them up and use them soon. Keep them out of the hot sun and on a hot day don't mix too much chum for it will stand around for hours and turn bad.

Weakfish and Sea Trout

Northern weakfish are caught best by chumming with grass shrimp. It is important to be quiet and make no unnecessary noise and to keep your chum line steady with no stops or breaks.

Northern weakfish in the surf and bays can be caught on a wide variety of baits. Sandworms or clamworms, grass shrimp and jumbo shrimp, strips of squid, shedder crab, and whole small baitfish or pieces of larger fish can all be used.

Big sea trout can often be seen feeding in the shallows, and then you can cast to them. They are usually "loners" or are found in small schools. Smaller sea trout run in larger schools, and when feeding, they will often swirl on the surface.

The best time to catch sea trout during the summer months is early in the morning, in the evening, and on cloudy days. Of course, fishing at night is often the best of all.

A good combination lure for sea trout is a gold spoon and a trailer with a white bucktail jig about 10 in. behind it. When cast into a school of sea trout, it will often hook two fish at a time.

Sea trout like lures with a lot of pink, yellow, orange, and red, probably because they resemble some of the shrimp on which these fish feed. So saltwater flies, jigs, and plugs with these colors should be used for them.

If you are drifting for sea trout in a boat and using live shrimp, don't just drag it through the water. Instead cast across the current and let the bait drift naturally. The sea trout will usually grab the shrimp before the line straightens out.

A flooding tide is good for sea trout on shallow flats since that is when these fish move in to feed.

When sea trout run along the beaches in the surf in the Carolinas and Georgia in the late fall and early winter, they can be caught on underwater plugs and bucktail jigs.

One of the best lures to use for big sea trout in Florida is a long, slim plug that imitates a needlefish.

If you are fishing for sea trout in shallow water and hook one or two fish and land them, it pays to leave that spot and move to a new one. The noise and commotion of fighting the fish will usually chase away other sea trout or make them wary, so they won't bite.

During the winter months fish for sea trout in inlets and work the points, drop-offs, eddies, and deep holes.

Most sea trout fishermen use live shrimp for bait. But strips of mullet about 3 or 4 in. long can also be used when drifting over grass flats.

CHAPTER 16

Tuna, Swordfish, Marlin, Sailfish, Dolphin, Albacore, and Bonito

TUNA

These days the smaller tuna are fished hard by commercial fishermen and sports fishermen. So they often break up into smaller schools and tend to be boat shy. Too many boats running around will put them down. Your best bet is to approach a school of tuna slowly along the edges and troll small feathers, spoons, or jigs.

Natural baits or live baits trolled on or near the surface usually work best when the giant tuna are actually showing or chasing fish on top.

If you are chumming for tuna with ground bunker, try forming some of the chum into "balls" and drop them into the water gently. Watch them sink to see whether tuna are taking them. When tuna arrive in numbers and start gulping the balls, make up a ball with a hook in it, wrapping it with fine thread several times to hold the chum together. Then dip it in the chum can to saturate it with the bloody chum, put it into the water, and drift it out toward the waiting tuna.

School tuna often travel on top of the water in schools with their tails and fins showing above the surface. These fish usually refuse to strike the regular tuna lures trolled at the normal fast speeds. One trick that sometimes works is to change to spoons and troll them at a slower speed in front of the school.

A good way to catch Allison tuna in Bermuda waters is to anchor and chum with anchovies or hog-mouthed fry. When you see the tuna in the chum slick, send out a hook baited with an anchovy or a few fry.

School tuna are often seen swimming or leaping during the middle of the day, but they don't hit too well. Usually they are not actually feeding then. You can often get better results if you fish early in the morning or in the late afternoon.

When fishing for school tuna, it's a good idea to have a couple of rods rigged and ready and equipped with butterfish jigs. Then if you hook any tuna, the rods can be grabbed and the jigs let out and jigged to hook other tuna near the boat.

The best way to jig or "bail" school tuna after you hook a fish or two and want to hold the rest of the school near the boat is to let out about 30 to 40 ft. of line and allow the lure to sink. Then you jig the lure and keep doing this as long as the lure stays below. If the lure rises to the top, reel it in fast and let it out again so that it sinks down.

There are times when giant tuna stay deep and a good distance from the anchored boat when you are fishing and chumming for them. At such times it's a good idea to let your bait drift way out and sink toward the bottom. You may have to let out 150 or 200 ft. of line to get out far enough and deep enough.

When using live tinker mackerel as bait for school tuna off the New Jersey coast, use small hooks similar to the "albacore" or "yellowtail" type hooks used on the live-bait boats on the West Coast.

If school tuna refuse to strike a trolled lure, try stopping the boat and rig some rods with diamond jigs. When a school of tuna shows up near the boat, lower the jigs and start working them up and down. This often draws strikes from the tuna. You can also use a surf-casting rod and cast big plugs, metal squids, or jigs into the fish.

Another trick to try when school tuna are showing but refuse to strike is to run the boat behind the school and speed up to chase the fish. Go right over the school and make them sound. Then slow the boat down and let the fish come up again to see the lures in your wake. This often excites the fish and makes them hit.

SWORDFISH

Although swordfish are usually baited with a whole squid, they will also take whole mackerel, bonito, bluefish, whiting, small dolphin, and rigged eels at times. All of these baits are best if they are fresh and kept in plastic bags on ice until used.

With swordfish being chased all over the ocean by commercial fishermen, harpooners, and sports fishermen these days, they tend to be boat shy. So when presenting your squid bait or any other bait to a sword, let out at least 150 or 200 ft. of line.

When choosing a bait for swordfish, don't pick one that is too big. A smaller squid, whiting, mackerel, or other bait is more likely to be mouthed and swallowed. A larger one is likely to be deflected by the fish's bill and will often result in a missed strike or a fish that is foul hooked.

If you come too close to a swordfish, he will often go down below the surface. When this happens stop the boat, shut off your engine and wait. Usually the fish will come to the surface again.

When presenting a bait to a swordfish, try to swing it well ahead of his bill. And there should be enough slack in your line dropped into the water so that the bait comes to a stop in front of the swordfish, giving him a chance to see and grab it.

If a swordfish takes your bait but fails to get hooked or if the bait pulls out of his mouth, don't reel in immediately but let the boat stay near the fish. The sword will sometimes pick up the bait a second time.

When you are hunting for swordfish, bring along or catch some live bait such as mackerel, whiting, or even porgies or other fish. There are times when swords refuse a dead bait but will go for a live one.

When the water is rough, it is difficult or impossible to sight swordfish. At such times try trolling a rigged eel or a squid anyway. Swordfish have been known to strike such baits blind at times.

If you do hook a swordfish, take extra care while fighting him. Strong-arm methods, tight drags, or horsing are out. The swordfish has a very soft mouth and flesh, and hooks pull out easily. Also, many swordfish are foul hooked outside of the mouth in the head, back, or dorsal fin.

MARLIN

Blue marlin often feed on false albacore and black fin tuna, so trolling well offshore in areas where schools of these fish are numerous is a good bet.

Blue marlin fishing is usually best when the current in the Gulf Stream is running strong. They also tend to rise to the surface more often when the water is rough and the day is overcast or dark. Late afternoon is best for surface trolling.

If you raise a blue marlin that hits the bait, but fails to get hooked, reel in quickly about 10 or 15 ft. then throw the reel into free spool and drop back the bait again.

Watch for man-of-war birds when searching for white marlin in tropical waters. When the birds get excited, head for that area, since it usually means the marlin are driving baitfish to the surface.

A good bait for white marlin is a live mackerel. But they pick it up and take their time about swallowing it. So let the marlin run with the bait for a while before trying to set the hook.

The striped marlin of the Pacific will often hit feather lures. These should be trolled at faster speeds than natural baits such as flying fish.

A whole natural eel from 18 to 24 in. long makes a good teaser for white marlin. Attach two eels without hooks in them to stout lines and let them out from the stern to skip just ahead of the baits that do have hooks.

More and more white marlin are being caught these days on the plastic imitations of eels, squid, ballyhoo, mackerel, or other fish.

Although most billfish anglers approach their fish at a slow or moderate speed in order not to frighten it, Mexican skippers deliberately speed up their boats and race in front of the surfacing striped marlin to provoke strikes.

Birds can lead you to blue marlin in many waters. If they are hovering, diving, or sitting on the water, it pays to troll in that spot. It's almost a sure sign that there are baitfish present, which attract dolphin, bonito, albacore, or mackerel, which in turn attract the blue marlin.

More white marlin would be caught off New Jersey and Long Island, N.Y., if anglers made longer runs offshore. The fish are often seen up to 50 or 60 miles or more offshore feeding on schools of mackerel and other fish.

In a pinch you can use almost any fish as blue marlin bait. Bonefish and ladyfish are often used in southern waters. Big mullet are good, and even small barracuda have caught these fish.

In the Caribbean white marlin often drive such baitfish as sardines to the surface and make them form into compact schools. At such times trolling a small 7 or 8 in. ballyhoo in your wake about 20 or 30 ft. from the boat is most effective.

If you are looking for blue marlin and see a weedline, troll your baits along these weeds. Dolphin hang around under the weeds and attract the blue marlin, which often feed on them.

When a big marlin is following a bait but refuses to strike, try gutting a small tuna, albacore, bonito, or other fish on board and dump the entrails and blood into the water so that the marlin swims through it. This often excites the marlin and makes him hit the bait.

The bigger marlin can swallow big baits. A 13 ft. black marlin contained a 4 ft. yellow-fin tuna that was estimated to have weighed 157 lb. in its stomach!

SAILFISH

Along Florida's east coast sailfishing is usually best along the "edge," where the green coastal waters mix with the deep blue waters of the Gulf Stream.

Some of the fastest fishing for sailfish takes place when they are "balling" the bait, such as ballyhoo and pilchards, into tight compact balls by circling around them. This usually takes place in December and January along Florida's east coast.

Fish early in the morning for sailfish, especially when a northwest wind is blowing during the winter months. A choppy or moderately rough sea is preferred to a flat calm.

Sailfishing with kites is becoming popular and highly effective when used with live baitfish. You need some wind to take out the kite. On days when there is no wind, you can inflate a balloon with helium and tie it on top of the kite to take it up.

When fishing for sailfish with live bait such as blue runners from a drifting boat, keep watching your line to make sure the baitfish doesn't try to hide under your boat. If it does, you can speed up your boat until the line and bait is some distance away, then resume drifting. You can also troll the baitfish very slowly to keep it away from the boat.

You can also catch sailfish on a live bait below a float. A piece of styrofoam is best for this. (See tip in Chapter 11.) Add the float a few feet above the hook. Bait the hook with a live blue runner, mullet, or pinfish. Let it out from a drifting boat.

For years it has been believed that sailfish first strike a trolled bait to stun it before actually taking it in their mouths. Now many anglers believe that this doesn't happen very often. Instead they grab the bait in their mouths, like most fish, but do not swallow it immediately. So it is still a good policy to allow a "drop-back" of slack line so that the sail can swallow the bait.

When using a live blue runner for sailfish, hook it through the head right above the eyes. This tends to make the bait swim on its side when it is trolled slowly, causing it to flash and attract the sails from the depths.

DOLPHIN

Dolphin are found offshore where the blue waters of the Gulf Stream meet with the green inshore waters. Look for them around buoys and floating objects and along weedlines. The best method is trolling surface-skipping baits such as mullet, ballyhoo, spoons, and feathers.

Dolphin will often hit a small surface plug cast with light tackle around floating objects or weedlines.

If you see a sea turtle on top, try trolling near him because dolphin often lurk beneath such turtles.

Dolphin can be caught on strip baits cut from the sides of tuna, bonito, albacore, and other fish. Skip these on top from outriggers for best results.

You can hold dolphin around a boat by chumming. Cut up small fish and throw the pieces into the water. This works best from a drifting or slow-moving boat.

ALBACORE

If you are trolling for false albacore, let out a longer line behind the boat than you would for school tuna.

While false albacore will take pieces of butterfish or bunker used for bluefish, you'll often do much better if you bring along some spearing and place one on a small hook so that the hook is almost completely buried.

False albacore and bonito are fast-moving fish, and quick action is required to intercept them when you see a school.. When trolling, try to swing the boat in front of them. If you are casting, send the lure into the school and reel as fast as you can.

BONITO

When trolling for bonito, run the boat at a fast speed and use a small feather lure about 100 or 150 ft. behind the boat.

Bonito and albacore will often hit streamer flies if they have some silver on the shank of the hook or along the sides. Mylar strips are good for this. But instead of trolling the flies, get the fish up to the boat by chumming with ground bunker in the Atlantic or live anchovies in the Pacific.

CHAPTER 17

Tarpon, Snook, and Bonefish

TARPON

Tarpon usually show on top by swirling or rolling. If you are fishing for them and don't see any tarpon come to the surface, move to another spot where you do.

A good time to catch tarpon is at sundown, regardless of the stage of the tide.

A top lure for big tarpon is a large underwater plug cast or trolled in the rivers, deep channels, and passes. Best results are obtained by reeling slow and deep. If the current is strong, the plug will have plenty of action.

During the winter months tarpon are more active during the warmer days. If the water temperature is around 70 degrees or higher, they will be more likely to show and feed.

When mullet are migrating along the beaches of Florida's east coast, tarpon come into the surf to feed on them. This usually happens during the fall months. Best fishing usually occurs when there is a good surf or stormy weather.

When fishing from or under a bridge for tarpon on moonlit nights, fish the dark "dark side"—where a shadow is cast.

If a school of tarpon is showing on or near the surface, you can cast a live baitfish such as a mullet, pinfish, or squirrel fish into the school and let the bait swim around among them. Keep your reel in free spool. If a tarpon takes the bait, let him run until he swallows it before setting the hook.

When using a long, limber rod such as fly rod or spinning rod, you have to set the hook hard to make it stick in the tough jaws of these fish.

When searching for tarpon on the flats, look for muddy or roiled patches of water. This usually indicates the presence of mullet, and tarpon are likely to be in the area feeding on these baitfish.

In mangrove country tarpon like to lie in the shady pools or holes under the mangrove bushes, especially during the heat of the day. At such times they won't move far for a bait or lure, but one that is cast right in front of them will often bring a strike.

A good way to fish for big tarpon from a boat is to anchor on the upcurrent side of a bridge and drift a live pinfish, grunt, or mullet toward the bridge.

Small tarpon hit faster than the big ones, and here you have to set the hook as soon as you see the flash underwater or the fish hitting. If you wait until you feel a strike, you'll fail to hook the baby tarpon.

Tarpon often lie under bridges waiting for baitfish or crabs moving with the tide. Here a good technique is to cast your lure on the up-current side of the bridge and reel it toward the bridge with the tide. This is tricky because you have to reel quickly enough to bring out the action of your lure but slowly enough so that a fish can get the lure.

If you see a trawler or shrimp boat dumping trash fish or shrimp scraps overboad in a bay or inlet in southern waters, fish behind such boats. They act as chumming boats and attract tarpon to the scene.

Big tarpon should never be gaffed when they are still green. They may suddenly go wild next to the boat and drive a hook into your hand or body or leap into the boat and wreck it. Play the fish until it quits and turns over on its side before gaffing or releasing the tarpon.

SNOOK

When you are fishing for snook with a plug and get a strike that misses, toss the plug back to the same spot and retrieve it fast. This often draws a solid strike from the snook.

One of the top baits for big snook is a live pinfish used in the inlets or passes and deep holes, especially during low tide periods.

Look for snook during the winter months in Florida in the upper sections of headwaters of mangrove-lined rivers and creeks, where the water is brackish.

When snook are actively on the prowl and feeding, they cruise along shorelines, seawalls, and bars and over grass and oyster flats.

A good combination rig for snook is a long yellow feather tied on a hook and a shrimp hooked through the head. This works best in a current or when cast out with a spinning outfit and reeled in slowly.

If you want to catch a big snook in the Everglades area of Florida, try a small, live ladyfish for bait. You can catch the ladyfish on a jig, spoon, or tiny plug.

Big snook under bridges or piers are tough to hold on light tackle. Here you should use heavy bait-casting rods with 20 or 25 lb.-test lines, two-handed spinning rods with 20 or 25 lb.-test line, or conventional boat or light surf rods with 30 or 40 lb.-test lines.

Snook are partial to plugs that are yellow or have some yellow on the body. Poppers, darters, and underwater plugs in yellow are highly effective.

If snook don't strike a surface plug retrieved steadily, try this trick: Cast the plug to a shoreline or snook hangout and let it float without moving it for at least a minute. Then give it a light pop and let it lie still for a few more seconds. Then start the regular retrieve. Usually the strike will come as soon as you start working the plug back after the two pauses.

During low water look for snook in the deeper holes, but at high water try the mangrove shores, sandbars, oyster bars, beaches, drop-offs, and points.

Big snook will often hit rigged eels, eelskin lures, and plastic eels cast from bridges or piers or trolled in waters where they are found.

Most of the larger snook hang around near the bottom and the best way to reach them is with a bucktail or feather jig. Don't be afraid to let the jig bounce bottom at regular intervals.

Snook that are migrating or moving fast through a pass or channel are usually not inclined to feed or take a lure or bait.

One of the best times to fish for snook is from about an hour before sunset right up until midnight, especially if there is an incoming tide during this period.

Snook like a fast-moving tide or rip when feeding. This usually occurs during the so-called spring tides, when the moon is new or full.

Snook are caught all year round in Florida, but the best fishing usually occurs during the late spring and the summer months.

Snook feed only for brief intervals at certain periods, and this usually depends on the presence of bait, the tide, and the time of day. You have to wait for them to start feeding or figure out when this will happen and be there at the right time.

Big snook often lurk in the shadows of bridges, docks, and piers. They like to lie or feed among the pier or dock pilings. Or alongside or in front of the bridge supports.

Trolling is one of the best ways to locate snook. Once you hook a fish you can drift or anchor and cast in that spot. The fishing guides or "regular" snook anglers who know an area, however, don't waste time trolling but head straight for the spot and try a few casts. If it doesn't produce, they head for another one.

Too much boat traffic will scare and scatter snook in shallow, confined waters and make it harder to catch them. It pays to slow down and approach the fishing grounds quietly when fishing in shallow, narrow creeks and channels. And if boat traffic is heavy in your favorite fishing area in the daytime, try a quieter spot or come back in the evening, at night, or early in the morning.

Tides are very important in snook fishing and have to be studied carefully in the area being fished to determine the best tide at that particular spot. In some places, usually bridges or inlets, an outgoing tide is best; others produce on a flood tide, and still others have to be fished at low water.

Snook will often drive mullet or other baitfish into the surf and can be hooked from the beach or piers. If big ones are around, use your heavier surf-fishing tackle to land them.

Snook lying on the bottom around bridges, piers, docks, jetties, along drop-offs, and under mangroves are usually not feeding actively in the daytime and are not too inclined to strike. However, they can be "teased" into hitting at times if you work the lure in an enticing manner or if you can maneuver a big live shrimp, pilchard, mullet, or pinfish near their noses.

BONEFISH

Bonefishing is best if the temperature of the water is above 70 degrees. If it is colder, the fish usually leave the flats for deeper water.

Smaller bonefish often travel in schools, but the big ones are usually seen alone, in pairs, or in groups of four or five fish.

A good time to fish for bonefish is early in the morning or in the evening, when the tide is flooding. You not only will catch more fish then but will also avoid the hot, bright sun during the middle of the day.

When you hook a bonefish and he makes his first long run, hold the rod tip high above your head. This keeps most of the line out of the water or on the surface, where it has less chance of getting fouled on weeds or cut on the coral or rocks.

Although bonefish come onto the shallow flats to feed, they may avoid such waters during the hot months, especially where there is little tidal flow and the water warms up too much. At such times, fish near high tide, when the water is cooler and deeper.

Bonefish are less spooky when they are "tailing" or "mudding"— actually feeding. Then the lure or bait can be cast closer to the fish. But when they are swimming or moving steadily, you have to cast your lure well ahead of them in order not to frighten them. Often a cast of 20 to 25 ft. ahead of the lead fish is required.

If you see a sting ray feeding on a flat, keep a sharp lookout for bonefish, which will often follow or swim alongside the ray hoping to grab tiny crabs, shrimp, or other sea creatures uncovered or disturbed by the sting ray.

When using jigs for bonefish, try adding a small piece of shrimp to the hook.

After a hooked bonefish makes one or two long runs, he usually starts circling, keeping his side to you. Then you should turn with the fish, always facing him and maintaining a tight line to avoid any slack line.

If bonefish are spooky and are frightened by lures cast near them, try casting well ahead of an approaching fish or a school of fish and let your jig settle to the bottom. Then as the fish approach the lure, raise the jig off the bottom.

One problem when fishing for bonefish in thin water—very shallow water—is hanging up in the weeds or grass. Then it's a good idea to use flies tied on weedless hooks. A pork chunk shaped like a small frog attached to a weedless hook also works well on such shallow flats.

CHAPTER 18

Saltwater Bottom Fishes

FLOUNDERS

Look for flounders on bottoms that are a mixture of black mud and sand containing tiny shellfish or worms. When you bring up this mud on your sinker or anchor, it should be smooth. Flounders usually avoid polluted or dirty mud that has a bad smell.

Scallops can be used as flounder bait. The stringy mantle or "lips" are the part to use on a hook. The shells, with bits of meat sticking to them, can be scattered around the boat as chum.

Years ago flounder hooks with red "whiskers" were popular. You can still use color to attract the flatties by adding red, orange, or white yarn or feathers to a hook near the eye. Then add the worm bait. You can also paint your sinkers red, orange, or yellow.

When using bloodworms or sandworms for flounders, "thread" about a 2 in. portion of the worm on the hook, leaving a short piece dangling. Don't use too big a piece of worm on a hook so that it

411

bunches up into a ball or lump. Flounders have small mouths and cannot swallow too big a bait.

Early in the year look for flounders in shallow bays and tidal rivers over muddy bottoms. Such waters warm up sooner than deeper waters and flounders emerge from the mud to feed. Fishing on sunny days, especially during the middle of the day, is better than on raw, cold, cloudy days.

The trend nowadays when fishing for winter flounders is to chum with crushed mussels or clams. This isn't so important if the fish are plentiful and only a few boats are fishing. But if the fish are scarce and there are a lot of boats all using chum, then it's smart to do the same thing. Otherwise the other boats will attract fish with the chum and catch most of the fish.

If you are fishing for flounders, do not jerk or lift your rod too sharply or violently. This may take the bait away from the fish or frighten them away. Instead lift your bait gently, but if you feel no fish, you can drop your sinker quickly to the bottom so it raises some mud.

A good flounder chum can be made by taking some clams, shucking them, and grinding them up in a meat grinder. Now boil some rice and mix it with the clams. Almost one-third rice to two-thirds clams will do the trick. You can scatter this around the boat or lower some of the mixture to the bottom in a chum pot.

If you are going to fish for flounders in a strange area and do not know which bait is best, play safe and bring two or three different kinds of bait. In some waters bloodworms are best; in other areas sandworms are better. In still other places you may find that clams or mussels should be used.

Although small baits are best for flounders, you can use somewhat larger baits if you don't want to be bothered by the smaller, "postage stamp" size flounders. They have small mouths and can't swallow big baits.

One trick that will enable you to catch more of the big "snowshoe" flounders off Block Island, R.I., is to feed some slack line and lower your rod tip when a wave or the tide threatens to lift your sinker and rig off the bottom. Snowshoe flounders may take some time to locate your bait and swallow it, so the bait that remains on the bottom at all times is more likely to be picked up by the fish and swallowed.

When fishing for snowshoe flounders, use the larger Chestertown hooks and skimmer clams, cutting the hard part into long narrow pieces and stringing only one narrow piece of clam on the hook. You can also use the mantles of the clam, piercing them in three or four places when putting them on the hook.

FLUKE

Rigs used for fluke or summer flounders can be plain hooks with bait or with spinners ahead of the baited hook. Usually, when fishing for the smaller fluke over a sandy or smooth bottom, a spinner can be used to attract them. Spinners are also good when fishing from a drifting boat in a strong wind or tide and when the water is a bit murky or roiled. The plain hook with bait is best for big fluke, especially over a rocky or broken bottom, where many rigs are hung up and lost. It is also good to use a plain hook when fishing from an anchored boat or when drifting in a weak tide or when there is little or no wind.

The bait usually used for fluke is a whole baitfish such as a killy, spearing, or sand eel. But long, narrow strips cut from almost any fish, such as a mackerel, porgy, herring, or shad, can be used.

Off the New Jersey coast the biggest fluke are caught over rocky bottoms. It's a good idea to drift near lobster pots. Use big baits such as smelt or 8 in. strips cut from a smaller fluke. And bring along plenty of rigs and sinkers to replace those lost in the rocks.

Most fluke are caught on natural baits, but they will also hit lures, and one of the best is a metal spoon with white or yellow feathers around the hook. Spoons with strips of pork rind or squid on the hook are also effective. Any lure used for fluke should be reeled or trolled slowly along the bottom.

Fluke should always be netted and never lifted into a boat. And bring a wide net if you expect to hook any big "doormats" running over 5 or 6 lb.

HALIBUT

When using live anchovies for California halibut, you often miss a lot of fish that strike at the tail or body and fail to get hooked. Then it's a good idea to use a tandem hook, one pentrating the anchovy's nose and the other going through the tail of the bait.

Pacific halibut will often hit artificial lures such as plugs, spoons, jigs, and pork-rind lures.

COD

When going codfishing, it's a good idea to make up your rigs in advance and have them ready. It takes time to tie up a rig on a boat, especially if your fingers are numb from cold. By tying them in advance, you'll have them coiled and in individual envelopes ready for immediate use.

If you run out of bait when codfishing, cut a strip of skin and meat from a fresh-caught cod. This often works, and when cod are numerous and hungry, they'll also take pieces of white rag on a hook.

When codfishing, it pays to know several good spots or wrecks in the same area. It doesn't take long for a fleet or even a few boats to clean out a spot. If you know of another spot nearby, you can run over and fish it. Some days you may have to try several spots before you locate the cod.

If you are using skimmer clams for cod, try soaking them in cod liver oil before putting them on a hook.

Examine your bait often when codfishing. Blackfish, bergalls, and crabs soon shred or steal a clam and leave either a bare hook or just the hard part of the clam. Cod bite better on a clam that has the softer portions and strings dangling.

If you catch a bergall, whiting, or ling, cut some fillets and use them for cod. They are less likely to be stolen by pests or crabs and make tough baits.

During the late fall, when spiny dogfish appear in large numbers on the offshore grounds, it's an indication that the water has turned colder. You can look forward to the appearance of the first cod soon after the dogfish appear.

A sure way to locate cod is to look for commercial boats dredging for sea clams. In working the offshore clam beds, these clam boats stir up the bottom, exposing food for cod. They also throw back small clams, broken clams, crabs, trash fish, and other marine creatures. This is really chumming on a big scale and attracts cod to the scene.

Although the common bait for cod is clams, they will also take strips of squid, pieces of whelk or conch, crabs, baitfish such as spearing, sand eels, shiners, smelt, herring, mackerel, and almost any other small fish.

When fishing for cod from an anchored boat, you might hit it right on the nose and get action the minute your bait is lowered to the bottom. Other times you might have to wait some time for action. Chumming with skimmer clams helps to bring the cod sooner and in larger numbers.

Cod are usually hungry and take the bait without fooling around too much. They generally hit better if the bait has some movement. Thus a drifting boat is good. If fishing from an anchored boat, you can raise and lower your rod to attract cod. But there are times when they prefer a bait that isn't moving and then you can let it lie on the bottom.

POLLOCK

Although cod will often take a big gob of skimmer clams—often two or three clams on a hook—pollock are more dainty feeders, and for them half a clam or a 3 or 4 in. strip of squid makes a better bait.

The diamond jig is one of the best lures to use for pollock. It can be lowered from a drifting boat to the bottom, reeled in a couple of feet, then jigged up and down. A variation is to let the jig down to the bottom, then reel it in slowly 50 or 60 ft. If you don't get any strikes, let it drop back to the bottom and repeat.

A good way to fish for pollock is to anchor above a tidal rip or a spot where pollock are present and use a hook baited with a strip of squid. A sinker just heavy enough to get the rig down to the bottom is used. When the sinker hits bottom, you reel the bait in slowly. Pollock will often chase and grab the squid bait.

Pollock usually show on the surface at high water or low water. Then they can often be seen breaking on top as they chase baitfish in the rips and currents. At such times you can catch them by casting popping or underwater plugs, metal squids, heavy spoons and jigs. The best procedure is to run the boat above the breaking fish and drift through them.

BLACK DRUM

Black drum usually bite best when the tide is running fairly strong. The top fishing periods usually occur during the new moon and full moon periods, when tides are highest and strongest.

Want to locate black drum? Listen for the "drumming" noise they make under the boat. Or try to feel the vibrations from this noise against your feet on the bottom of the boat.

Chumming often works when fishing for black drum. Cracked mussels, clams, oysters, and crabs can be scattered around the boat or lowered to the bottom in a chum pot or bag.

Black drum are usually caught on clams. Shedder crabs also make a good bait. One trick is to offer them a "cocktail" of clam and crab on the same hook.

Look for black drum over oyster, clam, and mussel beds, since the drum feed on the shellfish. But at times they will also be found along sandy beaches and inlets, bays, and rivers.

A good bait for big black drum is a blue crab. Use either half of a big crab on a hook or a whole, smaller crab.

BLACKFISH

When fishing for blackfish in an area where there are submerged boulders, cast your sinker and bait on top of a boulder and then yank it so it drops off the rock into the deeper water alongside. Blackfish like to gather in such spots.

If you want to catch big blackfish, use a heavier rod and stronger line than you do for the small ones. When hooked, blackfish try to run into a hole or crevice or around a rock. You have to stop them from doing this, and it calls for a stout rod and heavy line.

SNAPPERS

Red snappers are often smart and will not hit a terminal rig with a lot of hardware and a short leader. So when rigging for them, use a longer leader of mono or wire.

Red snappers in the Gulf of Mexico are often present in shallow water of 10 to 15 fathoms. But here they stay in the deeper holes. When found in deep water of 30 to 50 fathoms, however, they stay on the shallower plateaus or "banks," which rise higher than the surrounding terrain.

When fishing for mangrove snappers, use the lightest monofilament leader that is practical and drift your bait down naturally without any weight or sinker. If you must use a sinker because of the depth or strong tide, use the lightest weight that will do the job. A sliding egg sinker is best for this fishing.

Mangrove snappers can be attracted to an area by chumming. Use ground fish, tiny pieces of shrimp or crab, or even canned sardines. Scatter some of the chum in the water and drift a hook baited with a live shrimp into the slick.

Mangrove snappers will take lures, and one of the best is a tiny plug. They will also hit jigs. These can be cast with a light spinning outfit.

You'll find mangrove snappers over a wide variety of bottoms and in different kinds of waters. They frequent the outer reefs, wrecks, mangrove creeks, channels, inlets, bays, docks, and bridges.

SHEEPSHEAD

Sheepshead are usually caught on natural baits such as fiddler crabs, shrimp, and sand bugs, but they will also hit a bucktail jig if you add a piece of shrimp to the hook.

Sheepshead hang out in protected waters, so look for them under piers, docks, and bridges, over oyster bars, mangrove shores, and channels, and in deep holes in inlets, passes, river mouths, and creeks.

When you are fishing for sheepshead under piers, offshore oil rigs, bridges, and jetties and you hook a big fish, he will try to run your line around a pile, bridge support, or rock. So use a tight drag and snub a sheepshead as soon as you hook him, to keep him away from such obstructions.

CROAKERS

Croakers are most numerous in holes and along the drop-offs. Here they often congregate in big schools, and you can have some fast fishing.

Croakers will hit small bucktail jigs worked up and down along the bottom. This works best from a drifting boat in fairly shallow water.

SILVER HAKE OR WHITING

Whiting bite best on nights that are cold and still with not too much wind. Along the Atlantic coast a north, northwest, or west wind is best since it blows from land and cuts down or flattens the sea. A strong onshore wind is bad because it creates big waves and dirty water, which keeps the whiting away.

If you catch any herring, cut long, narrow strips from the belly or sides and use them for bait. Whiting will also take strips cut from mackerel and other fish.

You'll catch more whiting if you move your rod up and down to give your bait some action.

Most whiting are caught on natural baits but at times they will hit small metal lures, underwater plugs, and streamer flies.

VARIOUS BOTTOM FISHES

A prime bait for black sea bass in the Pacific is a whole mackerel on a big hook. Run the hook through the mackerel's back and lower it with a sinker to the bottom.

White sea bass caught along the California coast bite best at night. A natural squid can be hooked and lowered near the kelp beds or rocks where these fish feed.

A good rig for grouper when trolling over reefs down deep is a fillet or half of a mullet hooked on three hooks behind a feather lure. Troll it on a weighted or wire line for best results.

Rockfish in the Pacific are often found along the beaches in the surf and rocky shores. But they prefer the deeper tidal pools and coves sheltered from the waves.

When fishing for jewfish or big grouper, use a live fish such as a grunt, snapper, or jack crevalle. You can also try a live catfish with the sharp spines clipped off.

The best time to fish for jewfish or giant grouper from bridges or in channels or deep holes is just before and after the slack tides. These big fish don't like to fight strong currents and are more likely to venture out to search for food when the tide weakens or gets slack.

One of the toughest small fish in the sea is the Bermuda chub. A piece of spiny lobster makes a good bait for them.

If you want to catch surf perch along the Pacific coast, fish for them during the winter months, when they come close to shore to spawn. If you see baby perch among the kelp or rocks, it is a good indication that the larger perch are in deeper water but usually within casting distance.

CHAPTER 19

Other Saltwater Fishes

PACIFIC SALMON

To locate Pacific salmon, look for drop-offs where the shallow water suddenly deepens. Feeding and migrating salmon swim along this edge. Strong tidal currents, rips, and eddies where baitfish are trapped are also prime spots.

When fishing with herring bait for Pacific salmon, don't try to set the hook too soon. Usually a salmon merely nips or bumps the bait in an attempt to cripple it. When this happens, wait until you feel a strong, steady pull before you come back with the rod to set the hook.

Big chinook or king salmon like to lie behind rocks, especially in channels or rivers where the current is strong. Then a lure or bait must be trolled close and deep as possible next to the rock to get a hit.

When casting for salmon from a boat or shore with a spoon, let it sink and flutter, then raise it and let it sink and flutter again. This imitates a crippled herring or smelt, which the Pacific salmon feed on.

While Pacific salmon can be caught throughout the day, the peak fishing periods are usually early in the morning and toward evening.

Look for silver or coho salmon in salt water near patches of seaweed or kelp. Then troll your lures close to these weed beds.

Pacific salmon usually hit best when the tides are strongest. For best results, fish the tide changes about an hour after high or low water. Salmon will be more active and hit lures or baits more readily when currents are swift.

One trick salmon anglers use is to paint a herring bait with red stripes of Merthiolate.

Trolling for silver or coho salmon along shore with flies or lures is best when the water is ruffled or choppy. It isn't as productive when the water is glassy smooth.

When mooching for Pacific salmon, lower your bait to the depth to be fished as the boat is drifting. Then run the boat for 15 or 20 ft., cut the motor and drift again. Keep repeating this maneuver. It causes the bait to rise when the boat is running, then lets it sink when it is drifting. This often entices the salmon, especially the chinook.

Young salmon, called "jacks," come into tidal rivers and can often be caught. Look for leaping fish, usually when the tide changes at high or low water, especially around daybreak or dusk. This is also the best time to catch these young salmon.

You can locate Pacific salmon by looking for baitfish being chased to the surface or try to find schools of bait just below the surface. These are usually revealed by dark patches. You can also look for birds working over the schools of baitfish.

SHARKS

Small sharks often venture on the bonefish flats in southern waters and can be caught on light tackle and lures. Use a fly rod with big streamers or a spinning rod or bait-casting rod with a small surface plug.

When trolling a whole-fish bait for sharks, run the boat at a slow speed. Most sharks are slow swimmers and have poor eyesight. So you have to give them a chance to see the bait and grab it. It also helps to give the bait some additional action with your rod tip when you see a shark near it.

When hooking a long fish such as a mackerel or ladyfish to use as bait for sharks, use a two-hook rig and run one hook through the lips or head and the other hook into the body closer to the tail.

You can't beat a live fish as bait for sharks. When hooked, such a fish gives off vibrations in the water, which attracts sharks to the scene. One trick you can use is to cut part of the tail fins off your bait so that it is off balance and keeps moving and flashing in the water.

When fishing for sharks from shore or a pier, it is desirable to get a bait out quite a distance into deeper water. Then it's a good idea to attach a toy balloon to the leader a few feet above the bait.

BARRACUDA

Big barracuda often steal fish from an angler's line by biting it off just behind the head. If you want to catch them at such times, put a live fish on a hook attached to a wire leader.

Barracuda can be caught by trolling along mangrove-lined shores. You can run right in close to the mangrove trees. High tide is usually most productive in such areas.

A good way to catch barracuda on light tackle is to wade the flats in the Florida Keys and cast flies, jigs, or plugs.

Once you catch a barracuda, you have plenty of bait. Just cut a strip from its belly and troll it to catch more barracuda.

Barracuda in clear, shallow, calm water are more suspicious and cautious than in deeper water. Then they are often harder to fool and hook. Best results are obtained if you cast as far as possible and try to get the fish to hit at a distance. You'll get more strikes from barracuda on days when the water is ruffled than on calmer days.

Barracuda are a lot of fun on a fly rod. They'll hit poppers and large-size streamer flies if they are worked fast through the water.

Barracuda are often curious and are attracted to the wake of a moving or drifting boat. Trolling is a good way to catch them, as is casting behind the boat.

One trick anglers use to bring barracuda around a boat is to circle around a spot where they are present before starting to fish.

AMBERJACK

Amberjack are usually caught on live-fish baits. One of the best is a small yellow-tailed snapper hooked through the back.

You can often bring amberjack up to the surface around a boat by hitting the water with a rod tip, oar, or pole to create some commotion or splash on the surface.

Amberjack will often hit lures that are trolled or cast. Plugs, jigs, and spoons will draw strikes from these fish. Strip baits can also be trolled. Troll slower and deeper for them than for other fish.

When you catch an amberjack from a school, hold it in the water near the boat or tie it to the boat with a heavy line. This will often hold the rest of the school around the boat and give you a chance to hook more fish.

You can also hold amberjack near a boat by chumming with good-size chunks of cut fish or small whole ones.

When hooked over a reef, big amberjack often dive toward the bottom and cut your line off on the coral or rocks. So when fishing in such waters, use a stiff rod and strong line to turn or slow down the fish.

California Yellowtail

The easiest time to fool yellowtails is around daybreak, when they can't see the hook or leader. When it gets light, they may still be around but tend to shy away from baits.

When fishing for yellowtail down deep, try a strip cut from the belly of a mackerel. It should be about 6 or 7 in. long, an inch wide, and about ⅛ in. thick. Let this down to the bottom on a hook and sinker from a drifting boat.

If yellowtail are chasing baitfish on top, they will sometimes hit a surface plug that is reeled very fast.

On days when yellowtail are "boat shy" or laying off some distance, use lighter lines and cast the bait out as far as possible from the boat.

Once you catch a yellowtail, you can make a good bait from the fish by cutting a wide strip from its belly or side, shaping it like a squid. It can be about 9 in. long and 2 in. wide. The head part of the flat squid bait can be slit for about 3 in. to form several tentacles. The 4/0 or 5/0 tuna hook can be forced into the tail.

You can also use a whole small natural squid when yellowtail are feeding on them or when they refuse the regular sardine and anchovy baits. Hook the squid through the tail and allow it to sink deep. Then retrieve it with short jerks.

When fishing for yellowtail, use only the liveliest sardine on your hook. If the bait weakens or dies, remove it immediately and replace it with a fresh, lively one.

PACIFIC ALBACORE

If you are using live anchovies for long-fin albacore, they are often difficult to cast. Then you can add a ⅜ or ¼ oz. rubber-core sinker about 2 or 3 ft. above the hook.

If you are fishing on a live-bait boat for long-fin albacore and fish are sighted or the mate starts chumming, get ready with your rod and put a live anchovy on the hook so that you are ready to cast as soon as the fish move in. Usually the first baits in the water are taken quickly by the albies.

Pacific albacore like clean, blue water with a temperature between 60 and 65 degrees. When such favorable waters cover a wide area in the ocean, the fish will be scattered or spread out. When the favorable waters are narrowed down, the albacore will be more concentrated in compact schools and easier to locate.

Cobia

When in cobia waters, try trolling slowly or drifting and scan the water behind and under the boat. Cobia will often follow a boat closely and then you can try to catch them.

A live blue runner can be used to catch cobia. For best results, use the baitfish on a short line and let it splash around on top of the water.

Cobia are often found around buoys and channel markers outside the inlets or passes.

Cobia fishermen often take the first fish caught and tie it on a strong line under the boat, to act as a decoy. This draws other cobia under the boat, and then you can fish for them.

A large feather or bucktail jig is a good lure for cobia. This should be cast just in front of and a little beyond a swimming fish and then jigged. If a fish starts to approach the lure, let it settle or sink so he can grab it.

Common Mackerel

Although most mackerel off Long Island and New Jersey are caught by chumming and jigging, you can also try casting or trolling for these fish. A light spinning outfit is ideal for casting. Use tiny diamond jigs, metal squids, spoons, or spinners. Sometimes the mackerel show on top when chasing bait. Then you can cast into them. But most of the time you have to cast blind, let the lure sink a few feet, then reel it back fairly fast with some rod action.

Mackerel usually bite better when the water is choppy or even rough than when it is smooth and glassy.

A good rig for mackerel is a small diamond jig on the end of the line and three or four short droppers with tiny plastic tube lures on each one. By jigging this in a chum slick, you can often catch two or three mackerel at the same time.

Mackerel often come close to shore in Maine to feed on herring. The best time to catch them is in the evening or on overcast days.

To attract mackerel in Pacific waters, use ground-up anchovies as chum. Then you can catch them on mackerel rigs made up of three or four hooks dressed with red and yellow yarn and a ½ oz. sinker on the end.

King Mackerel

A live shrimp makes a great bait for king mackerel. Let the shrimp down under the boat as it drifts. If the tide is slow or the wind is weak, no sinker is needed, but if the tide is strong or the wind causes the boat to drift fast, a clincher sinker may be needed above the hook.

Look for king mackerel where there are "edges" and "drift lines." This usually occurs where two currents meet or clash. You can often locate such areas by looking for changes in the color of the water or watching for debris and weeds floating in a line or streak.

Most of the larger king mackerel, over 20 or 25 lb., are caught by drifting or slow-trolling with live baits such as blue runners, pinfish, grunt, and other small fish.

A good king mackerel lure is a nylon jig weighing about 1½ or 2 oz. Add a second hook to this and then a mullet strip about 5 or 6 in. long over both hooks, as shown. Let this jig down to the bottom from a drifting boat, then reel it back with a lot of rod action.

Ballyhoo trolled on top catch a lot of king mackerel, but it's a good idea to troll them about 90 or 100 ft. behind the boat so that when you turn the boat the baits sink below the surface. This often gets strikes from the kings.

When king mackerel are not on top or not hitting lures trolled on the surface or just below, try deep trolling with spoons, using weights or wire lines to get the lure down.

When fishing from piers, one of the best baits for big king mackerel is a live bluefish. But they'll also take other live fish, such as whiting, mullet, or small jacks.

Troll a ballyhoo or lure for king mackerel until you start getting strikes or hook a fish. Then you can anchor and start chumming with pilchards or ground-up or cut fish and later drift a live shrimp or fish out in the slick.

King mackerel tend to stay in schools of the same-size fish. Thus if you are catching only small kings on top, try deep trolling or jigging for bigger ones. Or head for a different spot, where you may run into bigger fish.

Spanish Mackerel

One of the best lures for Spanish mackerel is a white bucktail jig. But the sharp teeth of the mackerel chew up the hair on the jig, and after you catch a few fish, you need a new lure. So bring along plenty of white bucktails if you are after these fish.

If two or three anglers are casting lures for Spanish mackerel, wait until one angler hooks a fish, then the other anglers should cast near the hooked fish. Usually there are other fish around the hooked one, and they'll often hit other lures cast to them.

When you locate a school of Spanish mackerel, troll for them by circling around the school. Avoid running through the school.

One good way to catch Spanish mackerel is to chum for them with ground bunker or other oily fish. When they appear in the chum slick, cast lures into them.

Reel your lure as fast as possible with some rod action if you want to hook Spanish mackerel. Small spoons or jigs work best for these fish.

WAHOO

If you see wahoo swimming around the boat, you can often make them hit a jig by casting toward them with a spinning or bait-casting rod. But have plenty of line on the reel to take care of those long, fast runs. And a wire leader is needed to keep their sharp teeth from cutting your mono line.

Wahoo have been known to hit shiny swivels or snaps on a leader, so it's a good idea to use black or dull hardware when fishing in waters where these fish are expected.

Wahoo often hit a fish bait or strip bait at the tail end and bite it off. So when rigging for these fish, place the hook toward the rear of the bait.

POMPANO

The best bait for pompano is a live sand flea or bug. Use a whole big bug on a hook or two or three smaller ones. Pompano will also take small live shrimp or chunks of bigger shrimp.

Pompano feed along sandy beaches, but they prefer the rocky areas, reefs, holes, and sloughs in such places.

You can sometimes locate pompano by watching for flashes underwater as the fish turn over on one side. This is best done from an elevation such as a bridge or pier. Along the sand beaches, when the water is calm and clear, you can often see pompano swimming. The fish themselves are difficult to detect here, but you look for the shadows they cast on the sand bottom.

When pompano are in shallow water, they are wary and easily frightened by a boat or even lures cast near them. Best results are obtained by fishing for them in deeper water, where they are not so scary.

You can locate pompano just inside inlets and passes on the incoming tide. When the tide turns to go out, fish just outside the inlet.

Some of the best pompano fishing in the Gulf of Mexico is found around the oil-drilling platforms, especially during the winter months.

When using a tiny jig for pompano, add a tiny piece of shrimp to the hook. And tie the monofilament leader directly to the eye of the jig instead of using a snap.

In choosing a jig for pompano, pick a nylon or bucktail type with a small 1/0 or No. 1 hook and a short skirt, which doesn't extend much beyond the bend of the hook. The best colors in jigs are yellow, off-white, tan, or sand, which imitate the sand bugs pompano feed on.

When fishing for pompano from a boat, do not run it over the area you plan to fish. Instead circle around until you get above it, then cut your motor and drift quietly into the spot.

PERMIT

Good permit spots can be located by looking for trails or grooves cut in the bottom sand by the bellies of permit swimming along the bottom.

An effective lure for permit is a small spoon. This can be trolled in channels and passes adjacent to sandy and grassy flats.

Permit are often scarce, but one of the best ways to attract them is to anchor your boat and chum an area where they have been caught in the past. Spiny lobster or crayfish tails make the best chum and can also be used for bait.

VARIOUS FISHES

Jack crevalle can be caught in the surf, especially when there are mullet or pilchards or other baitfish along the beaches.

A choice lure for big jack crevalle is a surface plug that makes a lot of commotion on top.

Tripletail are tough fighters and can be caught in Florida waters around channel markers, buoys, and floating objects and debris. Bucktail jigs are fine lures to use for them.

To catch palometa or gaff-topsail pompano in Bermuda waters, try chumming with dry bread and, when the fish start feeding on the bread, cast your lures to them.

Herring can often be caught during the winter months from piers, bridges, and shore. They provide a good fight on light tackle. Use a tiny spinner, spoon, or piece of spearing on a hook. They bite best at night, especially under a light.

Mullet can often be caught on rod and reel, especially in rivers or canals in brackish water or even fresh water. Here they will often take a small wet fly. At times they will also take doughballs, bread, moss rounded into a small ball, worms, and cheese.

Ladyfish bite well at night, especially around bridges and piers on an outgoing tide. Here the best technique is to cast your lure upcurrent and retrieve it with the tide, to imitate a shrimp coming down with the current.

CHAPTER 20

Other Saltwater Tips

Dolphin aren't the only fish that are attracted to floating objects or debris. Such fish as yellow-fin tuna, skipjack, cobia, triggerfish, various jacks, and other species also investigate or hang around such objects.

Pacific salmon can often be caught from shore or a beach, especially at river mouths, inlets, entrances to bays, and other spots where there is a deep channel and strong tides within casting distance. Plugs, spoons, and herring strips can all be used in this fishing.

Shrimp boats working in the Gulf of Mexico attract king mackerel, cobia, dolphin, bonito, sailfish, and sharks when they dump trash fish overboard. So fishing is often good around such boats found anchored offshore.

At night you can often locate saltwater fish by looking for phosphorescent streaks indicating feeding or swimming fish. This is most noticeable from the banks or shores of bays, inlets, and rivers. In a fast-moving boat, you can often see fish scattering in front of you.

Sailfish aren't the only fish that will cause baitfish to "ball" up into a compact school. Jack crevalle, barracuda, and other fish do the same thing. These baitfish balls can be located by watching for ripples on top of the water or by looking for brown or dark patches. Cast your lure close to the baitfish and let it sink under them.

A good spot to fish in a saltwater canal is under a bridge. Tarpon, snook, and sea trout like to lie in the shade, especially during the daytime when the sun is bright.

You can create your own fishing spot quickly in the ocean by mooring a balsa raft or even sheets of black plastic cloth in the water, then coming back a few days later to fish the spot.

Chumming from beaches or shore, especially in tropical waters such as the Bahamas, Bermuda, and parts of Florida, will attract pompano, bonefish, snappers, and other fish that come into shallow water.

The most natural way to fish a bait is to let it drift, without any sinker or weight, with the current or tide. This, of course, is most practical in shallow water, in creeks, rivers, inlets, canals, and in the surf along some beaches, especially where there are jetties or high rocks. You can also drift a bait from a boat in shallow water over reefs. Chumming helps to bring fish up to the surface, where they will see the bait.

Buoys and channel markers can be used to locate many fishing spots in salt water. They can be used during the day to line up a fishing spot and are especially valuable at night when landmarks may not be visible. Of course, it's a good idea to have a spotlight on your boat or to bring along a powerful portable light to locate the buoys or markers in the dark. Or you can arrive at dusk and locate the buoys or markers while it's still light.

Early in the spring in northern waters, fish the shallow sections of a bay or tidal river. The water here warms up sooner than the deeper water and attracts shrimp, baitfish, crabs, and bigger fish.

Fish seem to sense the approach of a storm and often feed just before it. So if you get a forecast of a northeaster or hurricane, do your boat fishing or surf fishing before it hits. Striped bass especially will feed not only before a storm but during it and right after it if the water is rough but not too dirty.

Hickory shad in salt water provide great sport on light tackle and will hit small metal squids, spoons, jigs, and streamer flies.

When searching for such fish as bonefish, permit, redfish, or tarpon in shallow water, it is best to approach an area with the sun at your back. Then you can see the fish more easily, especially when they turn on one side and the light reflects on their silvery scales.

A small creek entering a bay is a good spot to fish for striped bass, weakfish, and other saltwater gamefish, especially on an outgoing tide. Small baitfish, crabs, and shrimp are swept out by the tide or current, and gamefish congregate at the mouth to wait for this food.

One way to get ground-up fish chum down deep in a hurry is to mix the chum with sand and form a ball. Then drop it under the boat, and it will sink pretty deep before the sand dissolves and releases the chum.

Even in bottom fishing a moving bait attracts more fish than one that is lying still on the mud or sand or is buried in the weeds or rocks. Thus the best fishing usually occurs when the tide is running or the boat is drifting, giving the bait some movement. That is also why most bottom fishermen keep bouncing their sinker on the bottom by lifting and lowering the rod tip. They feel they are fishing deep enough on the bottom and at the same time the bait rises and drops attractively.

Two or three days of strong winds will often ruin the fishing in shallow waters, the flats and bays. You can then try deeper waters or wait until the wind dies down and the water starts to clear.

Fish at night for spotfin and yellowfin croakers and corbina in the surf along the Pacific coast. These fish come in closer to shore then, are less wary, and bite better.

If you are fishing with two or more hooks for porgies, sea bass, or whiting in deep water and don't want to reel in just one fish, try for a double or even a triple. When you get your first bite, hook the fish and let it stay there. Its struggles will usually attract another fish, which will often grab the second bait. Then set the hook and reel in both fish.

"The terns are back!" That's a sure sign each spring along the North Atlantic coast that there are baitfish around in the inlets, along the beaches, and in the bays. And with these baitfish present, it means that the striped bass, bluefish, weakfish, pollock, and mackerel will start hitting lures.

If sharks or porpoises are thick in an area you are fishing, you might as well leave and head for another spot. Fishing is usually poor for most species when sharks and porpoises are around in numbers.

To locate saltwater fish, it's a good idea to study the bottom where you will be fishing. Some fish, such as flounders and ling, will be found over a mud bottom. Others, such as cod, sea bass, porgies, and blackfish, like a rocky bottom. Shellfish beds of clams, mussels, and oysters will attract these same fish. Striped bass and weakfish like eelgrass in bays, and stripers along rocky shores hang around kelp beds. If you get some U.S. Coast and Geodetic charts of the area you plan to fish, they'll show the type of bottom found there.

When trolling for striped bass and bluefish, best results are usually obtained in strong rips and tides. This calls for weights or wire lines to get the lures down deep, often near the bottom, in the strong currents.

Offshore anglers along Florida's east coast favor a northeast wind for the best fishing. Almost any wind is better than no wind for billfish.

When surf fishing, look for baitfish hugging the shoreline, or acting "nervous," or remaining in the same spot for any length of time. This usually indicates that larger gamefish are lurking nearby or were chasing the baitfish recently. Often they will return and start feeding on the baitfish again, and then you can cast there.

Corbina are caught in the surf in California using sand crabs as bait. After you cast out the bait, let it sink to the bottom, wait a minute or two, then reel it in 2 or 3 ft. Wait again and reel once more, and so on until the bait is near shore.

When fishing for snook, tarpon, and striped bass at night under piers and bridges, you'll get most of your strikes in the shadows of the structures or along the edge of a shadow line.

When wading and fishing the saltwater flats in Florida and along the Gulf of Mexico for channel bass or sea trout, look for feeding or cruising fish and cast ahead of and beyond them. Then reel fairly fast and hold your rod high so that the lure travels on or near the surface, clear of the weeds or the bottom.

Snook are very similar to striped bass in their habits. Both fish like strong tides and rips, feed under bridges, and are active at daybreak, at dusk, and during the night.

While fishing during the full or new moon may be good in the open ocean or surf, it is often poor in bays, tidal rivers, and inlets. The extra-high tides and strong currents wash out seaweed, sea lettuce, wood, dried grass, and other debris and junk. This often fouls up an angler's line, hooks, bait, and lures.

Fish can often be located at night by listening for the breaks or splashes they make when feeding on baitfish. On moonlit nights you can even see the fish breaking or the baitfish leaping.

When there is a strong wind blowing, you often get a "belly" in your line when reeling in a lure. You may get a strike but fail to hook the fish because of this belly. When this happens, it's a good idea to hold your rod tip low, almost touching the water, so that most of the line is submerged and can't be blown by the wind.

If you are bothered by smaller fish or pests that steal your bait when bottom fishing, try putting a larger piece of bait on your hook. This will take longer to clean off the hook, and in the meantime a larger fish may come along, chase away the smaller fish, and grab the bait.

Using lure at night requires a sense of "feel" or "touch," which salt-water anglers develop so they know when the lure is working right. By feeling the vibrations, pulls, and movement or action of the lure, they can tell when to slow down or when to speed up the retrieve.

Coiling surplus fly line on the bottom of a boat can cause tangles around rods, oars, outboard motors, tackle boxes, and other objects. One way to avoid this is to coil the excess line in a basket or small plastic garbage can.

When trying to locate school tuna or false albacore or bonito, troll four to six lines of different lengths behind the boat—lines with different size and color lures. Once you hook a fish and find out what they are hitting and how far out the lure should be, you can adjust all the lines to the same length and change the lures to match the one that caught the fish.

Almost all species found in salt water will hit a jig. This includes even the so-called bottom fishes such as fluke, porgies, and sea bass up north and grouper, snappers, and grunts down south. The best way to work the jig is to let it sink to the bottom and then bounce it along with brief pauses as the lure settles in the mud or sand. This gives the slower-moving bottom species a chance to grab the lure.

Offshore fishing for billfish is often poor after a big storm that dirties the water. It pays to wait until the water clears up before going after the big fish.

When fishing for Pacific halibut from a pier or an anchored boat, cast out your baited rig and reel it slowly along the bottom to give the bait some movement.

Before using saltwater flies for striped bass, bluefish, albacore, bonito, school tuna, or other fish, try dipping them in a fish oil like bunker oil. For small sharks on the flats you can soak the flies in blood.

It's good to fish for sea trout in the surf at the top of an incoming tide and the start of the outgoing tide. Then they come across the bars and move in closer to the beach and into the sloughs to feed.

One reason why chunks of cut fish or fish strips are so effective as bait is that they give off more flavor, juices, and blood than a whole fish or preserved bait. That is also why it's a good idea to replace washed-out baits with fresh ones.

Fish often swallow natural baits deeply, and a hook disgorger helps to remove the hook. But to save time when the fish are hitting fast, cut the leader near the hook and leave it inside the fish's mouth. Tie on a new rig or hook and get it out quickly to catch more fish. The hooks can always be easily removed from the dead fish when you are cleaning them.

If you are fishing from the front of a jetty or breakwater at an inlet or river mouth, you can often let your lure out with the tide up to 400 or 500 ft. Then reel it back very slowly against the current.

Chumming can be very effective when done from a pier. In fact, some pier operators do this to bring fish around for their angler customers. Or you can bring some of your own clams, mussel, and ground fish and toss a handful overboard from time to time to attract fish to your spot under the pier.

To catch big sea trout at night, fish a long, slim surface plug at a snail's pace. In fact, the sea trout will often hit a plug that is just drifting with the tide.

To give a lure some side action when trolling, hold the rod tip low and move it from side to side. This causes the lure to dart from one side to the other rather than just travel in a straight line as in ordinary trolling.

When fishing canals, rivers, inlets, or other spots where the tide or current is strong and you can't hold bottom with a sinker or get a lure

down deep enough, try waiting or coming back and fishing the same
spot around slack water when the tide or current gets weaker.

A good place to fish for surf perch and other fish in the surf in the
Pacific Northwest is along beaches where people have been turning
over the sand in search for clams. This exposes all kinds of marine life,
which attracts fish when the tide comes in.

Bonito have soft mouths and the hook often pulls out, so fish them
with a light drag and limber rods. Lures with treble hooks also hold
them better than those with single hooks.

When fishing saltwater flats or in clear, shallow water, the main
strategy is to spot feeding or swimming fish before they see you. Such
fish are spooky and take off in a hurry if they see you first.

If you see a school of feeding fish on top, such as tuna or albacore
in Pacific waters, run your boat up to the edge of the school. Then
circle the school and toss out live anchovies every 50 or 75 ft. After you
complete the circle, kill your engine, throw out some more baitfish,
and cast a hook with a live anchovy right into the middle of these
baitfish.

Mangrove-lined shores create good fishing because the trees and
roots provide shade and hiding places for snook, redfish, tarpon, sheepshead, mangrove snappers, and other southern species. You can cast
lures toward the roots or troll along the edges for these fish.

Not every spot on a pier offers good fishing. It depends on the species
running and the presence of baitfish, crabs, and other foods. Some fish
prefer the end of a pier and deeper water, others the middle sections,
and still other fish come into the shallow surf or the breakers. Depending on the wind and tide, one side of a pier is usually better than the

other. And often you have to cast out to a certain spot where coral, oyster, and mussel bottoms attract fish.

Mullet can often be attracted to an area by baiting it with bread, cornmeal, soybean cakes, canned corn, and cereals. Do this before you plan to fish the spot.

When using chum such as ground bunker or other fish, try adding strips of tin foil or tinsel. Then as the chum spreads, the shiny strips of foil or tinsel will flutter attractively and look like baitfish swimming around.

When trolling for billfish with surface baits, head the boat toward the sun or have the sun on either the port or the starboard side of the boat. Avoid having the sun directly behind the boat since the glare on the water makes it difficult to watch and see the skipping baits.

When fishing sunken wrecks, it is important to anchor the boat so that it lies directly over the highest section of the wreck. This is where cod and pollock are found. On windy days it may be necessary to use two anchors to prevent the boat from swinging away from the wreck.

When the ocean is rough, troll your baits or lures on shorter lines than when it is calm. Fish aren't as boat shy then, and you can control your lines better in the big waves and avoid tangled lines.

Most predatory gamefish such as striped bass, snook, and tarpon feeding under bridges like to lie near the fast tides and currents to intercept any food such as crabs, shrimp, or baitfish being swept toward them. But at the same time they prefer to wait in somewhat quieter water and eddies, where they don't have to fight or buck the strongest currents. That is why they usually choose to lie in front of or behind obstructions such as bridge pilings or abutments.

When using light tackle or spinning outfits for sailfish, white marlin, or striped marlin and these fish pick up the bait, let plenty of line run off the reel as the fish swallows the bait. Then set the hook with several short jerks. The longer line in the water and the short jerks help to take up some of the shock and prevents a break-off when setting the hook in a billfish.

If you are fishing over reefs with your bait down deep near the bottom, many of the hooked fish will try to run your line around coral or rocks or into a hole or crevice. One way you can avoid this is to chum heavily to bring the fish closer to the surface, where you can hook them and keep them away from the bottom.

Undercut sod banks in tidal creeks and estuaries are good places to fish. The water is usually deeper here and baitfish and shrimp and crabs are swept alongside such banks. Gamefish lurk there to feed on this food. Cast your lures or baits close to such undercut banks.

A good way to use a jig in southern waters is to let it sink to the bottom, then reel it back to the surface with plenty of rod action.

When chumming on a windy day, it's a good idea to use two anchors to hold the boat broadside to the tide or current so that it doesn't swing back and forth away from the chum slick.

Index

Albacore, 126, 158, 191, 220–221, 226, 401–402, 443; in bait strips, 162, 164, 217; false, 401, 402, 441; gulls and, 236; lines for, 233; Pacific, 427–428

Alcatraz Island, 146

Alewives, 372, 384

Algae, 284

Allison tuna, 395

Amberjack, 131, 425–426

Anchors, 112, 203, 227, 238

Anchovies, 124, 157, 372, 374, 414, 443; albacore and, 158, 220; California yellowtail and, 219, 220; striped bass and, 146, 153

Atlantic coast, 167, 185, 189, 217, 236

Atlantic salmon, 90–91, 106, 321–322

Azores, 178

Bahamas, 190, 213

Bait: floats, 29–30, 36, 102, 109, 142, 145, 164, 194–195, 212, 217; freshwater, 31–43, 71, 88, 89, 93 (panfish, 79, 80–81, 82, 84, 86); odor of, 113, 174, 233; rigs and, 23, 29, 142, 143; rods and, 1–2;

Bait (cont.)
    saltwater, 130, 151–165, 202–214 *passim,* 228 (*see also specific fish*); *see also* Chum; Lures; *and see specific kinds of bait, e.g.,* Insects

Bait-casting reel, 251–252

Bait-casting rods, freshwater, 250; saltwater, 343

Baitfish, 7, 153–161, 181, 193, 370–374, 385, 437, 438, 439, 440, 443; bottoms and, 236; coves and, 236, 239; dead, 371–372, 374; lights and, 178, 228; plug imitations of, 124, 166, 196–197; rigs and, 137, 138, 141, 189; schooling, 231; shallow water and, 173, 175; storms and, 234, 238; streamers and, 12, 13, 198; *see also specific varieties*

Baitfish balls, 436

Baits, natural, freshwater, 279–285, 309, 334; crayfish, 281–282, 382; frogs, 280–281; insects, 282–283; minnows, 279–280, 384; worms, 279; saltwater, 370–382; baitfish, 370–374, 385, 437, 438, 439, 443; chum, 380, 390, 411, 412, 437, 444; crabs, 375–376,

Tuna, 126, 180–185, 191, 217,
226, 394–396, 435, 441, 443;
gulls and, 236; moonlight
229; school, 395, 441; yellow-fin,
435

Umbrella rig, 369

Vancouver Island, 217
Virginia, 174

Wahoo, 190, 432
Walleyes, 75–77, 81, 310–312,
335; bait for, 31, 35, 39; lures
for, 16, 17, 18, 76–77, 104;
rigs for, 23–24, 26, 76
Warmouth, 79
Water dogs, 284
Weakfish, 152, 161, 169, 178–179,
227, 391–393, 437, 438;
feeding time, 234; lures for,
132; moonlight and, 229; rigs
for, 138, 145; rods for, 115,
116
West coast. *See* Pacific coast
Wet flies, 17, 89, 258–259, 339;
rigs and, 22, 23, 25; trout
fishing and, 3–4, 10, 11, 44–
45, 46, 47, 49, 51, 105
Whelk (conch), 151, 164, 201, 211

White bass, 84–85, 106, 114, 317–
318
Whitefish, 97, 332
White marlin, 186–187, 445
White perch, 81–82, 316–317
White sea bass, 420
Whiting, 167, 170, 175, 212–213,
415, 419–420, 438; bait, 161,
163, 171; cod and, 211;
mackerel and, 222; rigs for,
145; shark and, 217; tuna and,
180, 182, 184
Wigglers, 32
Worms, 22–24, 31–32, 79, 80, 81,
279 (*see also specific
varieties*); bass fishing and,
63, 170, 171, 172; saltwater
fishing and, 130, 133, 137,
138, 161, 166, 202; saltwater
bottomfish and, 209, 213,
214, 236; suckers and, 97–98;
trout fishing and, 46, 48, 49,
55

Yellowfin croakers, 438
Yellow-fin tuna, 435
Yellow perch, 80–81, 106; bait for,
32, 34–35, 42, 85, 315–316
Yellowtail. *See* California
yellowtail.